Early Childhood Care and Education and Equality of Opportunity

Kaspar Burger

Early Childhood Care and Education and Equality of Opportunity

Theoretical and Empirical Perspectives on Social Challenges

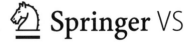

Kaspar Burger
Sion, Switzerland

Dissertation University of Fribourg, 2012

ISBN 978-3-658-01211-3 ISBN 978-3-658-01212-0 (eBook)
DOI 10.1007/978-3-658-01212-0

The Deutsche Nationalbibliothek lists this publication in the Deutsche Nationalbibliografie; detailed bibliographic data are available in the Internet at http://dnb.d-nb.de.

Library of Congress Control Number: 2012955557

Springer VS
© Springer Fachmedien Wiesbaden 2013
This work is subject to copyright. All rights are reserved by the Publisher, whether the whole or part of the material is concerned, specifically the rights of translation, reprinting, reuse of illustrations, recitation, broadcasting, reproduction on microfilms or in any other physical way, and transmission or information storage and retrieval, electronic adaptation, computer software, or by similar or dissimilar methodology now known or hereafter developed. Exempted from this legal reservation are brief excerpts in connection with reviews or scholarly analysis or material supplied specifically for the purpose of being entered and executed on a computer system, for exclusive use by the purchaser of the work. Duplication of this publication or parts thereof is permitted only under the provisions of the Copyright Law of the Publisher's location, in its current version, and permission for use must always be obtained from Springer. Permissions for use may be obtained through RightsLink at the Copyright Clearance Center. Violations are liable to prosecution under the respective Copyright Law. The use of general descriptive names, registered names, trademarks, service marks, etc. in this publication does not imply, even in the absence of a specific statement, that such names are exempt from the relevant protective laws and regulations and therefore free for general use. While the advice and information in this book are believed to be true and accurate at the date of publication, neither the authors nor the editors nor the publisher can accept any legal responsibility for any errors or omissions that may be made. The publisher makes no warranty, express or implied, with respect to the material contained herein.

Printed on acid-free paper

Springer VS is a brand of Springer DE.
Springer DE is part of Springer Science+Business Media.
www.springer-vs.de

Contents

I   Executive summary 11

II   Introduction 15

1   Early childhood care and education today 15
2   Equality of opportunity in view of social inequalities: what early childhood care and education strives for 17
   2.1   Social inequalities 17
   2.2   Equality of opportunity 17
   2.3   Early childhood care and education as a means to combat inequalities . 18
3   Research in early childhood care and education: disciplines and methods 19
   3.1   Scientific disciplines 19
   3.2   Research methods 20
4   Terminology 27
   4.1   Use of terms in international research 27
   4.2   Use of terms in Switzerland 27
5   Early childhood care and education: a unified concept 28
6   Ideological divide between childcare and education for young children 30
7   Use of extra-familial early childhood care and education 32
   7.1   Rates of use in Switzerland 32
   7.2   Rates of use in OECD countries 33
   7.3   Determinants of the use of early childhood care and education 33
8   Why early childhood care and education has evolved in economically developed countries 34
   8.1   Development of female labor force participation 35
   8.2   Immigration and fertility rates 35
   8.3   Gender equality 37
   8.4   Child poverty and social disparities 39
9   Characteristics of effective early childhood care and education programs ... 40

9.1	Program duration	40
9.2	Program intensity	42
10	Regulation of early childhood care and education	44
11	The role of the family in early childhood care and education	44

III New contributions to early childhood care and education research 47

How does early childhood care and education affect cognitive development? An international review of the effects of early interventions for children from different social backgrounds 49

1	Research objectives	51
2	Effects of socio-economic status on the development of children	52
3	Early education and care and equality of opportunity	53
4	Related analyses and main focus of the present analysis	53
5	Systematic review	54
6	Empirical evidence	70
7	Conclusion	99

Do effects of center-based care and education on vocabulary and mathematical skills vary with children's sociocultural background? Disparities in the use of and effects of early childhood services 105

1	Introduction	105
2	Previous research	107
3	Nursery provision in Switzerland	110
4	Objectives of the study and its contribution to research	111
5	Research questions	112
6	Method	113
7	Results	118
8	Discussion	128

A social history of ideas pertaining to childcare in France and in the United States 135

1	A brief comparison of France and the U.S. today	136
2	The beginnings of institutional childcare	137
3	Initial reception of institutional childcare	140
4	The evolution of institutional childcare	141

5	Institutional childcare prior to the Great Depression	146
6	Institutional childcare during the Depression and World War II	147
7	Institutional childcare after World War II	148
8	Conclusions	151

Begehren, Sprache und Bildung: Pädagogische Reflexionen über «Die gerettete Zunge» von Elias Canetti 157

1	Autobiographie als Bildungsbiographie	158
2	Methodische Vorüberlegungen zum Verhältnis von (autobiographischer) Literatur und Pädagogik	160
3	›Die gerettete Zunge‹ als Untersuchungsgegenstand pädagogischer Forschung	161
4	Zum erziehungswissenschaftlichen Diskurs über Bildung	163
5	Sprache und Bildung	164
6	Sprache und Bildung bei Canetti	166
7	Canettis Bildungsprozess als Annäherung an das Fremde und das Begehren nach Sprache	167
8	Das Begehren	171
9	Die prägende Funktion des sozialen Rahmens	172
10	Literatur und Sprache	175
11	Abschliessende Betrachtung	178

IV   Synopsis 181

1	Equal opportunities in the light of social disparities: a persistent challenge for early childhood care and education	182
2	How early childhood care and education can influence children's skills	184
3	Implications of the present research for practice	186
3.1	What type of early care and education should we implement?	187
3.2	For whom should we implement early childhood care and education?	188
3.3	Should early childhood care and education be regulated?	188
3.4	Why should practitioners be sensitive to social and cultural context characteristics?	189
3.5	What should parents know?	190
4	Prospects for future research	191
4.1	Ensuring multiple methodical approaches and disciplines in early childhood research	191

4.2	Avoiding ethnocentric description of children: technological challenges 192
4.3	Challenges in comparative-historical research.. 193
4.4	Equality of opportunity: Defining the scope of responsibilities of early childhood institutions 195
4.5	Generalizability of findings from research on literary accounts............. 196
5	Concluding remarks 197

Acknowledgements **201**

References **203**

«Education is the point at which we decide whether we love the world enough to assume responsibility for it and by the same token save it from that ruin which, except for renewal, except for the coming of the new and young, would be inevitable. And education, too, is where we decide whether we love our children enough not to expel them from our world and leave them to their own devices, nor to strike from their hands their chance of undertaking something new, something unforeseen by us, but to prepare them in advance for the task of renewing a common world.»

Hannah Arendt in «Between past and future: Six exercises in political thought» (1961, p. 196)

I Executive summary

Early childhood is a unique and precious stage in the human life cycle. Children's environments and experiences impact on child development and contribute to shape children's behaviors, intellect, and well-being. The significance of positive development during early childhood years for later educational achievement, successful interpersonal relationships, and positive adult citizenship is widely recognized. Societies therefore have a responsibility to ensure safe, healthy, nurturing and responsive environments for their youngest members. They need to be mindful of children's needs as young children require daily nurturance and guidance of adults in order to thrive. Institutional early care and education has a long history in Western societies, the roots of which can be found in the 19th century when industrialization and urbanization began to break up traditional family structures with fathers as breadwinners and mothers as caregivers due to an increasing entrance of mothers into the industrial workforce. Nowadays, the provision and use of early childhood care and education varies across countries. However, there is broad consensus that early care and education services should provide the fundamental requirements for children's care, health, safety, socialization, and education and that they should be made available to support in particular those children who grow up in unfavorable learning environments and are therefore at risk of detrimental development.

The present research focuses on a number of key issues in early childhood care and education, adding pedagogical, historical, and sociological perspectives to a body of research in education that has neglected important questions to date although these questions pose a challenge to societies that aim to provide for socially equitable education systems. First, research has not reviewed the latest studies into the effects of early childhood care and education on children from different social backgrounds across countries systematically. Second, the effects of center-based care and education on direct measures of children's skills have not been analyzed in Switzerland. Third, researchers have made no systematic attempts to account historically for present-day differences in the use and provision of childcare institutions in France and the United States. Finally, the intricate interrelations between desire, language and educational processes have not yet been studied. The present research essentially consists of four studies that address a variety of questions relating to the above-mentioned research desiderata. The following overview briefly summarizes the overarching research objectives as well as the methodical approaches of each of these studies.

(1) The first study is titled «How does early childhood care and education affect cognitive development? An international review of the effects of early interventions for children from different social backgrounds». The objective of this study is to determine how early childhood care and education programs influence children's cognitive development and whether these programs help to compensate for disparities among children from different social backgrounds. Methodically, the study systematically reviews findings from studies that looked at the effects of center-based programs enhancing child well-being, development and learning. All those studies were published after 1990 in diverse national contexts.

(2) The second study is titled «Do effects of center-based care and education on vocabulary and mathematical skills vary with children's sociocultural background? Disparities in the use of and effects of early childhood services». This study examines whether, in Switzerland, effects of center-based care and education on primary school children's vocabulary and mathematical competence vary with children's sociocultural background. In addition, it analyzes disparities in the use of early childhood care and education services among children from different families. Quantitative statistical analyses including multiple hierarchical regressions are used to address these questions. To date, no study has assessed the effects of early childhood care and education on direct measures of children's skills in primary school in Switzerland. Thus the study makes an added-value contribution to the research literature and it attempts to establish whether political measures are required to counteract social inequalities.

(3) The third study, «A social history of ideas pertaining to childcare in France and in the United States», raises the question whether differences in the use of and societal attitudes toward childcare in France and in the United States can be explained historically. It traces the social history of ideas pertaining to childcare in France and in the United States, illustrating major processes in the evolution of two corresponding daycare facilities, the French crèche and the American day nursery. The study adopts a comparative-historical methodical approach. By enlightening discursive paradigms about childcare and childcare policies since the inception of the first formal childcare institutions, the study analyzes societal and political conditions under which early childcare institutions

I Executive summary

and practices evolved. It thereby seeks to contribute to the understanding of current approaches in institutional childcare in both France and the United States.

(4) The fourth study is titled «Desire, language and education: pedagogical reflections on «The tongue set free» by Elias Canetti». This analysis investigates the interplay of desire, language development, and educational processes in early childhood as delineated in the first part of Elias Canetti's autobiography «The tongue set free». Methodically, a systematic theoretical approach is adopted. The study uses a literary document as a source of historic-pedagogical research in order to reflect upon the relationship between desire as a driving force of an intellectual engagement with the self and the world, language as a means to appropriate unintelligible, alien, experiences to oneself, and educational processes which consist in developing a specific, adjusted relationship between a reflecting self and a continually changing exterior world. (The original German title of this article is «Begehren, Sprache und Bildung: Pädagogische Reflexionen über «Die gerettete Zunge» von Elias Canetti.»)

By looking at different phenomena pertaining to early childhood care and education from various methodical angles, the present studies yield multiple important findings. They highlight effects of both early childhood care and education and family background on children's cognitive development, disparities in the use of services, diverging historical trajectories of institutions in different countries, and a complex interplay between desire, language development and educational processes. The findings point to the importance of appropriate pedagogical intervention in early childhood services for the lives of children. Moreover, they suggest that in research and policy-making in the field of early childhood care and education, special emphasis ought to be placed on children from socially disadvantaged backgrounds since well-designed early childhood programs can help establish social equity and equalize educational opportunities among different children by compensating for disadvantage and vulnerability resulting from factors such as socioeconomic status, ethnicity, gender, or minority status. However, such effects are more sizeable in the short term than in the long term. Furthermore, it has to be noted that in addition to the effects of early childhood care and education services, socioeconomic background factors contribute substantially to the development of children.

In addition, the present research shows that different policy frameworks, societal and political discourses, and cultural as well as economic structures impact on the provision and use of early childhood care and education systems. Relative to French traditions, for instance, American customs and policies of childcare have been underpinned by an ideology of domesticity, that is, a high value placed on individual responsibility and a philosophy of limiting government interventions in matters related to child-rearing and the family. As a result, U.S. Americans have assigned the responsibility of childcare and child-rearing to a greater degree to families, notably to mothers, whereas the French have tended to share responsibilities between the family and some structure of society such as public childcare institutions.

In literary and autobiographical works, specificities of educational processes in early childhood often are not described in mainstream or scientistic ways. Tracing such processes in this literary genre allows for generating insights that may differ from those based on scientific analyses. The study of Elias Canetti's work reveals how desire manifests itself as a result of a lack of a given object or condition. Desire, originating in a state of deprivation, aspires for phantasmagoric completeness, that is, for desired objects or conditions. One source of desire can be a perceived deficiency in the mastery of language and, consequently, incapacity to partake in the realm of language shared by others. The perceived difference between the actual command of language and the potentiality of perfect language proficiency constitutes a source of desire for language enhancement and may prompt an individual's efforts to acquire language skills. Since educational processes essentially take place in the medium of language, the advancement of language can also entail educational processes.

II Introduction

1 Early childhood care and education today

Early childhood care and education has become the subject of considerable debate and interest in both private and public sectors and the significance of early care and education to fostering children's early learning and development has been recognized widely. Across many countries, economic development and social change have transformed traditional family and child-rearing patterns. Parental work habits, for instance, have affected family life to the effect that enrollment in some form of early childhood care and education program is becoming a reality for many children before the onset of official schooling. In the member countries of the Organization for Economic Cooperation and Development (OECD) approximately 80 percent of three-to-six year-olds are enrolled currently in some form of early childhood program and the proportion using programs under the age of three amounts to about 25 percent (UNICEF, 2008). Moreover, programs have been applied in countries in Asia, Africa, and South America and enrollment rates in programs for children below school age are estimated at around 30 percent to 40 percent in some less industrialized countries (Weikart, 2000, p. 9). Besides, in recent decades, more systematic attention has been paid to the importance of early learning experiences as a foundation of child development. Sensitive periods have been assumed for the development of various behaviors and acquisition of capabilities, that is, short parts of the early life cycle during which the developing organism is uniquely sensitive or responsive to specific environmental influences. It has been hypothesized that outside this period, particular competences cannot be acquired as easily as during the period (Shaffer, 1994). Empirical findings from neurobiology, developmental psychology, and educational sciences highlight that early childhood care and education can be crucial for skill formation, including school readiness skills and later school outcomes (Phillips & Shonkoff, 2000). Furthermore, children have been considered as citizens with their own rights and needs, including the right to education. With a view to achieving this right progressively and on the basis of equal opportunity, the states parties to the Convention on the Rights of the Child shall promote and encourage international cooperation in matters relating to education (United Nations, 1990, article 28). In this regard, early childhood care and education has been seen increasingly as a first integral part of the education system and it has been advocated by scientists, policy-makers, and international organizations such as the World Organization for Early Childhood Education (OMEP), the United Nations Educational, Scientific and Cultural Organization (UNESCO), and the United Nations International Children's Emergency Fund (UNICEF).

Various key actors in different societies have started using early childhood care and education as a means to tackle current social challenges. Through investing in early care and education services, governments of OECD member countries, for instance, have aimed not only to increase female labor force participation, but also to reconcile work and family responsibilities on a more equitable basis for men and women; to tackle growing demographic challenges faced by industrial countries such as falling fertility rates, population decline, and ageing of populations; to counter exclusion of immigrant and second-language children among the school-entry population; and finally, to address issues of child poverty and educational disadvantage which concern a significant proportion of young children even in a number of developed countries (OECD, 2006, pp. 19–43). Poverty analyses make use of poverty lines, yet there is no categorical qualitative difference between being poor and not being poor or between being unable and being able to achieve personal goals due to economic circumstances. Participating in society is not an all-or-nothing ability. Rather, contemporary standards for what constitutes poverty or mainstream living conditions are nodes along a continuum of material well-being. Yet huge disparities exist between different people's struggles to convert their material resources into some sort of social participation (Rainwater & Smeeding, 2003). For instance, children who grow up in economically underprivileged milieus tend to have fewer life chances than their more advantaged peers. Such inequalities raise political and economic challenges (OECD, 2008). Commonly, societies are considered to be socially more equitable where equality of opportunity reigns supreme as an ideal to be striven for, that is, where everyone has the right to compete on equal footing for benefits such as prestige, wealth, celebrity and other privileges. Ideally, all children in such a society, no matter how humble their origins, can – as a consequence of their own talent and diligence – grow up to be anything their efforts and abilities allow them to be (cf. Molnar, 1985).

The present research addresses important open questions in early childhood care and education research, contributing new pedagogical, historical and sociological insights into the field. Specifically, the research reviews the latest studies into the influence of early childhood programs on children; it analyzes the effects of center-based care and education on children's skills as assessed in primary school in Switzerland; it provides a historical account of childcare in France and in the United States and thereby accounts for current disparities in the use and provision of childcare in these countries; and it illustrates the interplay between desire as a psychological driving force of human behaviour, language development, and educational processes in the early years of life.

2 Equality of opportunity in view of social inequalities: what early childhood care and education strives for

2.1 Social inequalities

In stratified societies, the resources available to individuals as well as the access to social goods including education, health, income, and social participation vary considerably (e.g., Bertelsmann, 2011). Social inequality is not a new phenomenon. Anthropologists and archeologists have long contrasted egalitarian and non-egalitarian societies, characterized either by largely equivalent roles, rights, and privileges for all members or else by ranking and stratification which served to define each individual's position in a societal hierarchy. Yet the fundamental transition to hierarchical societies occurred long before the advent of written history and civilization (Price & Feinman, 1995). Although the pursuit of equality has had a high value for large portions of mankind and has characterized almost all modern secular ideologies in particular in the last few generations (Boulding, 1975), social inequalities continue to exist in at least six key areas: education, work, income, living standards, health, and social participation (OECD, 2011b). A part of the present research focuses specifically on questions surrounding socioeconomic inequalities in early childhood care and education.

2.2 Equality of opportunity

According to our common cultural understanding, we cannot play our social roles or participate meaningfully in communities without the basic resources necessary to carry out our activities. Yet how can individuals gain access to desired goods? Michael Levin's answer to that question is axiomatic: "Everyone agrees that opportunities should be equal" (1981, p. 110). Equality of opportunity is one of the foundational principles of meritocratic societies. Unlike cast societies, where the access to goods and assignment of individuals to social positions is fixed by birth, meritocratic societies are based on the tenet that the distribution of goods and positions is to be subject to some form of competitive process, and all members of society are eligible to compete on equal terms (Arneson, 2009). Often, it is supposed that equality of opportunity is to create a level playing-field where people's social circumstances should not differentially affect their life chances in any serious way (Mason, 2004). In these terms, equality of opportunity exists where everyone is accorded the same chance to develop his or her capabilities and to be acknowledged for personal accomplishments regardless of characteristics such as gender, religion, political stance, color of the skin, or social background, that is, characteristics which are not related to personal performance (e.g., Hradil, 2001).

2.3 Early childhood care and education as a means to combat inequalities

Yet in practice, social background does impact on personal opportunities and success including educational attainment as shown in studies such as the Program for International Student Assessment 'PISA' (2001, 2004, 2007) and the Trends in International Mathematics and Science Study 'TIMMS' (e.g., Baumert et al., 2000; Gonzales et al.; 2009; Schnabel & Schwippert, 2000). From the very beginning, for instance, schools acknowledge and reward skills and knowledge that children learnt not only in school but also in other social settings outside school (Burger, 2011b, 2011c). Hence the extent to which equal opportunity is given for individual members of any given society is questionable. Consequently, early childhood care and education has been proposed to offset the negative impacts of socioeconomic disadvantage and inadequate learning environments on children's development and school achievement since a broad range of high-quality early childhood programs have produced some positive effects on a variety of cognitive, social, and schooling outcomes (Burger, 2010a, 2010b; Karoly, Kilburn, & Cannon, 2005; Yoshikawa, 1995). Many governments have begun to invest in early care and education programs specifically in order to counteract social inequalities and establish equality of educational opportunity for children at the beginning of their school career. By fostering the development of children in the early years, early childhood programs aim to ensure that all children – regardless of their social, cultural, or ethnic background – have the prerequisites for a successful start at school (e.g., Siraj-Blatchford, 2004). Hence early childhood care and education services attempt to enhance those abilities

II Introduction 19

which constitute the basis for beneficial development. By enriching the learning experiences in particular of children at risk of less successful development, they strive to compensate for the unfavorable learning conditions that children face in families who provide less opportunity for informal learning (Barnett, 2011). Children from socioeconomically disadvantaged families and children with special needs, for instance, tend to experience more difficulties in elementary school than their more advantaged counterparts (Burger, 2009). Frequently, they begin school with less developed intellectual skills and they often cannot make up for their developmental delay over the course of the school years. Since many educational systems have not been capable of compensating for socioeconomic inequalities among children (Schütz & Wössmann, 2005a; Wössmann, 2004), efforts to provide early childhood care and education are crucial in particular for two categories of children: those with additional learning needs that are considered to arise mainly from socioeconomic, cultural, ethnic and/or linguistic factors; and those with special needs derived from physical, mental or sensory disabilities (OECD, 2006, p. 92; Stamm, Burger, & Reinwand, 2009; Stamm & Viehhauser, 2009).

3 Research in early childhood care and education: disciplines and methods

3.1 *Scientific disciplines*

On a societal level, early childhood care and education systems can reflect wider interests including respect for children's rights, diversity, social inclusion, and equality in society. These systems can be complex and unwieldy as a field of research and, as a consequence, multiple perspectives can be adopted and different disciplines can be engaged with the topic. Scientific interest in early childhood in general has a long history and pertinent contributions span virtually the full range of academic disciplines including philosophy, psychology, sociology, ethnology, anthropology, history, education, economics, law, biology, and (public) health research. Frequently, research on early childhood care and education in particular has focused specifically on provision, funding, administration, and quality of programs. Furthermore, relevant analyses have examined curricula, social practices, interpersonal relations and interactions, family support and parent involvement, child development and health, ethics in early education settings, or staff training and qualifications, to name just a few. The most common types of research include (longitudinal) evaluation of programs and children's development, policy research, research on theories and practices in early care and education, neuroscience, and economics of education. In addition to these domains of research, a more ample research perspective using a variety of methodologies, rationales and focuses has been witnessed recently. Among the more auspicious avenues of this research are, for instance, socio-historical analyses, cultural studies, and post-modernist research. This research examines the lessons from the past and origins of the present, cultural foundations of care and education, and dominant discourses revolving around early childhood, respectively.

3.2 Research methods

The present research draws on a number of methodical approaches which range from statistical analysis to systematic theoretical and comparative-historical methods. The choice of methods will be explained hereafter and the methods used will be contextualized within the broader field of early childhood research. This field comprises competing theoretical frameworks and methods that relate to differences in epistemological premises. Major methodical disparities exist, for instance, between qualitative and quantitative research which represent two distinct orientations to phenomena being studied. While qualitative research, originating in descriptive analysis, is essentially an inductive process, reasoning from specific situations to more general conclusions, quantitative research tends to be more closely related to deduction, reasoning from principles and theories to particular situations (Wiersma & Jurs, 2005, p. 13). However, quantitative and qualitative approaches are not entirely opposing methodologies; rather each methodical approach has unique strengths to bring to bear on a new generation of knowledge. Hence qualitative and quantitative research are to be viewed as complementary, providing an arsenal of methods with differing capabilities for addressing a given research problem (Goodwin & Goodwin, 1996, p. 5). Thereby, it has to be noted that different types of research methods may have their roots in societal trends and issues and can thus be (unduly) favored or criticized at times. In early childhood care and education research, a broad spectrum of methods is used. Different analyses drawing on a multitude of methods represent the wide variety of methodical strategies and corresponding analytic perspectives adopted in scientific research today. Thus an array of valuable methodical frameworks for research exists, the purpose of research dictating the type of methodical framework that is appropriate to answer specific questions. Although individual methods are far from inherently uniform, they are typically used to describe and analyze concrete topics and issues of research from particular angles – identifying research problems, clarifying their assumptions and consequences, throwing light on the limitations of their approaches, and venturing generalizations from specific techniques according to their own logics of research (Kaplan, 1964). As such, different sets of methods are linked (albeit to varying degrees) with distinct theoretical paradigms, that is, different schemes or patterns of thinking consisting of specific suppositions, theoretical concepts, and abstract propositions.

3.2.1   Quantitative research

Currently, quantitative analyses are predominant in early childhood research. Statistical analyses typically measure children's behaviors and competences, program characteristics, quality aspects and other characteristics by assigning scores and numerical ratings and analyzing these data by means of statistical procedures. The rationale of measurement can be traced to Thorndike's dictum: "If anything exists, it exists in some amount. If it exists in some amount, it can be measured" (1926, p. 38). The array of measures available today is vast. Yet the quality of research resulting from data measurement depends on the quality of the measures used and on the accuracy with which methods are applied and results are interpreted.

3.2.2   Qualitative research

As opposed to quantitative research, qualitative studies in early childhood tend to focus more on providing insights into the social, organizational and policy environments of early childhood care and education by illustrating how these services are, amongst others, embedded within larger socioeconomic structures, produced by labor market organization or coined by various advocates and their visions. Attention is given, for instance, to the historical change of thought and practice, issues of the comparability of concepts, linguistic equivalences, and cultural differences with respect to child-rearing and early childhood education. Unlike quantitative studies which use statistical methods, qualitative analyses including sociocultural and historical approaches draw on theoretical, hermeneutic, and historical methods, and the questions raised usually differ from those of researchers who use quantitative methods.

3.2.3 Methodical pluralism

Different types of (qualitative theoretical or quantitative statistical) methodical approaches allow for conclusions which may be complementary or compete against each other. They represent a constellation of techniques and views shared by particular communities of researchers. Insofar, they are constitutive parts of scientific paradigms, that is, disciplinary matrices of concepts, assumptions and premises that influence how we understand und conceive of particular phenomena (Bryant, 1975). As scientific evolution depends not only on paradigms but also on paradigm shifts, different paradigms must enter into a debate. Paradigms need to be contested and their validity proven. When they compete against each other, their role is inevitably circular. Each group of advocates for a paradigm uses its own paradigm to argue in that paradigm's defense. Proponents of traditional or mainstream paradigms and those of a revolutionary successor both provide exhibits of what scientific practice ought to look like, attempting to persuade each other on the basis of diverging assumptions. Paradigm choice eventually occurs by virtue of the assent of the relevant scientific community (Kuhn, 1996).

3.2.3.1 Methodical diversity as a means for paradigm development

Methodical diversity can be a means to avoid a predominance or undue persistence of certain paradigms and thus serves as a tool for paradigm development. Paradigm development thereby implies technological uncertainty related to the production of knowledge in a given discipline or scientific field. While technological certainty is characterized by wide agreement on certain methods, technological uncertainty is characterized by more intense disputes and varying clarity and straightforwardness in respect to methods and goals of research (Pfeffer, 1993). A given level of paradigm development within a field is linked with processes that maintain the level of development, that is, paradigmatically more developed fields - characterized by a greater number of coexisting paradigms - are likely to advance more consistently and rapidly than paradigmatically less developed fields. Since paradigms rely on assumptions and theories which are related to specific methodical approaches, methodical diversity seems desirable to promote paradigmatic development (Norgaard, 1989).

3.2.3.2 Methodical diversity as a means to avoid ethnocentrism and reductionist conclusions

Recently, early childhood research has been criticized increasingly for relying on ethnocentric perspectives and using identical methodical instruments in different cultural settings (e.g., Stamm, 2011c; Woodhead, 2005). However, children develop as members of cultural communities (Keller, 2011). For this reason, their development is best understood in view of the cultural practices and customs of their environments. Yet to date, research on human development has drawn largely on studies and theories stemming from Europe and North America (Rogoff, 2003). This research, albeit frequently assumed to be universally generalizable, may be culturally biased. For instance, measures of quality in studies on early childhood settings are cultural constructs and do not reflect local values and concerns of different communities systematically (Tobin, 2005). Several scales have been criticized for focusing exclusively on the assessment of practices and competences that are meaningful in one particular culture. Insofar, developmental accounts are tied to cultural assumptions about the developing human being, and they reflect the context and objectives for children's growth mostly within Western societies (Stamm, 2011c; Woodhead, 2005). Yet cultural differences should be respected in definitions of concepts, terminology, and tools to conduct research if ethnocentrism and intellectual provincialism is to be eschewed. Using a wide array of different approaches and methods that are sensitive to cultural differences and specificities in research may decrease the likelihood of culturally partial or ethnocentric assessments and conclusions, although it does not eliminate any risk of simplistic and biased thinking.

3.2.4 Methods applied in the research at hand

The methods adopted in the present studies range from hierarchical regression analyses to a comparative-historical research approach. Different analytical frameworks are chosen in order to answer distinct research questions and enlighten diverse aspects relating to early childhood care and education.

3.2.4.1 Research review

Systematic reviewing is used as a method of identifying and synthesizing the effects of early childhood interventions on children's cognitive development.

The goal is to summarize reliable and valid evidence in a rigorous manner so as to reach conclusions that can be considered more general and thus less context-dependent than those of individual studies. The systematic review of the effects of center-based early childhood care and education is undertaken through a staged process covering a definition of the review objective, research questions and protocol, search for relevant analyses, evaluation of the quality of these analyses and selection of the evidence, data extraction, and synthesis (cf. Victor, 2008). The evidence of individual analyses from the past twenty years is appraised and summarized in a concise overview in order to advance scientific research as well as evidence-based policy initiatives that are to promote children's development effectively.

3.2.4.2 Regression analysis

Multiple hierarchical regressions are used as a statistical technique that allows for assessing the relationships between several independent variables and one dependent variable (Tabachnick & Fidell, 2001). Associations between children's sociocultural background factors, participation in an early childhood care and education setting, and cognitive proficiency levels are analyzed on the basis of numerical data. Multi-item scales are used to assess children's cognitive skills. Specifically, one scale assesses mathematics and one scale assesses vocabulary skills. The results of regression analysis highlight which independent variables predict most of the variance in children's proficiency levels, thereby shedding light on the magnitude of influence of individual predictors.

3.2.4.3 Comparative-historical research

A comparative-historical research method is used as a tool to point out how varying sociopolitical and cultural framework conditions as well as societal discourses have contributed to shape particular approaches in the development of childcare institutions over time. This method allows contrasting country-specific viewpoints, pedagogical concepts, political developments and other factors affecting the practice and theory of childcare. Historical research within comparative discipline enables scholars to trace the conceptualization of ideas and information and the formation of knowledge over time and space (Nóvoa & Yariv-Mashal, 2003). This theoretical framework for comparative studies is dynamic and multidimensional, including all efforts to detect and comment on similarities and dissimilarities between forms of care and education in different times and spaces (cf., Fairbrother, 2005; Sweeting, 2005). The scopes of contrasting phenomena under differing circumstances are multifaceted. Among the purposes of the present comparative study are understanding countries' early childcare systems; improving, developing, and reforming these systems, policies, and practices; and expanding instruments to support any of these endeavors through the elaboration of theoretical schemes. Specifically, by comparing the historical trajectories of institutional childcare across nations, reasons for current disparities in enrollment rates and public funding of institutional early childhood services in France and in the United States are identified and conclusions are drawn regarding societal perceptions as well as purposes, funding, and administration of childcare institutions.

3.2.4.4 Systematic theoretical analysis

A systematic theoretical approach is a technique used to broaden analytic perspectives in domains that cannot be broken down into a number of variables. Theoretical research seeks to understand phenomena by considering a multitude of ideas and thus focusing on a comprehensive picture in one field. The objective is a holistic view and depth of understanding rather than a numeric assessment of data or illustration of results through effect sizes and variance components. A problem-centered approach whereby answers are sought to specific questions ensures an exclusive focus. This basic interpretative type of research draws heavily on document review and all kinds of written material such as autobiographies, reports, literary fiction, letters and so forth (Ary, Jacobs, Sorensen, & Razavieh, 2009). Although the process of conducting theoretical research is not as standardized as the stages of quantitative research, theoretical work must be methodologically explicit and rigorous and analytical concepts need to be defined accurately. In addition, consistency in the use of terms needs to be ensured and theorizations are to be carried out carefully and in accordance with scientific standards (cf., LaBrecque & Sokolow, 1982). The present study into complex interrelations between desire, language, and education draws on a literary work by Elias Canetti as well as on educational and psychoanalytic theories as sources of reflection. It theorizes about critical dimensions in early education and thereby expands current knowledge about driving forces of language development.

3.2.4.5 Methodical attention to cultural diversity

The research at hand attempts to acknowledge cultural diversity by avoiding to judge concepts, terms and viewpoints from varying cultures – defined as patterns of common standpoints, habits, customary practices, and values of a given group of people – based on a system of values and patterns of perception that are exclusively characteristic for Western mainstream society. It adheres to the tenet that beliefs and practices of different cultures cannot be evaluated meaningfully using criteria of only one culture as it seems methodologically unsound to attempt to understand varying cultural practices using the assumptions and categories of solely one culture (cf. Tobin, 2005). Two studies of the present research contrast evidence from different countries and thus to a certain degree different cultures: the review of studies into cognitive effects of early childhood programs and the comparative analysis of the history of childcare in the United States and in France. Both studies are committed to respond to the cultures experienced by the children they describe. They seek to avoid both overgeneralization and 'anything-goes' cultural relativism. However, while striving for value-free description, the analyses are, to a certain extent, inevitably culture-bound themselves. The most effective way of dealing meaningfully with this paradox is by maintaining a high level of self-reflection throughout the analyses. That is, conclusions are questioned against the background of different epistemological premises and thus put into perspective according to these premises. However, a limitation needs to be acknowledged for the international review of effects of early childhood programs as well as for the study into the effects of center-based care and education in Switzerland. Both studies are based on a set of measuring instruments designed to assess cognitive skills as conceptualized by contemporary researchers mostly from the United States and Europe. All of the studies included in the systematic review and in the analysis of center-based care and education in Switzerland were published in English, German, or French. Consequently, the analytic concepts are restricted insofar as they are based on notions typical for communities that speak these languages and they do not necessarily reflect the way other cultures would conceive of cognitive development. This has to be borne in mind when the findings of these studies are interpreted.

4 Terminology

4.1 Use of terms in international research

One of the critical challenges facing studies into any aspect of early childhood care and education consists in using terms accurately because various forms of early care and education have been distinguished including preschool, nursery school, prekindergarten, day care, child care, day nursery, early childhood education, family day care etcetera (Kagan, Tarran, Carson, & Kauerz, 2006). In the vast majority of cases, the term early childhood care and education is used as a collective term to cover any kind of formal institutional programs and services that share the objective of nurturing children's development, growth, and learning under compulsory school age or up to approximately eight years even though these programs and services may draw on a variety of approaches and are funded, operated, and regulated by different administrative bodies. It has to be noted that there is no universally recognized consensus on the age period to which early childhood refers. While the World Organization for Early Childhood Education defines early childhood as the age span from birth to eight years of age, the focus in certain countries is on the period from birth to five or on the age phase immediately prior to mainstream compulsory schooling (Riley, 2008).

In place of the collective term early childhood care and education, a number of shorter terms are used in some cases such as the terms early childhood program and early childhood services. In general, these terms refer to center-based services as distinguished from parental care and informal care by relatives, nannies, or babysitters in private homes. Although in practice, different approaches may focus either more on custody and supportive and nurturing care of children's development or on education in terms of intellectual stimulation, the notion of early childhood care and education suggests that care and education are not separate processes for children during their first years of life. For instance, purely didactic efforts that aim to enhance solely children's intellectual development are likely to undermine what they attempt to improve wherever physical and emotional needs are neglected (UNICEF, 2008).

4.2 Use of terms in Switzerland

In Switzerland, a distinction exists between early childhood services or 'extra-familial care' for children from birth to four years ('Frühbereich') and preschool services for children from four to six years ('Vorschulbereich'). Preschool services are called 'Kindergarten,' 'école enfantine' and 'scuola dell'infanzia' in the German-speaking, French-speaking and Italian-speaking part of the country, respectively. The canton of Tessin constitutes an exception as children in this canton are entitled to participate in preschool services as of three years of age. For both age periods, formal services are differentiated from informal services. Formal services thereby include daycare centers ('Kindertagesstätten') such as daycare, play groups and nurseries ('Krippen,' 'Spielgruppen,' 'Horte'), family day care and institutions for out-of-school care ('schulergänzende Betreuung') such as all-day kindergarten and lunch services. Informal services encompass relative care and privately hired 'Au Pairs' (i.e. youths as of 15 years of age who help a host family with several household chores in a foreign-language region in Switzerland), nannies (i.e. qualified child minders in private homes), domestic aids, child-care services, and private family daycare. These services differ primarily with regard to opening hours, admission criteria, and the type of care that children receive (Stamm et al., 2009).

5 Early childhood care and education: a unified concept

Across most countries, policies on infant care and policies on education have had distinct historical trajectories, developing separately with different conceptions of young children's needs and fractured systems of governance. In most cases, the division of auspices is mirrored by a two-tier organization of services with child care for children from birth to three years and early, pre-primary or preschool, education for children between three and six years (OECD, 2006, p. 46). In many instances, programs are not connected by a comprehensive vision encompassing both support of working parents and learning as well as developmental objectives. Instead, many programs tend to place emphasis on either one goal or the other and thus pursue diverging missions. As a consequence, a service delivery system has emerged with disparate scopes and administrations. Service providers frequently define their own quality standards, staff requirements, and eligibility criteria for children and families (Hansen, 2003).

Even within individual subsystems of provision, disparities can be identified. In some countries, for instance, child care for children below three years of age can be described as a system divided by the socioeconomic background of the families who use it. One tier of child care embraces a custodial system established to care for lower-class children, the purpose of this category of care being to ensure a safe and clean space for children while their parents are at work. A second tier of child care is designed to provide additional socialization and education to children of more wealthy families (Weinraub, Hill, & Hirsh-Pasek, 2001, p. 235). While the first tier tends to be described as a social welfare program, the second tier is frequently labeled as an educational service.

Where a distinction is made between child (or infant) care and early education, child care typically refers to the non-parental care of children by family members, friends, child-care providers, or center-based child-care providers. Early education, in turn, embraces more formal programs that rely on curricula with specific educational scopes below the age when compulsory schooling begins, generally encompassing kindergartens, pre-kindergartens, and pre-schools. A good percentage of the world's child care depends on informal arrangements. In most instances, these arrangements are unlicensed and unregulated and the quality provided can therefore vary considerably (Lally, 2007, pp. 442ff.). As the provision for children is typically characterized by a combination of informal and formal, private and public services, access to a coherent system of early childhood care services is not a given and divergences exist in terms of eligibility, funding, programming, staffing, and regulation, even within countries. Early childhood education in terms of pre-primary education for three-to-six-year-olds, on the other hand, tends to form part of national early childhood systems in most OECD member countries. In these countries, the coordination of early childhood services with education is relatively advanced; accessibility or eligibility criteria of such services are similar to those pertaining in the public educational system (OECD, 2006, p. 58).

Recently, an increasing number of authors have acknowledged the need for integrated early care and education (e.g., Stamm, 2010a). According to the National Research Council in the United States, for instance, "education and care in the early years are two sides of the same coin" (Bowman, Donovan, & Burns, 2001, p. 306). Children need to be well-cared-for in order to develop intellectual skills; and they need education not only to exploit their learning potential but also to develop social skills (Hansen, 2003; Stamm & Edelmann, 2010). The relatively recent coining of the neologism 'educare' acknowledges and corroborates this perspective although it does not specify the exact content of the services and pedagogical approaches that the term aims to describe (Caldwell, 1991). Instead, the term attempts to convey a unified concept describing a broad and inclusive type of service for children that operates along a continuum of time. By introducing the term 'educare,' advocates of a broad concept covering the full range of common services for children aimed to prevent a profusion of labels for primarily one type of program that includes conceptually what is required for early development rather than excludes either one or the other aspect of service and thus fosters the endorsement of an artificial dichotomy between care and education. The 'educare' concept thereby intends to communicate the idea that services should offer components of both programs previously conceptualized as disconnected and distinct. Since this concept is not established firmly in research, policy, or practice, and most research literature continues to use the term early childhood care and education, the present studies draw on the term early childhood care and education where applicable, defining it as a uniform, coherent concept that embraces all the aspects that children need in early childhood programs.

6 Ideological divide between childcare and education for young children

Extra-familial early childhood care and education is an ideological issue insofar as diverging viewpoints are adopted by different actors in society and while some of these viewpoints are underpinned by scientific evidence, others are not (Ahnert, 2010; Moss, Krenn-Wache, Na, & Bennett, 2004; Pungello & Kurtz-Costes, 2000; Randall, 2000). In Switzerland, for instance, along with attempts to implement a new school entry model (the 'Grund-/Basisstufe'), more intense debates have arisen recently as to whether a child ought to be cared for primarily at home by its parents or in an institutional setting (e.g., Stamm, 2009b, 2011a). Right-wing politicians have called for a strengthening of the family in the upbringing of children as well as for a mother who is to be constantly available for her children. They criticize the intrusion of the state in matters that they deem to be distinctly private and they raise concerns about the predominance and imperatives of a neoliberal market ideology that seems oblivious of traditional child-rearing practices in the family. At the same time, they fear an outsourcing of child-raising which will be organized and controlled by the state and allow for a manipulation of children's thoughts and behaviors. Left-wing politicians, on the other hand, have advocated a more extensive provision of early childhood services which are, amongst others, supposed to allow mothers to take on a gainful occupation. While opponents of early childhood services have emphasized that institutional care can be harmful to child development, proponents have argued that children can benefit from exposure to institutional services in terms of the acquisition of social and cognitive skills (Stamm, 2011b).

The discussions in Switzerland echo controversies in other Western countries. Elkind (1988, 1989), for instance, coined the term of the 'hurried child' and cautioned against overly achievement-oriented parents who unduly put their children under pressure as they intend to advance their development. Postman (1982) warned against the 'disappearance of childhood' in case social and cultural frameworks and attitudes do not protect the distinct status of children in society. Finally, Dollase (2007) summarized studies from the 1970s which analyzed the influence of early schooling of three-to-five-year-old children on academic learning, highlighting that the findings show no practical advantages of early schooling. On the other hand, advocates stressed the importance of institutional early childhood care and education in particular for those children whose home environments do not allow for a sound development of capacities (e.g., Campbell, Pungello, Miller-Johnson, Burchinal, & Ramey, 2001; Schweinhart & Weikart, 1997; Spiess, Büchel, & Wagner, 2003). Frequently, they call for an upgrading of early childhood professions and reforms in the education of professional staff (e.g., Robert Bosch Stiftung, 2011). An analysis of the history of institutional childcare in Great Britain, France and the United States of America indicates that there has been a changing pattern of approval and rejection of childcare institutions over time (Burger, 2011a). The disagreements between proponents and opponents revealed a great deal about the ongoing disputes about childcare, displaying diverging viewpoints and doctrines which characterized the overall dynamics of childcare movements (Burger, 2012, in press, a, b).

In Switzerland, the intensity of the political discourses varies widely across cantons and municipalities.[1] While German-speaking cantons tend to have political debates about childcare, the French- and Italian-speaking cantons hardly politicize this issue because childcare provided by people other than the parents is more common and thus less contested: more than 80 percent of children between birth and four years of age are attended to in early childhood services or by childminders in these cantons (Schulte-Haller, 2009). Moreover, different perspectives on child-rearing and childcare are mirrored by disparities in the demand for childcare in different regions of Switzerland. The highest demand for institutional childcare for children between birth and four years was identified in the urban areas of the Romandy and the Tessin (60%), followed by the demand in the rural areas in these cantons (47%) and by the urban areas of

---

1   Recently, five parliamentary initiatives called for an expansion of the childcare infrastructure on a federal level in order to increase the compatibility of family and work responsibilities and to promote beneficial development of socially disadvantaged children (Schulte-Haller, 2009, p. 30).

German-speaking cantons (45%). In rural areas of German-speaking Switzerland, finally, only 34 percent of families wished to use institutional childcare for their children (Iten et al., 2005). These results reflect different conceptions of and attitudes toward the organization of family life. In the German-speaking part of Switzerland, the traditional male-as-breadwinner model of family organization is more widespread than in the other parts of the country as shown, for instance, by a lower female labor force participation and by more traditional ways of voting when family policies are at stake (e.g., the vote on maternity insurance in 2004; see Schmid et al., 2011). In addition, differences in cultural values concerning family life can be assumed between rural and urban areas, since families in urban regions often choose more equitable forms of division of labor between men and women (Buchmann & Fend, 2002). According to a recent study, parents' convictions that mothers ought to be the primary caregivers for their children diminishes the use of extra-familial services for six-year-olds among these families. However, parental attitudes toward a gender-specific division of labor or toward parenting styles had no significant effect in this regard. Hence the fact that extra-familial care and education institutions are used more frequently in cities than on the countryside might depend primarily on the availability of services rather than on differences in cultural values and parents' ideals (Schmid, Kriesi, & Buchmann, 2011).

7 Use of extra-familial early childhood care and education

7.1 Rates of use in Switzerland

In 2007, 46.9 percent of two-parent families and 72.0 percent of single parents used extra-familial childcare for children below seven years of age in Switzerland: 24.4 percent of two-parent families used childcare for up to one day and 22.5 percent used childcare for more than one day per week; 26.1 percent of one-parent families used childcare for one day per week and 45.9 percent used childcare for more than one day per week (SAKE, 2010).[2] In 2009, children of two-parent families were cared for by relatives (53.2%), acquaintances and neighbors (5.4%), other persons such as nannies (3.4%), in-home daycare pro-

---

2 A statistic that did not distinguish between single-parent and two-parent families showed that out of the families who used early childhood services for their children, about 20 percent used them for one day, about 33 percent for two days, and about 20 percent for three days per week. Thereby, 64 percent of these children spent the whole day in the institutions whereas 33 percent spent half a day in institutions (BSV, 2010).

viders (14.1%), institutional settings such as daycare centers and all-day kindergarten (34.7%), out-of-home lunch and after-school care (2.0%) and other care (1.5%). These figures do not add up to 100 percent because some children were cared for in multiple settings (ibid.).

7.2   Rates of use in OECD countries

According to the most recent statistic published by the Organization for Economic Cooperation and Development (OECD, 2010b), the enrollment rates of children under five years of age in public and private early childhood care and education institutions in Switzerland are relatively low when viewed in international comparison. In 2008, 27.2 percent of children age four and under were enrolled in Switzerland (as a percentage of the population aged three to four years) whereas 46.9 percent of this population were enrolled in the United States of America, 110.1 percent of this population were enrolled in France, 101.5 percent were enrolled in Germany, and 71.5 percent were enrolled in the OECD member countries on average.[3]

7.3   Determinants of the use of early childhood care and education

To date, it has not been well researched in all of Switzerland how families who use institutional early childhood services differ from those who do not use any comparable services. Only one recent study analyzed characteristics of families who used extra-familial early childhood care and education institutions for six-year-old children (Schmid et al., 2011). This study investigated the proportion of children who were attended to in families and in formal early childhood institutions. In addition, it assessed the influence of provision of institutions as well as the influence of parental values on the patterns of use of early childhood care and education institutions in Switzerland. Although the study does not allow for conclusions regarding children below the age of six years, it can be interpreted as an indicator of familial backgrounds of the clientele of early childhood services. The main findings of this study are as follows: More than half of the six-year-olds were cared for exclusively in the nuclear family at home whereas 44.3 percent were cared for outside the nuclear family in addition, notably in infor-

---

3   For further information regarding the use of early childhood service in various OECD countries, see the Starting Strong report by the Organization for Economic Cooperation and Development (OECD, 2006).

mal care by grandparents or in formal institutions such as daycare centers and all-day kindergartens. Half of the children who were in extra-familial care spent less than two days per week out of home. Thereby, a number of factors influenced the use of extra-familial care: First, parents with higher workloads were more likely to use extra-familial care. Second, parents with higher educational degrees used formal extra-familial care more frequently than those with lower degrees. Third, families with higher household incomes were more likely to use formal extra-familial care.[4] Fourth, single-parent families used extra-familial care institutions more frequently than two-parent families. Fifth, the higher the supply of formal early childhood institutions in communities, the more families used the institutions. Sixth, while parental attitudes toward a gender-related division of labor or toward specific parenting styles did not influence the use of extra-familial care and education institutions, a traditional attitude toward motherhood – which involves the idea that the mother should be the primary caregiver for the child – diminished the use of extra-familial institutions. In sum, family characteristics predicted the greatest proportion of variance in the use of institutions for six-year-old children (notably parental workload, educational background and household income), followed by the local supply of institutions and by norms and values such as parental attitudes toward motherhood. This suggests that the analysis of social and cultural norms may prove instructive in studies into the use and structure of early childhood care and education within and across countries.

8 Why early childhood care and education has evolved in economically developed countries

The global early childhood care and education landscape (Hayden, 2000) is shaped by the political, economic, social, and cultural contexts of different countries. The development of services can be traced to at least four broad challenges. First, the increasing influx of women into salaried employment created a growing need for provision of early childhood care and education services. Second, demand for provision has arisen in response to increased immigration and falling fertility rates particularly in European countries. Third, the traditional model of child-rearing with a male breadwinner and a female care-

---

[4] The effect of household income varied with the density of the provision of formal early childhood institutions. In communities without daycare centers, the families with the highest household incomes were more than three times more likely to use (private) formal care than families with lower incomes.

II Introduction

giver has lost its dominant position in view of endeavors to reconcile work and family responsibilities on a more equitable basis for women and men. Finally, governments have become increasingly mindful of the importance of early care and education as a means to attempt to break the cycle of poverty and social inequality in society (OECD, 2006, p. 20; Riley, 2008). This sociopolitical context is illustrated very briefly in the following sections as it helps understand the four principal studies of the present research as well as their main conclusions in more depth. However, contextualizing research within social, political, economic and cultural frameworks is not only an academic virtue because it allows for interpreting results more carefully. It is also a means of recognizing that every child is born into a historically contingent context which influences the child's experiences and development.

8.1 Development of female labor force participation

Over the last decades, the labor force participation of women aged 25 to 54 years increased in most OECD member countries (OECD, 2011d). In the G7 economies (a group of seven industrialized countries with large economies including France, Germany, Italy, Japan, United Kingdom, United States and Canada), for instance, the average female participation rate in the labor market increased from 58 percent in 1993 to 66 percent in 2003 (OECD, 2006). The increase in female employment influences patterns of family life and modes of child-rearing. In several countries, the changes in female employment have driven policy-makers to modify policies regarding early care and education. Frequently, modifying policies has been recognized as a necessity because women alternate between labor, leisure, and home production including childcare and because the preferences for women's employment are high in many countries. In the member countries of the European Union, for instance, only one in ten couples with young children prefers the traditional male as a breadwinner and female as a caregiver model of family organization although this model is still more widespread in practice (Jaumotte, 2003).

8.2 Immigration and fertility rates

Two major demographic challenges further spur policymakers and educational authorities in economically more advanced countries to provide early childhood care and education services: first, large numbers of immigrant and second-language children among the population of primary school children; second, falling fertility rates and accompanying population decline.

8.2.1 Immigration and children's at-risk status

Research has shown that factors related to migration such as speaking a foreign native language can be regarded as a risk for beneficial child development. Frequently, children from immigrant families achieve poorer results than their native peers in a variety of standardized cognitive tests (Dubowy, Ebert, von Maurice, & Weinert, 2008). This is all the more problematic as children with a migration or minority background are often less likely than their native-born counterparts to participate in center-based care and education as compared to parental care prior to kindergarten (Turney & Kao, 2009). Yet such services could familiarize children with the official language as well as with the culture and customs of a given country. Both social and cognitive development can be influenced favorably through appropriate use of well-designed services. Recognizing that the probability of school failure increases with the number of at-risk indicators such as minority status, low parental education, parental unemployment, low social class of parents' occupations (including semi-skilled or unskilled workers) or a poor home learning environment (Pungello et al., 2010; Sylva et al., 2003), some host countries take measures to help immigrant children accustom more easily to the new society and thus overcome their at-risk status.

8.2.2 Low fertility and demographic decline

According to demographic forecasts, most OECD countries will not remain capable of guaranteeing future labor supply if they aim to maintain pension and public health obligations for their ageing populations unaltered (OECD, 2011c). In all member countries except Mexico and the United States, the birth rates are below replacement levels. Hence the ratio of the population of the over 65 year-olds to the total labor force is expected to increase in the future. This trend is supported by the fact that increasing numbers of women pursue education at higher levels (including the tertiary level) and working careers. The increase in women's labor participation has also been linked with a decline in fertility. Against the background of decreasing fertility rates, some governments have modified family and childcare policies in order to help couples to have children and to combine work and family responsibilities. Such policies include parental leave, subsidies to purchase childcare and family-friendly work practices (OECD, 2006).

8.3 Gender equality

In modern societies, a lack of equality among men and women persists. There are different dimensions to gender inequality. For instance, socially constructed conceptions of women menace the potential of women to obtain specific opportunities, positions and merits in society. Different forms of discrimination can deny women access to educational institutions, achievement in education, or a particular status in the job market. Legal and economic inequality exist in society and marriage and differences can be testified in terms of women's and men's empowerment as measured, for instance, by the percentage of women in parliament or the year when women earned the right to vote in democracies (Dollar & Gatti, 1999). Hereafter, three of the most outstanding challenges for women are considered in more detail: equal opportunity in the employment market, the opportunity to combine motherhood with a working career, and a more equitable sharing of child-rearing and household chores between men and women.

8.3.1 Equality of opportunity in the employment market

Among the profound labor market developments in the course of the post-World War II period has been the continued progress made by women. Female participation in the job market has expanded and the wage gap relative to men has narrowed in many countries. However, in spite of the advances societies have made to promote women's equality, significant inequalities continue to exist including unequal access to jobs and unequal occupational choices, earning gaps between the sexes, and, in some instances, tax penalties on women's work related to their husband's earnings or a loss of benefits and allowances for a second wage earner.

8.3.2 The opportunity to reconcile motherhood with a working career

For women with child care responsibilities, full and equal achievement in the work force is often less realistic (Bravo, Sanhueza, & Urzua, 2008; Frug, 1979). Women are more likely to be in part-time work that is more precarious and poorly paid. In addition, unemployment rates are higher for women than for men in many countries. Specifically, mothers of two or more children are considerably less likely to be in employment than women without children and their total earnings are therefore significantly lower than those of childless women (Clery, Lee, & Knapp, 1998; OECD, 2002, 2006). However, policies that increase employment flexibility such as part-time opportunities and reduce the costs of children (child benefits, parental leave, and subsidized childcare and early education) can counteract the negative correlation between fertility rates and female employment rates. For instance, in the Nordic countries where more generous social policies are implemented, fertility rates and women's market participation are both high whereas in Southern countries, where social policies are less supportive for women, both fertility and labor market participation are lower (Del Boca & Locatelli, 2006).

8.3.3 Sharing of child-rearing and household chores between men and women

Although an increasing number of women work in many countries, there has been little change in how social and family life is organized and there has been no comparable process of change toward a redistribution of domestic workload. As long as women bear the brunt where work and family duties are not reconciled, women experience significant limitations and discrimination such as barriers to their entering the labor market, fewer job opportunities due to fewer educational achievement, and lower income (ILO-UNDP, 2009). Adema and Whiteford (2007) demonstrated that women in full-time employment devote more time, on the whole, to work than men. Frequently, women face the challenge of holding a job, attending to household work and raising children. A distinct imbalance in gender roles was shown, for example, in France where mothers with children under 15 years of age devote 1 hour and 35 minutes per day to parenting whereas fathers devote only 31 minutes to parenting (OECD, 2004). Although gender-based discrimination at home cannot be combated directly or exclusively through policies, it would be desirable to encourage societal discourses which promote gender equity in families.

8.4 Child poverty and social disparities

Early childhood care and education has been used as a means to reduce child poverty and educational disadvantage among children from underprivileged families. Family poverty and social deprivation are related to poorer educational achievement and greater risk of school failure which increases the likelihood for a host of negative intellectual, social and professional outcomes among children, adolescents and young adults (Leone et al., 2003). The links between socioeconomic status and child development have been identified in numerous studies including the Program for International Student Assessment PISA (OECD, 2010c). Many associations between family background and children's performance are well understood (OECD, 2006, 2010). One main reason for disparities in the achievement of children from different social backgrounds may be the differences in the quality of the home learning environment and the number of opportunities for informal learning outside of schools. Children from middle- and upper-class families tend to have daily access to cultural resources, social codes and language patterns as well as vocabulary which are valued in mainstream education. In addition, better educated parents may choose to interact with their children in a manner that will help them succeed more easily at school. The availability of particular household possessions such as a quiet place to study can constitute an advantage for learning and acquiring intellectual skills. Finally, better-off parents are more likely to provide more educational resources at home, choose schools that will supply such resources, or pay for private tutoring. Children in higher-risk contexts, on the other hand, may not experience successful role models or acquire the basic competencies and motivations underlying learning processes such as language, adequate understanding of abstract concepts, and self-regulation. According to Leseman (2002), low socioeconomic status can be linked with poorer informal learning at home, resulting in children being less well prepared for formal schooling. Family background is also likely to be associated with intellectual performance and social development through community and neighborhood contexts. That is, more stimulating contexts influence school performance positively (Pong & Hao, 2007) whereas a lack of access of children in poor neighborhoods to adequate education institutions can be a source of poorer academic development. Even where access to adequate schools is guaranteed, the achievement gap between children from different family backgrounds can persist and become more pronounced over time.

Research demonstrates that early childhood care and education contributes to overcome the negative effects of poverty and cultural deprivation and to put at-risk children on the path to more success in school (Barnett, 1998; Jarousse,

Mingat, & Richard, 1992; Leseman, 2002; Plaisance & Rayna, 2004; Thorpe et al., 2004). While some studies found no benefits of early childhood services on children's development, a great deal of evidence suggests that positive effects can be expected in particular where programs are of high quality and designed to enhance vulnerable children's school-related behavior and achievement. In general, program benefits are most marked for children who suffer from some kind of socioeconomic or cultural disadvantage in a society that does not value their particular background characteristics. In some cases, the academic and behavioral gains children make in center-based programs can persist into the school years and even into young adulthood. However, it has to be noted that longer-term effects are unlikely to be identified unless well-funded, developmentally appropriate programs provide sustain support during subsequent school years (Brooks-Gunn, 2003). This holds true above all where children grow up in families and neighborhoods that do not provide adequate intellectual and social stimulation to support beneficial child development or where children end up attending poor-quality elementary schools.

9 Characteristics of effective early childhood care and education programs

The research literature concerning key features of effective early childhood care and education has been relatively consistent during the last decades, highlighting the importance of a number of features including duration, intensity, quality, curriculum and breadth of programs. As the international review of effects of early childhood programs as well as the empirical analysis of effects of center-based early childhood care and education on cognitive skills of children in Switzerland considers influences of duration and intensity, previous evidence about duration and intensity is illustrated in what follows.

9.1 Program duration

Although duration and intensity of program participation are frequently interrelated, some researchers have attempted to isolate the effects of these variables on child development in order to identify the ideal dosage of center-based services for children (cf., Stamm, 2010b). These studies are relatively rare. Typically, studies into the effects of duration have analyzed the number of months per year as well as the number of years of program participation. Up to now, pertinent research has not shown clear tendencies in the findings. While some studies suggest that a longer duration yield greater positive effects for program attendees (Büchner & Spiess, 2007; Caille, 2001; U.S. Department of Health and Human Services, 2005), others found that longer lasting programs do not necessarily bring about more beneficial development (NICHD Early Child Care Research Network, 2007, NICHD Early Child Care Research Network, 2001; Sammons et al., 2008c). For instance, Gullo and Burton (1992) found that a longer duration of participation in early childhood services boosts children's academic readiness in kindergarten. Jarousse, Mingat and Richard (1992) revealed that a longer duration of participation in the French preschool reduces the probability of retention in the first grade. The Effective Preschool and Primary Education project – Europe's largest longitudinal investigation into the effects of early care and education on children's developmental outcomes – revealed that the number of months a child attended an early childhood institution was associated positively with developmental progress until the start of primary school (Sammons et al., 2004). This effect was stronger for academic development than for social and behavioral development (Sylva, Melhuish, Sammons, Siraj-Blatchford, & Taggart, 2008). However, the positive result disappeared in subsequent years. At the age of eleven years, on all cognitive and social outcomes there were no longer significant net effects for duration of participation in preschool (Sammons et al., August 2008b). In Germany, Seyda (2009) established that a longer kindergarten attendance increased the likelihood of attending a higher level secondary school in Germany. Andersson (1992), in turn, found that the school performance and socioemotional development of children entering center care or family daycare before the age of one year was better at age thirteen. Overall, however, more sustained effects are more likely to appear where extended services over and above the preschool years continue to advance children's developmental gains (Reynolds, Temple, Robertson, & Mann, 2001).

A number of studies analyzed the impact of the enrollment age of individual children in programs. Note that these studies assessed the effects of program duration, explicitly taking into account children's age of entry into programs. A study conducted in France found that a starting age of two years was associated with a slightly better subsequent school achievement than a starting age of three years (Caille, 2001). This finding is in accordance with evidence from an U.S. American study whereby children who entered preschool at three or four years scored higher on a first-grade readiness test than children who entered preschool at five years of age (Gullo & Burton, 1992). However, using data from the NICHD study, Belsky repeatedly pointed out risks associated with early child care, demonstrating that early, extensive, and continuous nonmaternal care is linked with worse parent-child relations, heightened levels of aggression and noncompliance, poorer social adjustment, and distress during separations from the mother (Belsky, 1988a, 1988b, 2001, 2006). These results are not supported consistently by other studies (NICHD Early Child Care Research Network, 1998, NICHD Early Child Care Research Network, 1997). However, they indicate that factors other than the duration of programs including the intensity of programs also have significant effects on child development.

9.2 Program intensity

On the whole, two types of studies evaluating the influence of program intensity on child development exist. While the first type compares half-day with full-day programs, usually focusing on kindergartens, the second type analyzes the effects of specific units of time such as the number of days per week and the number of hours per day.

Research concerning the effects of full- versus half-day kindergartens typically comes from the United States and often analyzes academic gains. The evidence provided by this research has been ambiguous. A study by Fusaro and Royce (1995) showed that children who attended full-day kindergarten had higher scores on a reading test than their counterparts in half-day kindergartens although Sergesketter and Gilman (1988) found no such effect. The results from another study suggest that full-day kindergarten attendees demonstrate higher mathematics and reading achievement at the end of kindergarten, but this benefit disappeared by the end of kindergarten or by the end of the first grade and was no longer found in subsequent school years (Votruba-Drzal, Li-Grining, & Maldonado-Carreño, 2008; Wolgemuth, Cobb, Winokur, Leech, & Ellerby, 2006). This result is in line with the finding that readiness for the first grade is higher among full day attendees (Elicker & Mathur, 1997) as well as with a study concluding that full-day kindergarten is related positively to school performance at least through the first grade (Cryan, 1992). Other studies do not confirm the positive short-term effects (Hatcher, Schmidt, & Cook, 1979). However, a meta-analysis into the academic effects summarized that, on the whole, full-day kindergarten participants manifest greater achievement than half-day participants (Fusaro, 1997). On the other hand, although research into the social and behavioral effects is scarcer, there is reason to believe that the effects of full-day kindergarten on social and behavioral development are more inconsistent than those on cognitive achievement (Herry, Maltais, & Thompson, 2007). Studies investigating more specific units of time such as days per week and hours per day of program participation mostly focus on children below kindergarten age. A study by Loeb, Bridges, Bassok, Fuller and Rumberger (2007) established a positive association between the intensity of preschool and intellectual development although this effect varied with family income and race. Specifically, children from low-income families developed better academic skills whereas those from high-income families did not and English-proficient Hispanic children gained more than their white or black counterparts. On the other hand, a higher intensity of preschool was linked with more problematic behavior at the beginning of kindergarten. This held true in particular for children from high-income families whereas the behavioral development of children from low-income families was affected less negatively.

The NICHD study of early child care, a comprehensive longitudinal study examining how differences in childcare experiences are linked with children's social, emotional, and intellectual development, demonstrated no relations between a higher intensity of childcare and cognitive or language development (NICHD Early Child Care Research Network, 2000), but it established adverse effects on social development (NICHD Early Child Care Research Network, 2003). Notably, a high intensity of exposure to out-of-home childcare was related to heightened behavior problems according to caregivers at two years of age (NICHD Early Child Care Research Network, 1998) as well as to less harmonious mother-child interactions during the first three years (NICHD Early Child Care Research Network, 1999). More childcare hours also predicted more problematic social behavior, fewer prosocial behaviors, and more conflict as reported by caregivers up to 54 months of age (NICHD Early Child Care Research Network, 2006). Longer-term follow-ups showed that more extensive exposure to center care predicted more teacher-reported externalizing behavior problems up to twelve years (Belsky et al., 2007). This result was not moderated by age which means that the unfavorable effect did not dissipate as did other effects of amount of childcare on social functioning. A more recent study corroborated this finding, showing that more intensive non-relative care from birth to 54 months yielded greater impulsivity and risk taking until 15 years (Vandell, Belsky, Burchinal, Steinberg, & Vandergrift, 2010). However, the adverse effects can be mediated by other childcare characteristics such as the group size (McCartney et al., 2010).

10 Regulation of early childhood care and education

Examination of the history of childcare in France and the United States indicates that regulation of institutions offering services to young children is crucial not only to ensure quality of services but also to prevent institutions from being criticized and discredited by opponents in the long run. For instance, over time, institutions in France were regulated by departments or the state more strictly than institutions in the United States. As a consequence, many of their services tended to be more trustworthy and socially legitimized (Burger, 2012). As the number of children in early childhood care and education increases, the regulation of services increasingly becomes a public responsibility. The type and extent of regulation frequently varies not only between countries but also within countries as a function of regions and the nature of the programs. An effective regulatory system helps ensuring children's rights to care and education settings that protect them from harm and advance their health and development. In the United States, for instance, states with more effective regulatory structures supply higher-quality early childhood services (Phillips, Howes & Whitebook, 1992). Regulation is useful to define and enforce standards as well as to ensure some degree of equity for children and families in various neighborhoods. For instance, where regulations exist, administrations and governments may be more likely to supply poorer neighborhoods with financing, buildings, pedagogical materials and other structural inputs in order to provide for more social equity. Public regulation of early childhood services thereby represents a basic level of protection afforded to all children in settings outside their family. It also allows for national coordination of supply and facilitates the implementation of those program features that research and practice demonstrate as reducing harm and supporting child development.

11 The role of the family in early childhood care and education

Research often pays attention to questions revolving around institutional care and education. However, the present studies into the cognitive effects of center-based care and education highlight the significance of various family characteristics for child development (Burger, 2010b, 2011b). Hence families are as much a part of the process of early care and education as are caregivers, educators, particular facilities, different curricula, pedagogical practices, quality standards, and regulations etcetera. Research documents the importance of efforts to involve parents and families in many aspects related to early care and education since a number of family variables can influence children's school careers and well-being: these include parents' educational aspirations (Stamm, 2005a, 2005b), the frequency with which children engage in activities such as eating meals with the family, learning activities with the alphabet and numbers, being read to (Melhuish et al., 2008), parenting practices (Zupancic & Kavcic, 2011), different kinds of learning stimulation at home (Bradley, 2002; Bradley, Corwyn, McAdoo, & Coll, 2001; Broberg, Wessels, Lamb, & Hwang, 1997; Luster & Dubow, 1992), and families' socioeconomic circumstances (e.g., Burger, 2011b; McLoyd, 1998). An important lesson derives from a finding of the NICHD study of early child care investigating children in their first years of life, notably that family factors and processes are typically more predictive of child functioning than childcare factors and processes in childcare institutions for young children. Hence families contribute to children's wellbeing although this may be a function of both shared genes and environment effects (Belsky, 2001, p. 855). An investigation by Christian, Morrison and Bryant (1998) revealed that the family literacy environment (e.g., daily reading, taking children to the library, monitoring television etc.) had positive causal links with academic measures in kindergarten: Children of less educated mothers who scored high on the family literacy environment scale outperformed children whose better-educated mothers engaged in fewer literacy-promoting activities with their children. In Switzerland, the first results of a longitudinal study conducted at the University of Fribourg confirm the importance of family factors for children's intellectual development. In particular, they indicate that positive interactions with children impact beneficially on children's skills at three to four years of age (Negrini, Sabini, Knoll, & Stamm, 2011; see also Stamm, Knoll, & Sabini, 2011). On the whole, the family has an important place in the lives of children. Acknowledging that the family and early childhood institutions have complementary roles in the provision of early care and education is therefore crucial for children's development (Lumsden & Doyle, 2009, pp. 167ff.).

III New contributions to early childhood care and education research

The present research essentially makes four major contributions to the literature. Although numerous authors have investigated the effects of early childhood care and education on children's cognitive development, the results of more recent studies have not been reviewed systematically across national boundaries. The first contribution therefore provides a meticulous synthesis of the primary research that assessed cognitive effects of early childhood care and education programs in different countries, analyzing whether these programs helped to ensure equality of educational opportunity for children from various social backgrounds in these countries. Second, while empirical evidence about the influence of early childhood programs on children may be externally valid, country-specific biases cannot be excluded categorically since a majority of important studies have been conducted in the United States and in the United Kingdom. In Switzerland, for instance, there has been no study into the effects of center-based care and education on direct measures of children's cognitive proficiency levels as measured in primary school. For this reason, the second study assesses effects of early institutional care and education experience on the cognitive proficiency of first graders. Third, the standing of childcare institutions varies across societies. For instance, France and the United States differ markedly in terms of the use and provision of institutional childcare. Hence it is worth analyzing the reasons for these differences. The third study investigates the historical origins of those disparities and thus enhances the understanding of current approaches in and attitudes toward childcare in the two societies. Fourth, a lack of research into the connections between desire, language and education can be identified. The analysis of Elias Canetti's autobiography «The tongue set free» addresses this desideratum by studying the interrelationships between the analytic notion of desire as a driving force of human behavior, language development and educational processes.

This section encompasses the four original studies, presenting notably (1) the international review of the effects of early interventions for children from different social backgrounds, (2) the evaluation of the influence of center-based care and education on children's skills as measured in primary school in Switzerland, (3) the comparative-historical analysis of ideas relating to childcare in France and in the United States of America, and (4) the study into the interrelations between desire, language and education in Elias Canetti's work «The tongue set free».

How does early childhood care and education affect cognitive development? An international review of the effects of early interventions for children from different social backgrounds[5]

Abstract: A number of authors have investigated the impact of early childhood education and care programs on the development of children. Often they have focused on the effects on children from socio-economically disadvantaged families. To assess the effects of various preschool programs on cognitive development, recent key studies were reviewed. In addition, the extent to which these programs could establish equal educational opportunities for children from different social backgrounds was evaluated. Program start, intensity, and duration were considered. The findings indicate that the vast majority of recent early education and care programs had considerable positive short-term effects and somewhat smaller long-term effects on cognitive development and that in relative terms children from socioeconomically disadvantaged families made as much or slightly more progress than their more advantaged peers. Despite this, early childhood education and care cannot compensate completely for developmental deficits due to unfavorable learning conditions in disadvantaged milieus. Implications for research and policy are discussed.

Children from disadvantaged families often experience particular difficulties at school. They enter school with fewer academic skills than their more advantaged peers, and they often lag behind in their cognitive development during the later school years (Stipek & Ryan, 1997). During the 1960s, these difficulties were attributed to adverse learning conditions in families that do not provide their children with what is required for successful development in the early years. In 1965, U.S. president Lyndon B. Johnson therefore implemented Head Start, the most widespread compensatory education programs for disadvantaged preschool children. Since then, numerous early education and care programs

---

5 Reprinted from *Early Childhood Research Quarterly* with permission from Elsevier. Citation details: Burger, K. (2010). How does early childhood care and education affect cognitive development? An international review of the effects of early interventions for children from different social backgrounds. *Early Childhood Research Quarterly, 25*(2), 140-165.

have been launched in many countries and researchers have begun to investigate the effects of these programs on the development of children.

Most of the 30 member countries of the OECD - an international organization committed to democratic government and the market economy - became concerned about early care and education after the Program for International Student Assessment (PISA, 2001, 2004, 2007) had highlighted the close relationship between school attainment and student social background for a number of countries. Up to now, the educational systems have not been able to compensate for social inequalities (e.g., Schütz & Wössmann, 2005a; Wössmann, 2004). Many experts have therefore heralded preschool programs as a promising means of establishing equal educational opportunities for children from different social backgrounds. Early interventions have been assumed to reduce school readiness gaps among children from families with low educational aspirations and/or low socio-economic status. Recently, the United Nations have also considered preschool programs as a potential means of fostering school readiness. Within the scope of the six Education for All goals adopted at the World Education Forum in Dakar in 2000, the expansion and improvement of comprehensive early childhood care and education - especially for the most vulnerable and disadvantaged children-was declared to be the first of six goals of education for all (UNESCO, 2008). The priority given to early child support and development was justified by the claim that setting strong foundations for learning begins in the earliest years of life (UNESCO, 2007).

Hence there appears to be consensus that the early years are particularly important for the development of basic skills which will help children cope with everyday requirements later on. However, few reviews have been carried out of studies of the effectiveness of early interventions in different countries and with different pedagogical approaches. The present paper therefore reviews recently published key studies from Europe, North America, and Asia in order to explore the extent to which preschool programs affect the development of children across national borders. Most earlier reviews of preschool programs have focused on studies in the U.S. (Anderson et al., 2003; Barnett, 1995; Currie, 2001; Karoly et al., 1998; Karoly, Kilburn, & Cannon, 2005; Yoshikawa, 1995). By drawing on major studies from different countries, the present analysis goes beyond previous reviews insofar as it attempts to detect a pattern of effects which is not bound to a particular country, cultural context, or curriculum. Moreover, in contrast to narrative literature reviews (e.g., Ramey & Ramey, 1998; Rossbach, Kluczniok, & Kuger, 2008), it provides important details about the statistical results of the studies included. Since the effects of early interventions are manifold, an exhaustive overview cannot be given. Instead, the paper focuses on cognitive development. Cognitive development is only one of several indicators of a successful development. Others include social skills, motivation to achieve, self-esteem, health status, and attitude towards school. However, the early cognitive effects of participation in a preschool program carry over to school competence and educational attainment, thereby influencing longer-term social development (Reynolds, Mann, Miedel, & Smokowski, 1997). This makes analysis of cognitive development particularly interesting.

1 Research objectives

The present review explores the cognitive development of children who attended an early care and education program comparing target children's progress with children who may have participated in all kinds of alternative programs or have not been cared for in a formal preschool setting at all. Along with the general effects on the child's cognitive development, the paper analyzes whether early interventions help to overcome social inequality, and if so, whether these interventions can ensure equal educational opportunities for children from different social backgrounds. Hence two major questions are considered: (1) what are the effects of early childhood care and education programs on the cognitive development of children? And (2) can such programs help to overcome inequalities among children from different social backgrounds?

To simplify matters, the terms early (childhood) education and care and preschool education are used interchangeably in this review. Both terms are intended to refer to center-based early intervention programs that foster the cognitive and socio-emotional development of children between about two years and the official school entrance age. In most instances, these programs address children between three and six years of age. As opposed to parental care or informal care by relatives, nannies, or babysitters, early childhood education and care (as it is defined here) is carried out in institutions such as day care centers, nursery schools, pre-kindergartens, and kindergartens. Many of the early education and care programs have been designed specifically to increase the school readiness of children from socio-economically disadvantaged families. It is therefore crucial to ask to what extent these programs can reduce disadvantage by providing socio-economically deprived children with a better start at school. This is particularly important since it is well known that low socio-economic status can have a detrimental influence on the development of children (Barnett & Belfield, 2006).

2 Effects of socio-economic status on the development of children

Socio-economic status refers to the relative position an individual, a family or a group holds within a societal hierarchy according to its access to or power over valued goods such as wealth or social recognition and privileges (McLoyd, 1998). Under these terms, the members of a society can be classified into different social strata according to the status values they have acquired. Typically, parental occupation and education, family income, power, and prestige are important components of these values, and members of the different strata are also faced with different living conditions (e.g., Hurrelmann, 2000; Mueller & Parcel, 1981). Children of families with a low socio-economic status are frequently at risk of not successfully developing the skills they need to achieve at school (Duncan, Brooks-Gunn, & Klebanov, 1994; McLoyd, 1998). Since their skills are less developed in their early years (Moser, Stamm, & Hollenweger, 2005; Roberts, Bornstein, Slater, & Barrett, 1999; Taylor, Dearing, & McCartney, 2004), the school readiness gap for these children is greater than for children from families with a higher socio-economic status (Barnett, Brown, & Shore, 2004; Paxson & Schady, 2007; Schady, 2006). Considerable discrepancies in academic competencies persist during the subsequent school years (Evans & Rosenbaum, 2008; Korenman, Miller, & Sjaastad, 1995; Magnuson, Meyers, Ruhm, & Waldfogel, 2004; Moser, Bayer, & Berweger, 2008; Osborn & Milbank, 1987; Sammons et al., 2008b; Schneider & Stefanek, 2004).

As children from socio-economically disadvantaged backgrounds are prone to more unfavorable development, they are more likely to repeat grades, to develop special education needs in the course of their later school years, or to withdraw from school before completing their program (Goodman & Sianesi, 2005; Niles, Reynolds, & Roe-Sepowitz, 2008; Reynolds et al., 2007). This applies where low socio-economic status brings an impoverishment of the child's world so that the child lacks the basic social and cognitive stimulation required for optimum development. For this reason, researchers have examined informal education and school preparation at home, for example parents' teaching strategies when playing and their manner of conversing with their children. Their analyses have revealed differences between families that are associated with socio-economic status and identified these as a key cause of early differences between children in cognitive and language development, intelligence, and school achievement (Hoff, 2006; Hoff & Tian, 2005). Thus low socio-economic status can be associated with poorer informal learning at home, resulting in children being less well prepared for formal schooling (Leseman, 2002).

Effects of early childhood care and education on cognitive development   53

3   Early education and care and equality of opportunity

The aforementioned findings show that children from different social backgrounds have unequal skill levels when they enter school. The vast majority of early education and care programs strive to counteract such inequalities. By fostering the development in the early years, they aim to ensure that all children-regardless of their social background-have the prerequisites for a successful start at school (e.g., Siraj-Blatchford, 2004). If all children attain these prerequisites, they can be assumed to have comparable educational opportunities at the start of their school track. Hence early interventions attempt to enhance those abilities which are the basis for beneficial development. By enriching the learning environments of children at risk of less successful development, they aim to compensate for the unfavorable learning conditions children face in families that provide less opportunity for informal learning. Equality of opportunity exists where everyone is accorded the same chance to develop his or her capacities and to be acknowledged for personal accomplishments irrespective of characteristics such as gender, religion, political stance, color of the skin, or social background, that is, characteristics which are not related to their personal performance (Hradil, 2001). Equality of opportunity, however, is not given in practice. In view of such social inequalities, it is imperative to ask whether early interventions help to overcome differences between children from different social backgrounds.

4   Related analyses and main focus of the present analysis

Many specific questions have been analyzed in early childhood research. The following overview about research into the acquisition of skills and educational development of children may give insight into some of the most prominent research questions. So far, these questions have concerned the influence of time spent in preschool (e.g., Walston & West, 2004) and the differential effectiveness of different types of preschool provision (e.g., Schweinhart & Weikart, 1997). A number of authors have compared full-day with half-day kindergarten (e.g., Cryan, Sheehan, Wiechel, & Bandy-Hedden, 1992; Plucker et al., 2004; Votruba-Drzal, Li-Grining, & Maldonado-Carreño, 2008; Zvoch, Reynolds, & Parker, 2008). Others have analyzed the effects of preschool quality (e.g., Early et al., 2007; Fried, 2002; Fthenakis & Textor, 1998; Howes et al., 2008; Tietze, 1998; Vandell, Henderson, & Wilson, 1988), quality management (Spiess & Tietze, 2002), various program or process features (e.g., Guimarães &

McSherry, 2002; Marcon, 1992; Montie, Xiang, & Schweinhart, 2006), the role of schools in sustaining the effects of early childhood education and care (e.g., Entwisle, 1995; Magnuson, Ruhm, & Waldfogel, 2007a), the effects of parent support programs (Goodson, Layzer, St. Pierre, Bernstein, & Lopez, 2000), and the effects of state-funded preschool (Gilliam & Zigler, 2001). Still others have examined early training of cognitive competencies (e.g., Krajewski, Renner, Nieding, & Schneider, 2008; Pauen & Pahnke, 2008), the contribution of parent and peer support to children's early school adjustment (Bennett, Weigel, & Martin, 2002; Taylor & Machida, 1994), the role of the teacher-child relationship quality on preschoolers' academic readiness for kindergarten (Palermo, Hanish, Martin, Fabes, & Reiser, 2007), and comprehensive case management interventions (St. Pierre, Layzer, Goodson, & Bernstein, 1997). Finally, numerous researchers have focused on the return on financial investments in early education and care (e.g., Anger, Plünnecke, & Tröger, 2007; Bock-Famulla, 2002; Fritschi & Oesch, 2008; Fritschi, Strub, & Stutz, 2007; Heckman, 2006; Mackenzie Oth, 2002; Müller Kucera & Bauer, 2000; Pfeiffer & Reuss, 2008; Rauschenbach & Schilling, 2007; Spiess et al., 2002). The main focus of the present paper, however, is the overall influence of early education and care on the cognitive development of children and the extent to which early interventions can reduce social disparities among children. In addition, some of the questions addressed in other studies-such as the effects of age at entry, intensity, duration, and pedagogical focus of a program-will also be studied. However, although it would be interesting to relate differences in these variables explicitly to cognitive outcomes, this is not done here because well-grounded conclusions in these terms would require studies that have specifically focused on these questions. Instead, the review attempts to discover general and compensatory effects of program participation on several cognitive outcome measures.

5 Systematic review

In order to gain an overview of the relevant research, recent studies were analyzed using focussed categorizing of empirical findings. Systematic reviews and evidence-based conclusions are increasingly important for policy decision making. In education systems with rising demand and limited resources, methodical assessment of educational technologies is important for those who make resource allocation decisions. Moreover, reviews provide researchers with useful syntheses of the primary research literature guiding them to the principal contributions of the field and familiarizing them with the state of the art of a par-

Effects of early childhood care and education on cognitive development 55

ticular area of research. Reviews are an appropriate means to summarize the evidence of a given field, in particular when the data required for meta-analysis are not available exhaustively. Like meta-analyses, reviews can deal with certain heterogeneity of studies by paying attention to the methodological (and statistical) rigor of these studies. Reviews can organize and qualify conclusions by the type and quality of the studies. Hence good reviews weigh results by considering the elaborateness of the statistical approaches and by critically reflecting the scientific value of the studies included. Reviews range from highly qualitative methods which rely on subjective considerations about the research procedure and results to rather quantitative methods which include various statistical data from the literature. The present review attempts to draw on both a qualitative approach and inclusion of statistical results. Reviewing the literature is a scientific inquiry that needs a clear conceptual framework to preclude bias. This framework is specified hereafter.

5.1   Conceptual approach and criteria of including studies

The framework for the review consisted of three major steps: First, relevant studies were identified in computerized databases (like ERIC, PsycInfo, and PubMed), in various online research portals (e.g., ec.europa.eu/research/; forschungsportal.net; researchportal.ch), and in books; furthermore, non-refereed publications such as major research reports from educational authorities and research institutes were searched on the internet. Secondly, since any literature review will inevitably be selective, eligibility criteria were defined which studies had to meet to be included for further analysis. These criteria concerned the type of program analyzed and the study reports:

(1) The intervention must have begun during a child's preschool years, that is, before compulsory schooling. (2) The intervention was center-based and focused on the promotion of child well-being, that is, it was a promotion or prevention program. (3) The goal of this direct, child-focused approach was to enhance child development and learning by attending to the needs of children. (4) Center-based approaches involved several kinds of institutions offering early years provision such as preschools, childcare centers, crèches, playgroups, day-care nurseries, and nursery schools which served as alternative physical and social environments for care, development, and education. (5) Information was provided about characteristics of the type of service. (6) Studies were published after 1990; the only exception concerned the Child Health and Education study by Osborn and Milbank published in 1987 and included here because of its

particular importance for early education and care research in the United Kingdom. (7) Studies had well-defined average- to large-scale samples with at least 300 study participants. (8) Research was reported in journal articles or research reports and documented an evaluation of an early childhood education and care program. (9) The report provided information from a primary study, and was not a literature review. (10) Research methods, statistical analyses, and findings were sufficiently detailed to provide a basis for judgment about the robustness of the conclusions, that is, the research procedures and characteristics of the sample were specified in detail so that the validity of the results could be evaluated. (11) Outcome measures were indicators of the construct of children's cognitive development. (12) The evidence assessed linkages between participation in a program and cognitive outcomes. (13) A control (or comparison) group was given that either received no preschool education or had been assigned to another kind of program so that the effectiveness of different interventions could be compared. The present review does not aim to duplicate existing reviews like the ones by Anderson et al. (2003), Barnett (1995), Boocock (1995), and Currie (2001) and therefore largely omits the studies included in these thoroughly conducted previous reviews.

The third stage in the review was to summarize the evidence of effectiveness. Information was collected about outcomes of pre-specified interest concerning cognitive development measures rather than about all outcomes measured in a study. To this end, a data collection form was designed and used as a bridge between what was reported in the studies and what is reported here. It was linked directly to the review question and structured like tables 1 to 4 in this paper. However, statistical data from the original studies were recorded in more detail. For this review, four tables of evidence were defined in which various categories of information were included (see tables 1, 2, 3, 4). These tables are related and can be considered as one overall table with four parts. For studies that met the inclusion criteria, information was recorded about project period, age of the children at entry to the program, duration of program attendance, last follow-up of the study (for the time being), size of the original and the follow-up samples, cognitive achievement test outcomes and/or educational attainment, special education rates, grade retention rates, graduation rates, and number of years of school attendance whenever information about these indicators was provided in the publications. Furthermore, the capacity of projects to compensate for socio-economic disadvantage was specified by comparing developmental gains of children from more privileged families with gains of children from more disadvantaged families. When interventions targeted children from disadvantaged backgrounds exclusively, cognitive effects were assessed but no

Effects of early childhood care and education on cognitive development 57

conclusion could be drawn about the compensation for socio-economic disadvantage in the strict sense. In addition, a selection of the major measuring instruments was reported in table 3 together with the publications included in the review. Finally, table 4 reports on the statistical methods and effect sizes and evaluates the quality of the study designs.

The table of evidence was designed to allow conclusions about the two questions of interest, firstly the general effects of early interventions on cognitive development and secondly the capacity of interventions to overcome social inequalities among children from different social backgrounds. In order to answer these questions, the most pertinent results from the individual studies were extracted and structured in tables 2, 3, and 4 to make them directly comparable. Further information on methods for conducting systematic reviews is given by Briss et al. (2000).

5.2 Experimental versus quasi-experimental studies

The most accurate estimates of the impact of early education and care programs can be derived from random-assignment, controlled experimental studies. These contrast children who experience a particular form of preschool with children who do not experience any comparable program but are otherwise equivalent with regard to relevant background characteristics, thus ensuring that differences in development are attributable principally to the particular experiences in the program. However, randomized trials are generally conducted with small samples and at one single site only. For this reason, the majority of studies evaluating the effectiveness of preschool adopt a quasi-experimental design and investigate the impact of naturally occurring variations in different types of interventions. Similarly, birth cohort studies and large-scale representative surveys providing data on a wide range of information typically retrospectively compare children who have experienced some form of early intervention with children without this experience, while trying to control for other important background characteristics that could influence development.

The clearest evidence of the longer-term efficacy of preschool interventions, reaching into adolescence and young adulthood, comes from small-scale high-quality model programs such as High/Scope Perry Preschool (Schweinhart et al., 2005). These programs primarily enroll socio-economically disadvantaged children who are manifestly behind in their development compared to more privileged children. In addition, these programs generally use highly trained teachers and have low child-to-staff ratios in contrast to large-scale public programs. Hence they are designed to highlight the positive effects of early education and care. In fact it is well known that these model interventions have beneficial effects on the development of children (Barnett, 1995). However, while these programs illustrate how interventions could work, the present paper aims to explore how they do work. For this purpose, it is reasonable to examine the findings of quasi-experimental studies which analyze larger-scale programs. By mirroring more typical (real-world) experiences of children, these findings are more generalizable to other programs and children. As their external validity is superior to that of model program outcomes, they are analyzed in depth in this paper. Other authors have already reviewed studies of the effectiveness of preschool interventions (e.g., Barnett, 1995, 2008; Currie, 2001; Karoly et al., 1998; Rossbach et al., 2008). However, as Reynolds et al. (1997) observe, the majority of the empirical evidence comes from model programs. Unlike evaluations of model programs, the present review provides a synopsis of different average- to large-scale sample studies including curriculum comparison and birth cohort studies from different countries. The results of the Delaware Early Childhood Longitudinal Study (Gamel-McCormick & Amsden, 2002) included here were based on a sub-sample that was relevant to the present review. Hence we must avoid any assumption that the findings are nationally representative.

In sum, this review analyzes the effectiveness of early education and care interventions by drawing on quasi-experimental studies without random assignment of participants to an intervention or a control group. The Head Start Impact Study (U.S. Department of Health and Human Services, 2005) is the only one that used an experimental research strategy. Some of the studies used norm-referenced, age-standardized outcome measures to compare the achievement of children in early intervention programs with nationally representative norms. These measures were used for the evaluation of six projects, notably the North Carolina More at Four Pre-kindergarten Program (Peisner-Feinberg & Schaaf, 2008), the Head Start Family and Child Experiences Survey (FACES, 2006), the Universal Pre-kindergarten in Oklahoma (Gormley, Gayer, Phillips, & Dawson, 2005; Gormley, Phillips, & Gayer, 2008), the Georgia Early Childhood Study (Henry et al., 2003, 2004), the Dutch Public Preschool Study (van Tuijl & Leseman, 2007), and the Miami School Readiness (Winsler et al., 2008) projects. The outcome measures of all the other studies included here differ depending on the method applied. The analytic framework used in the present review reports the findings of empirical studies which conform to the eligibility criteria even if the methodological approaches differ. The selection of studies was based on their common overall research objective. Thus the studies were equivalent in respect of their research questions but varied as regards their statistical methods. The techniques applied include t-tests, χ^2-square tests, analyses of variance, regression (discontinuity) analyses, and instrumental variable estimates. An important issue in reviews concerns publication bias towards statistically significant results. This leads to an overestimation of positive results and poses a special challenge for interpretation. For this reason, the present review may have overrepresented positive findings so that some uncertainty may remain as to the effectiveness of early education and care programs. However, where nonsignificant findings were reported in the studies, they were included in the present review.

5.3 Program characteristics and research designs

Table 1 provides an overview of the projects included in the review. It indicates project names and periods, mean age of children at entry to the programs, mean duration of attendance, and mean age of participants at the last follow-up. It includes studies about eight European, one Asian, and eleven North American projects as well as three birth cohort studies from Great Britain and Canada. The characteristics of the early education and care programs analyzed and the research designs adopted in these studies are specified in the next section. The pedagogical concepts of the programs are outlined as defined at the time of inquiry; ongoing projects do not necessarily continue to operate according to the same principles. It should be noted that the programs reviewed were all center-based and child-focused. Their common overall goal was to serve children by helping them to acquire social and cognitive skills. However, given the number of programs reviewed, they differed in some points: some included special kinds of supports, and three of them included parent involvement, notably the Chicago Longitudinal Study Child-Parent Centers (Reynolds, Temple, Robertson, & Mann, 2001, 2002; Reynolds et al., 2007), Head Start (FACES, 2006; U.S. Department of Health and Human Services, 2005; Zill, Sorongon, Kim, & Clark, 2006), and the Early Childhood Development Study undertaken in rural Vietnam (Watanabe, Flores, Fujiwara, & Huong Tran, 2005) (see below). In the according studies, differences in cognitive outcomes between program participants and comparison groups must not be attributed exclusively to the influence of the programs carried out in the centers but may be affected by parenting strategies which can work as multiplicators of center-based effects. In the United States, parent involvement figures prominently in early childhood programming, and state and national agency regulations in this respect are more demanding than in most other countries (OECD, 2006). Hence they should not be left out completely in a review about the effects of center-based early education and care. However, program breadth appears to have an influence on child outcomes: Programs that adopt a multifaceted approach and provide more wide-ranging services including health and social services, transportation, neurodevelopmental therapies as needed, parent services and training, and a strong educational program for the children, usually produce larger developmental gains (Ramey & Ramey, 1998). Their results will therefore need to be weighed in the conclusions.

Table 1: Project features

Project	Project period	Age at entry	Mean duration of attendance	Age at last follow-up
Europe				
Effective Provision of Pre-School Education (EPPE, EPPE 3-11), U.K.	1997-2003 2003-2008	3 years	variable	7 years 11 years
Early Years Transition and Special Education Needs (EYT-SEN), U.K.	1997-2003	3 years	variable	7 years
Effective Pre-School Provision in Northern Ireland (EPPNI), NI	1998-2005	3-4 years	variable	8 years
Socio-Economic Panel (SOEP), DE	1984-ongoing	variable	a) 1 year, b) 2 years	a) 14 years, b) 12-14 years
Dutch Cohort Study of Primary Education (PRIMA), NL	1996-2000	4 years	60-240 days	10 years
Dutch Public Preschool Study (DPPS), NL	Not indicated	4-5 years	2.5 years	6-7 years
School Success of Immigrant Children (CH), CH	1998-ongoing	variable	variable	7 years
Panel 1997, FR	1997-ongoing	variable	variable	9 years

Table 1 – continued: Project features

Project	Project period	Age at entry	Mean duration of attendance	Age at last follow-up
USA				
Chicago Longitudinal Study - Child-Parent Center (CLS)	1985-ongoing	3 years	2 years	24 years
Early Childhood Longitudinal Study - Kindergarten Class (ECLS-K)	1998-ongoing	5 years	1 year	11 years
North Carolina More at Four Pre-kindergarten Program (Carolina)	2001-ongoing	4 years	2 years	6 years
Head Start Family and Child Experiences Survey (FACES)	1997-2010	3-4 years	1 year	a) 4 years, b) 5-6 years
Head Start Impact Study (H.S. Impact)	2002-2009	3-4 years	1 year	4-5 years
Albuquerque Child Development Centers, ACDC (Albuquerque)	1999-2006	3-5 years	1-2 years	13-17 years
Arkansas Better Chance Pre-kindergarten Program (ABC)	2005-2010	5 years	1 year	7 years
Universal Pre-kindergarten – The example of Oklahoma (Oklahoma)	2003, 2006	4 years	1 year	5 years

Table 1 – continued: Project features

Project	Project period	Age at entry	Mean duration of attendance	Age at last follow-up
Georgia Early Childhood Study (Georgia)	2001-2004	4 years	1 year	7 years
Delaware Early Childhood Longitudinal Study (Delaware)	1997-2002	4 years	1 year	8 years
Miami School Readiness Project (Miami)	2002-2007	4 years	1 year	5 years
Asia				
Early Childhood Development in rural Vietnam (Vietnam)	1999-2003	4 years	2 years	6-8 years
Birth cohort studies in Great Britain and Canada				
National Child Development Study (NCDS), GB	1958-ongoing	variable	variable	46 years
British Cohort Study (BCS), GB	1970-ongoing	variable	variable	34 years
National Longitudinal Survey of Children and Youth (NLSCY), CA	1994-2009	4 years	1-2 years	14-25 years

5.3.1 Programs studied in Europe

Several programs were studied in *Europe*: The early education and care services analyzed in the projects in the *United Kingdom* - the Effective Provision of Preschool Education (EPPE, 2004), the Effective Preschool and Primary Education (EPPE, 2008a, 2008b), the Early Years Transition and Special Education (EYTSEN, 2003), and the Effective Preschool Provision in Northern Ireland (EPPNI, 2004) - varied according to the institution offering the early years provision. These four projects explored nursery classes, playgroups, private day nurseries, local authority day care nurseries, nursery schools, and centers that combined education and care (so called integrated centers). Centers were selected randomly within each type of provision in each of six English local authorities in five regions and in Northern Ireland. The sample covered provision in urban, suburban, and rural areas, and a range of ethnic diversity and social disadvantage. The respective care and education programs differed with regard to the timing, duration, intensity, quality, and main pedagogical focus. Methodologically, these projects compared the development of children who had attended a preschool institution with home children who had not been cared for in a formal preschool setting. Individual preschool centers varied in terms of their effectiveness in promoting intellectual progress. Hence the results reported in this review reflect the average overall developmental benefits of the above programs. In *Germany*, the preschool provision analyzed in the Socio-Economic Panel (SOEP) was equally varied. The SOEP is an ongoing survey of private households providing information on all household members, consisting of Germans, foreigners, and recent immigrants. It is a wide-ranging representative study with annual follow-ups (DIW Berlin, n.d.). As they do today, the public kindergartens analyzed in the SOEP primarily targeted four- and five-year-olds. The kindergartens were designed to promote both the social and the cognitive development of children and they were mostly available on a half-day basis. In West Germany, where the studies were conducted, only about 20% of all kindergarten slots offered full-day care in 2001, for instance. For this, working parents usually need additional care arrangements which consist mainly of private provisions (neighbors, grandparents etc.), although by law, the German kindergarten is supposed to support parents' labor market participation and help parents meet their family life responsibilities, and it is seen as the first stage of the education system. Kindergarten is generally provided by the community or non-profit organizations. It is intended to prepare children for school even though it is not compulsory. Providers of kindergartens receive high public subsidies and kindergartens are supposed to be available for every child. In

Germany, family day care for children between four and five years plays a minor role and is rather used for toddlers (Spiess, Büchel, & Wagner, 2003). The main research question concerned the effect of kindergarten attendance on the probability of later attending a school with extended academic requirements, the so called "Gymnasium," or restricted requirements, "Realschule" and "Hauptschule" (Landvoigt, Muehler, & Pfeiffer, 2007; Spiess et al., 2003). In the *Netherlands*, a variety of early education and care programs was researched in the Dutch Cohort Study of Primary Education PRIMA (Driessen, 2004). The common aim of these different programs was to stimulate the socio-emotional and the cognitive development of children. Various institutions targeted different age groups between birth and eight years. Most of the programs were available on a part-day basis: Day-care centers provide child care for children between birth and four years of age. They are generally open every work day and usually funded and administered by local authorities or private organizations. However, based on their income, parents have to contribute to the cost of day-care centers. Preschools or preschool playgroups target children between two and four years and are available two to three half-days a week. They are financed by municipalities which usually charge a fee to parents. Early childhood education and care programs, finally, are special services typically aimed at children from disadvantaged backgrounds and usually conducted in preschools or elementary schools. The programs are intended for children up to eight years of age. Three-quarters of all programs are at least partly financed by municipal authorities, and one-quarter by the ministry of welfare. The Dutch Public Preschool Study (DPPS) drew on public preschools which are integrated in the primary school system, forming the first two grades of primary school (van Tuijl & Leseman, 2007). Their curriculum is predominantly developmental: Most preschools work with mixed-age groups; most time is spent in free-play activities and work lessons with children in small groups. Whole group activities are regularly provided as start, break, or closing activities during the day and include book reading, play, talking, and singing. In the second year of preschool, these activities are complemented by literacy and math activities (exploring letters and words, counting, measuring etc.). The vast majority of preschools adopt an eclectic, practical pedagogical approach. In *Switzerland*, Lanfranchi (2002) analyzed the effects of participation in day nurseries, playgroups, and kindergartens on the school success of immigrant children from Italian, Turkish, Portuguese, and Albanian families. Playgroups and day nurseries (for three- to four-year-olds) provided mainly custodial care and were attended on a rather irregular basis whereas kindergartens (for five- and six-year-olds) primarily fostered the socio-emotional development of children and were available on a regular basis as a half-day program. In these services, the promotion of pre-academic abilities was not stipulated explicitly but approved implicitly. In Switzerland, only kindergartens are subsidized entirely by public authority. In *France*, the Panel 1997 explored the influence of age at entry to the kindergarten on the grade retention rates of children up to the second grade of primary school (Caille, 2001). The French kindergarten, the "école maternelle," is available to all children from three to six years and it has an explicit educational mission although not all of the institutions analyzed in the Panel 1997 necessarily focused on the promotion of pre-academic skills (some primarily emphasized the promotion of social development instead). The French kindergarten is fully funded and organized by the State as it is part of the national education system. Furthermore, it is attended by almost 100% of three-to-five-year-olds (OECD, 2006).

5.3.2 Programs studied in the U.S. and elsewhere

The eleven *North American* projects represent a number of different early care and education institutions and pedagogical approaches. The research strategies in these projects are specified hereafter. Details about the early intervention programs and their characteristics are given in a subsequent section.

5.3.2.1 Research strategies

The Chicago Longitudinal Study (CLS) is an ongoing quasi-experimental investigation of low-income children (the vast majority of whom are African-American) comparing children who have completed preschool and kindergarten in Child-Parent Centers with children who participate in alternative full-day kindergarten programs available to low-income families (Reynolds et al., 2001, 2002; Reynolds et al., 2007). The Early Childhood Longitudinal Study – Kindergarten Class (ECLS-K) contrasts different types of early education and care in the year before kindergarten in nationally representative surveys, notably center-based day care including pre-kindergarten programs, preschools, nursery schools, Head Start, and other non-parental center-based care (Magnuson et al., 2004; Rumberger & Tran, 2006). Children who attended these programs were compared with children who had experienced parental care but no preschool care. This type of comparison was also carried out in three other studies in the U.S., those based on the Albuquerque Child Development Centers (ACDC), the

Arkansas Better Chance Pre-kindergarten Program (ABC), and the Delaware Early Childhood Longitudinal projects: In the Albuquerque study (Boyle, 2007; Boyle & Roberts, 2003), a comparison was made between children who had attended ACDC programs (these children were from families with household incomes of less than 175% of the national poverty line) with similar children who had attended federal free lunch programs (families with incomes below 135%), reduced price lunch support programs (incomes between 136% and 185%), and no support programs (incomes above 185% of the national poverty line). Similarly, children from at-risk, low-income families in ABC pre-kindergarten programs were contrasted with comparable children without pre-kindergarten experience (Hustedt, Barnett, & Jung, 2008). Finally, the Delaware study also assessed the effectiveness of interventions modelled after the federal Head Start program for children living in poverty (Gamel-McCormick & Amsden, 2002).

Unlike these analyses, the evaluation of five other projects drew on age-standardized norm-referenced measures, namely the North Carolina More at Four Pre-kindergarten project, the Head Start Family and Child Experiences Survey FACES, Oklahoma's Universal Pre-Kindergarten project in Tulsa, the Georgia Early Childhood Study, and the Miami School Readiness Project: The North Carolina project was an evaluation of a pre-kindergarten program for at risk children from families with an income of up to 75% of the average income or up to 300% above the national poverty line where longitudinal growth models were used to estimate whether the achievement gains of the children included exceeded national norms (Peisner-Feinberg & Schaaf, 2008). FACES is a research initiative of Head Start providing nationally representative longitudinal data on the outcomes of children served as compared to national norms (FACES, 2006; Zill et al., 2006). In the same way, Oklahoma's Universal Pre-K project assessed the effectiveness of typical pre-kindergartens (Gormley et al., 2005; Gormley et al., 2008) and the Georgia study investigated the effectiveness of pre-kindergarten, Head Start, and private preschool or childcare centers as described below (Henry et al., 2003, 2004). The research goal of the Miami project was to assess the extent to which ethnically diverse (i.e. mainly Hispanic/Latino, Black/African-American, and White non-Hispanic/Caucasian) children from low-income households who are at significant risk in the areas of language and cognition made school readiness gains in their pre-kindergarten year in terms of relative standing compared to national norms (Winsler et al., 2008). The Head Start Impact Study, finally, used an experimental methodology and assigned newly entering Head Start applicants randomly to either a treatment group that had access to Head Start services or a comparison group that could receive any other non-Head Start services chosen by their parents (U.S. Department of Health and Human Services, 2005).

5.3.2.2 Pedagogical concepts

The following section summarizes the pedagogical concepts adopted in the different early education and care programs listed above, hence it relates to the North American studies cited above. The Child-Parent Centers investigated in the Chicago Longitudinal Study provide educational and family-support services for children between three and seven years. The intervention emphasizes the acquisition of basic cognitive skills through relatively structured but diverse learning experiences that include teacher-directed whole-class instruction, small-group work, and individualized activities. Major elements of the intervention include furthering educational attainment, parenting education, home visits, and health and nutrition services. Parents are expected to participate in the program for up to half a day per week. The program is run on a half-day basis whereas the subsequent kindergarten program is provided on a part-day or full-day basis during the school year.

The early childhood education and care programs analyzed in the other studies include a wide range of part-day and full-day programs that have an education and/or social welfare focus. Across the country, private family day care and center-based early education and care constitute 90% of provision for children between birth and three years. The most usual forms of provision for these children are private, giving way gradually to publicly-funded pre-kindergarten and kindergarten provision by school districts which are typically made available to four- and five-year-old children (OECD, 2006). Overall, three broad types of provision exist: the purchase of service systems which is composed of private centers and family day care homes, the public school system which is under the responsibility of each State and generally offers free, half-day kindergarten for five-year-olds and mostly preschool in addition, that is, publicly funded pre-kindergarten programs for three- and four-year-olds, and Head Start, that is, comprehensive child development programs that have the overall goal of increasing school readiness of children from low-income families and children with disabilities or developmental delays from birth to five, enrolling primarily three- and four-year-olds.

In state programs, program content and pedagogical approach are generally left open for each center to decide, and therefore many eclectic practices exist. Nevertheless, some more detailed information can be given: The U.S. *pre-*

kindergarten is typically a part-day educational program situated within public schools. Some additional services are usually offered, including meals, but few programs provide a full array of comprehensive services. Almost all pre-kindergarten initiatives target children deemed in need of education due to the economic disadvantage of their families or other recognized risk factors. Accordingly, public schools with high ratios of children from disadvantaged families are more likely to have pre-kindergarten programs than other schools. The ABC pre-kindergarten, for instance, provided early care and education services for children from at-risk, low-income families. While the majority of the ABC participants were served in public schools, programs also operated in other locations such as educational cooperatives, Head Start facilities, and private child care services. *Universal pre-kindergarten* programs, on the other hand, are non-targeted services that do not require children to meet specific eligibility criteria. Oklahoma's universal pre-kindergarten programs, for instance, offer part- or full-day early education to any child who has turned four, and classes are held at local public schools. *Head Start* is a federally funded early education program that uses a comprehensive approach to service delivery, including nutrition programs and health check-ups, social services, such as assistance by lawyers, and parent involvement. The majority of Head Start programs operate part-day and part-year, but some also provide full-day education and care to support parents in the labor market. Traditional *preschools and nursery schools* mainly provide early education for three- and four-year-olds. They are usually available part-day and part-week, serving sometimes for longer hours for families with working parents. Unlike preschools, center-based day care programs are typically open up to ten hours a day and five days a week and the facilities may accept children of all ages (see also Magnuson, Meyers, Ruhm, & Waldfogel, 2004).

One of the projects included in the review was carried out in *Asia* (Watanabe et al., 2005). The early childhood development intervention in rural Vietnam was conceptualized as a program that built on a nutrition intervention and strengthened existing center-based preschools. It added material and trained teachers in child-focused teaching methods. And it supported parental behavior with monthly training sessions for parents on different topics relating to child care and development. The intervention included the establishment of a small local library for parents and also promoted play corners in the homes of the participating families. It targeted children aged four to five years who had previously been exposed to a nutrition intervention. This early intervention project was evaluated through a comparison of children who had received a nutrition program from birth to three years with children who had received the same nutrition program together with an additional early childhood development program at four and five years of age.

As can be expected in large-scale surveys, the types of early education and care provision examined in the *birth cohort studies* included in this review varied widely. A range of preschool and pre-compulsory education centers were analyzed in Great-Britain in the National Child Development Study NCDS (Goodman & Sianesi, 2005) and in the British Cohort Study BCS (Feinstein, Robertson, & Symons, 1999; Osborn & Milbank, 1987), as well as in Canada in the National Longitudinal Survey of Children and Youth NLSCY (Lipps & Yiptong-Avila, 1999). As a result, these cohort studies reflect a broad overall picture of the effectiveness of various early education and care programs. The NCDS is a continuing, multi-disciplinary longitudinal study which takes as its subjects all the people born in Great Britain in one particular week in March 1958. It analyzes the effects of pre-compulsory education (any form of formal education before the compulsory school entry at age five, including premature school entry) and pre-school education (attendance of a crèche or playgroup, independently of premature school entry) as opposed to informal care. That applies to the BCS as well. The BCS is a continuing, multi-disciplinary longitudinal study which takes as its subjects all the people living in Great Britain who were born in one week in April 1970. Finally, the NLSCY is a long-term study that follows the development of Canadian children from birth to early adulthood. In 1994, it included children between birth and eleven years as well as their parents and it follows these children until the age of 14 to 25 years in 2008 and 2009 (the current data collection began in September 2008).

6   Empirical evidence

Table 1 provides general information on the selected studies. For age at entry, there was variability among the different programs. Typically, children were between three and five years of age when they participated in early education and care programs. The mean duration of attendance varied between less than one year and more than three years with a majority of children attending a program for one to two years. Most of the research projects reached at least into the primary school years. Some projects also followed the participants well into adulthood, that is, up to 46 years. Table 2 documents the size of the original and the follow-up samples, cognitive achievement test outcomes, educational attainment, and special education rates. Treatment groups are indicated by an upper case *T*, comparison groups are indicated by an upper case *C*. An upper case N refers to the overall number of participants in a study; this is reported when no information about the number of participants in treatment and comparison groups was found in the studies. Most of the samples were deemed to be large, the largest being the original sample of the British Cohort Study which comprised more than 12,000 participants, 72% of whom attended some form of preschool provision (Feinstein et al., 1999). However, a large sample size does not guarantee that a survey is nationally representative. In fact, only five studies-based on the SOEP, the Panel 1997, the ECLS-K, the FACES, and the Head Start Impact projects-used nationally representative samples.

Additionally, many studies were plagued by problems of attrition. Loss of participants over time is particularly serious when there is selective drop-out of a specific subgroup of participants. In this case, attrition is a severe threat to both the internal and the external validity of a study, and it can invalidate the outcomes so that they lose their generalizability to the larger population. In some studies, a relatively high proportion of participants were retained until the last follow-up survey reported here. Nevertheless, all of the outcomes were partially flawed as a result of sample attrition. The lowest attrition rate was measured in the Chicago Longitudinal Study: when the participants were 24 years old, 90.3% of the original sample still had valid data on educational attainment. The PRIMA study, on the other hand, appears to have suffered substantially from a loss of participants since over time there was selective drop-out of children who had scored lower on language and mathematics at the beginning of the study.

Another difference between the European and the North American studies concerns the early childhood services. According to a recent league table established by UNICEF (2008), most of the European countries from which studies were selected for this review currently meet more quality standards than the services in the United States. While the services in the United States only meet the standards of 'subsidized and regulated child care services for 25% of children under three years of age,' '50% of staff in accredited early education services having tertiary education qualification,' and 'a minimum staff-to-children ratio of 1:15 given in preschool education,' many European countries such as Germany, Netherlands, the UK, and France (excluding Switzerland) additionally meet standards such as 'subsidized and accredited early education services for 80% of four-year-olds,' '80% of all child care staff trained,' and '50% of staff in accredited early education services having tertiary education qualification' as well. When interpreting the results of the studies in this review, this should be kept in mind.

Table 2: Study samples and outcomes

Project	Samples	Cognitive achievement test outcomes and/or edudational attainment	Special education rates
EPPE	2004: T = 2,857, C = 314 (a) 2008: T = 2,701, C = 276 (b)	a) At age 7: T > C: in pre-reading, language, and early number concepts b) At age 11: T > C: in English and math	
EYTSEN	2003: T = 2,857, C = 314 (c)		c) At risk of special needs: at age 6: T = 21%, C = 51%; at age 7: T ≈ 25%, C = 42%
EPPNI	2003: T = 683, C = 151	At age 8: T (nursery class/school) > C: in numeracy and literacy, T (reception groups, private nurseries) ≈ C: in numeracy and literacy	
SOEP	2003: T = 266, C = 50 (a) 2007: T = 1,272, C = 60 (b)	a) At age 14 at schools with extended requirements: T (64.4%) > C (41.4%) b) At age 12 to 14 at the highest secondary school track: T > C	
PRIMA	1996: T = 10,097, C = 1,509 2000: N = 3,596	At age 10: T ≈ C: in math and language	
DPPS	t1: N = 333 t2: N = 312	At age 6-7: significant verbal and fluid intelligence gains relative to age-norms	Referrals during investigation: until age 6-7: 2.24%

Table 2 – continued: Study samples and outcomes

Project	Samples	Cognitive achievement test outcomes and/or edudational attainment	Special education rates
CH	1998: T = 98, C = 216	At age 7: T > C: in cognitive capabilities and language	
PANEL1997	1997: N = 9,260 2001: N = 8,661		
CLS	1985: T = 989, C = 550 2004: T = 902, C = 487	a) At age 23: College attendance: T (29.4%) ≈ C (27.4%), 4-year college attendance: T (14.7%) > C (10.0%), Highest grade completed: T (11.73) > C (11.44)	c) At age 18: T (14.4%) < C (24.6%)
ECLS-K	2004: T = 10,680, C = 2,124 (a) 2006: N = 11,468 (b)	a) At age 7: T (center-based care) > C (parental care): in reading and math, T (Head Start) < C (parental care): in reading and math	b) Until age 9: T (Head Start) = 1.14%, T (Non-Head Start) = 0.49%, C (parental care) = 0.91%
Carolina	2003-2005: N = 514 (cohort 1) 2005-2007: N = 478 (cohort 2)	At age 6: T > national norms: in language, literacy, math, general knowledge	

Table 2 – continued: Study samples and outcomes

Project	Samples	Cognitive achievement test outcomes and/or edudational attainment	Special education rates
FACES	1997: N ≈ 3,200 (cohort 1) 2000: N ≈ 2,800 (cohort 2) 2003: N ≈ 2,400 (cohort 3) Control group: -	a) Percentage of gap between 4-year-old children and national norms closed between fall and spring of Head Start year in cohorts 1, 2, and 3: In early reading: cohort 1: -11%, cohort 2: 7%, cohort 3: 10%*. In vocabulary: cohort 1: 28%*, cohort 2: 27%*, cohort 3: 22%* b) At age 5-6: Significant positive effects on vocabulary, early math, and writing	
H.S. Impact	2002: T = 2,783, C = 1,884	At age 4 or 5: T > C: in pre-reading, pre-writing, vocabulary, literacy, T ≈ C: in oral comprehension, phonological awareness, early math	
Albuquerque	2000: N = 3,943 2006: N = not specified	Among the best two-thirds of students in reading in 2006: ACDC: 60.5%, Free lunch program: 48.7%, Reduced price: 63.5%, No support program: 80.3%	Not learning disabled in 2006: ACDC: 93.4%, Free lunch: 91.4%, Reduced price: 93.2%, No support: 94.7%

Table 2 – continued: Study samples and outcomes

Project	Samples	Cognitive achievement test outcomes and/or edudational attainment	Special education rates
ABC	2005: T = 530, C = 218 2007: T = 451, C = 190	At age 7: T > C: in calculation and letter-word-identification, T ≈ C: in receptive vocabulary, applied math problems, math fluency	
Oklahoma	2003: T = 1,461, C = 1,567 (a) 2006: T = 1,264, C = 1,492 (b)	a) T > C: in letter-word-identification, spelling, math applied problems b) T > C: in letter-word-identification, spelling, math applied problems	
Georgia	2001: T = 630, C = 225 2004: T = 466, C = 204	Mean scores of 1) Pre-K, 2) Head Start, and 3) private program attendees at age 4 versus age 7, and 4) scores of control group at age 7 (x = 100, SD = 15). All cognitive gains over time were statistically significant: Letter/word recognition: 1) 103 vs. 112, 2) 95 vs. 103, 3) 109 vs. 116, 4) 114, Language: 1) 93 vs. 99, 2) 83 vs. 90, 3) 98 vs. 104, 4) 103, Applied problems: 1) 97 vs. 110, 2) 90 vs. 102, 3) 101 vs. 114, 4) 114	

Table 2 – continued: Study samples and outcomes

Project	Samples	Cognitive achievement test outcomes and/or edudational attainment	Special education rates
Delaware	2002: T = 42, C = 109	School grades in 1st, 2nd, and 3rd grade satisfactory: T (83.0%) > C (71.0%) Meeting reading standard at age 8: T (69.1%) > C (48.7%) Meeting math standard at age 8: T (61.9%) > C (45.8%)	
Miami	2003, 2004: N = 3,838	Cognitive and language skills in national percentile ranking in pre-kindergarten: at entry: 32nd - 43rd percentile < at end of program: 47th - 52nd percentile	
Vietnam	2004: T = 141, C = 170	At age 6-8: T > C: in cognitive test scores	
NCDS	1974: T = 6,605, C = 4,343 (a) 1974: T = 9,266, C = 1,684 (b)	At age 16: a) T (pre-compulsory) > C: in math and reading, b) T (preschool) ≈ C: in math and reading	At age 7: a) T (pre-compulsory) < C. b) T (preschool) ≈ C

Effects of early childhood care and education on cognitive development 77

Table 2 – continued: Study samples and outcomes

Project	Samples	Cognitive achievement test outcomes and/or edudational attainment	Special education rates
BCS	1980: T = 5,029, C = 3,380 (a) 1980: N = 3,568 (for math) (b) N = 3,227 (for reading)	At age 10: a) T > C: in British Ability Scale and Picture Language Test score, reading, math, and communication b) T (preschool) ≈ C: in math; T (preschool) < C: in reading	
NLSCY	1996/1997: N = 8,600	At age 6 or 7: Outcomes of children 1) in ECEC programs, 2) cared for by a person other than the mother, 3) cared for in the family environment by a parent at age 2 and 3 years: Very good math skills: 1) 34%, 2) 18%, 3) 25%, Very good reading skills: 1) 27%, 2) 25%, 3) 16%, Overall achievement: 1) 26%, 2) 25%, 3) 21%	

Note – ACDC stands for Albuquerque Child Development Centers, Reduced Price stands for Reduced Price Lunch Support Programs, ECEC stands for early childhood education and care. Further information about programs and outcome measures is given in the text. <, >, and * indicate statistically significant results at the $p < 0.05$ level at least.

Almost all the studies measured academic performance with standardized academic achievement tests. A list of the most important tests is given in table 3. In some surveys, official reports were consulted and school records were interpreted to provide a measure of cognitive development. The academic achievement tests in the qualifying studies generally measured basic or advanced cognitive abilities with a special focus on language and mathematics development as assessed through reading, vocabulary, writing, and math scales. Compared with IQ tests, these scales primarily assessed academic accomplishment and the acquisition of what is taught in early education and care programs or schools. Along with cognitive achievement test scores and special education rates, a range of other indicators for cognitive development have been used in early childhood research. The most common ones are grade retention and school graduation rates or years of school attendance. These indicators are illustrated in table 3 wherever they were included in the studies.

Finally, study design characteristics were evaluated. Three categories of quality were defined (good, fair, limited) and studies were classified along this dimension by taking account of four criteria: (1) Methodological quality was assessed by determining whether a study used retrospective reconstruction of data on early intervention use with post-test measures only or a sophisticated longitudinal design with pre- and post-test data. This distinction is important as lack of pre-test measures increases selection bias threats if children are not assigned randomly to treatment and control groups. However, lack of pre-test data can be acceptable if random assignment is given or if a regression discontinuity design is used where incoming younger cohorts serve as control groups for incoming older cohorts (see Cook, Shadish, & Wong, 2008, for an analysis which contrasts estimates from a randomized experiment with those from a regression discontinuity analysis providing evidence for comparable findings). (2) Specific investigations of effects of clearly defined early interventions were distinguished from general-purpose panel studies with data about early intervention use. (3) The extent of attrition was determined wherever applicable. And (4) sample size as well as representativeness of the study for a larger population were assessed. In the following, the effects of early education and care programs on children's cognitive development are discussed.

Effects of early childhood care and education on cognitive development

Table 3: Study outcomes, selected measuring instruments, selected publications

Project	Grade retention; Graduation from school; School years	Compensation for socio-economic disadvantage	Selected measuring instruments	Selected publications
EPPE EYTSEN		Partially	British Ability Scales;Reading and math tests	a) EPPE (2004) b) EPPE (2008a) c) EYTSEN (2003)
EPPNI		Partially	British Ability Scales;	EPPNI (2004)
SOEP		Yes	Official reports	a) Spiess et al. (2003) b) Landvoigt et al. (2007)
PRIMA		Not analyzed	Student profiles; Concepts test; Ordering test	Driessen (2004)
DPPS		Yes (targeted intervention)	Revised Amsterdam Child Intelligence Test RAKIT	van Tuijl & Leseman (2007)
CH		Not analyzed	Teacher reports	Lanfranchi (2002)

Table 3 – continued: Study outcomes, selected measuring instruments, selected publications

Project	Grade retention; Graduation from school; School years	Compensation for socio-economic disadvantage	Selected measuring instruments	Selected publications
PANEL1997	Grade retention until age 9: Children who entered kindergarten: at age 2: 9.2% <, at age 3: 12.3% <, at age 4 or older: 23.4%	Partially	Tests about general and specific cognitive abilities	Caille (2001)
CLS	c) Grade retention by age 15: T (23.0%) < C (38.4%) c) School dropout by age 20: T (46.7%) < C (55%) a) High school completion by 23: T (71.4%) > C (63.7%)	Yes (targeted intervention)	School records; Family and participant surveys; Administrative records	a) Reynolds et al. (2007) b) Reynolds et al. (2002) c) Reynolds et al. (2001)

Table 3 – continued: Study outcomes, selected measuring instruments, selected publications

Project	Grade retention; Graduation from school; School years	Compensation for socio-economic disadvantage	Selected measuring instruments	Selected publications
ECLS-K	a) Grade retention until first grade: T (center-based care) < C, T (Head Start) ≈ C	a) Yes b) Partially	Academic Rating Scale	a) Magnuson et al. (2004) b) Rumberger et al. (2006)
Carolina		Yes	Peabody Picture Vocabulary Test-III; Woodcock Johnson-III Tests of Achievement	Peisner-Feinberg & Schaaf (2008)
FACES		Yes (targeted intervention)	Peabody Picture Vocabulary Test-III; McCarthy Draw-A-Design task; Woodcock-Johnson Test	a) Zill et al. (2006) b) FACES (2006)

Table 3 – continued: Study outcomes, selected measuring instruments, selected publications

Project	Grade retention; Graduation from school; School years	Compensation for socio-economic disadvantage	Selected measuring instruments	Selected publications
H.S. Impact		Yes (targeted intervention)	As in FACES	U.S. Department of Health and Human Services (2005)
Albuquerque	Not retained until 2006: ACDC: 73.0%, Free lunch: 67.0%, Reduced price: 75.3%, No support: 75.5% High school graduation on time: ACDC: 31.0%, Free lunch: 23.0%, Reduced price: 38.0%, No support: 43.0%	Partially	Kindergarten Development Progress Report; School records	Boyle (2007) Boyle & Roberts (2003)

Table 3 – continued: Study outcomes, selected measuring instruments, selected publications

Project	Grade retention; Graduation from school; School years	Compensation for socio-economic disadvantage	Selected measuring instruments	Selected publications
ABC		Not analyzed	Peabody Picture Vocabulary Test; Woodcock Johnson Tests	Hustedt et al. (2008)
Oklahoma		Partially	Woodcock-Johnson Tests of Achievement	a) Gormley et al. (2005) b) Gormley et al. (2008)
Georgia	Retention of pre-K children: in kindergarten: 5.3%, in first school year: 9.8%	Partially	Oral and written language scale; Woodcock Johnson-III Tests; Comprehensive Test of Phonological Processing	Henry et al. (2003, 2004)
Delaware	Grade retention until age 8: T = 6.67%, C = 16.5%	Not analyzed	Delaware State Testing Program	Gamel-McCormick & Amsden (2002)

Table 3 – continued: Study outcomes, selected measuring instruments, selected publications

Project	Grade retention; Graduation from school; School years	Compensation for socio-economic disadvantage	Selected measuring instruments	Selected publications
Miami		Yes (targeted intervention)	Learning Accomplishment Profile-Diagnostic	Winsler et al. (2008)
Vietnam		Not analyzed	Raven's Progressive Matrices Test	Watanabe et al. (2005)
NCDS	Level 2 qualification by age 33: a) T (pre-compulsory) > C b) T (preschool) ≈ C Higher education by age 33: a) T (pre-compulsory) ≈ C b) T (preschool) ≈ C	Yes	Different tests for math and reading/language development and an overall measure	a), b) Goodman & Sianesi (2005)

Table 3 – continued: Study outcomes, selected measuring instruments, selected publications

Project	Grade retention; Graduation from school; School years	Compensation for socio-economic disadvantage	Selected measuring instruments	Selected publications
BCS		Yes	English Picture Vocabulary Test; British Ability Scales; Picture Language Test	a) Osborn & Milbank (1987) b) Feinstein et al. (1999)
NLSCY		Partially	Peabody Picture Vocabulary Test-Revised	Lipps & Yiptong-Avila (1999)

Note – Level 2 qualifications are usually obtained at age 15-16 years. Further information about programs and outcomes is given in the text.

6.1 Evidence of the effectiveness of the programs

Table 2 summarizes the key findings of the studies. Scepticism towards the comparison of children's learning progress in different programs is comprehensible because these programs do not necessarily pursue identical objectives and the children served in different institutions possibly differ according to their social backgrounds. All of the longitudinal studies included in the review provided pre-test data. However, the few cross-sectional studies (based on the CH, Delaware, and SOEP projects) and the birth cohort studies reviewed used a retrospective, two-group, post-test-only design. The differences in outcomes between children who did or did not attend preschool can therefore not be attributed unambiguously to the influence of preschool. It should be noted, for instance, that the factors affecting attendance are not known in these studies. Moreover, predictive validity of early academic test scores may differ across assessments as a function of test type, construct being assessed, length of prediction, and administration procedures (Kim & Suen, 2003). For this reason, the results must be treated with caution. Direct comparison of North American and European interventions, for instance, is problematic since children in the American programs typically suffered from greater economic disadvantage than the children in Europe (McLoyd, 1998). In most instances, early education and care programs in Europe are open to all children and are attended by children from both disadvantaged and more favored families whereas programs in the U.S. are frequently open primarily for the socio-economically disadvantaged. In many instances, particular preschool projects were evaluated by more than one study. In these cases, the authors usually drew on different data collections.

In tables 1, 2, 3, and 4, lower case letters - (a), (b), and (c) - indicate from which publication the information is taken in cases where more than one publication was analyzed. The authors of the publications are listed in the last column of table 3. The sample sizes of these studies also differ. Where authors have carried out multiple follow-up examinations of a particular project, the findings are not reported exhaustively. The focus here is on the results of the latest investigation. Two major types of studies are included in this review. One type comprises studies that compared children in treatment groups with children without any treatment or "home children" in comparison groups. The other type comprises studies that compare different programs or curricula and measure academic achievement in comparison to national norms. The results reported in tables 2 and 3 are arranged as follows: Directly interpretable parameters such as age-standardized mean scores and percentages are reported as a common measure of different studies. Their statistical significance - at the $p <$

0.05 level at least - is indicated by the symbols <, >, or *, whereas statistical nonsignificance is indicated by the symbol ≈, whenever information about statistical (non-)significance was given in the original studies. The results of statistics such as t-tests, χ^2-square tests, regression analyses, analyses of variance, or multilevel analyses, in contrast, are indicated merely by the two symbols < and > where they are statistically significant, and are denoted by the symbol ≈ where they are not statistically significant.

The results of the 32 studies (concerning 23 projects) analyzed in this review are outlined and summarized below. They are based on studies that used different statistical methods. The included studies were therefore categorized according to their methodological rigor in studies that used (1) only descriptive measures like mean scores and percentages, (2) bivariate measures such as χ^2-tests and simple correlations, or (3) multivariate measures such as binary probit models, (multiple) regression analyses, multilevel analyses, (multivariate) analyses of (co-)variance, or instrumental variables estimates (see table 4). Of the 32 studies, 27 (or 84.4%) used multivariate measures, four (12.5%) used bivariate measures, and one (3.1%) used descriptive measures exclusively. These methodological differences have to be considered when it comes to drawing conclusions based on the results reviewed. Furthermore, effect sizes are listed in table 4. Effect sizes are estimates of the magnitude of the relationship or difference between two or more variables and help to determine the size of an observed relationship. In the present review, no clear differences can be identified between effect sizes in studies that were published in peer-review journals and studies that were published in research reports or books. Out of 14 studies published in peer-review journals, six reported effect sizes whereas eight did not. Likewise, among the 18 studies published in reports and books, six recorded effect sizes whereas 12 did not. Effect sizes reported in peer-review journals do not appear to be higher than those reported in research reports. Apart from the impact of preschool experiences on cognitive development, the impact on the development of children from families with varying socio-economic status is discussed. Across the majority of studies, the results are comparatively consistent and constitute evidence that early childhood care and education can improve the cognitive development of children.

Table 4: Statistical methods, effect sizes, and quality of the studies

Project	Statistical methods	Effect sizes	Quality of design
EPPE	(3) a) Multilevel analyses, b) Multilevel analyses	a) Pre-reading: 0.28; language: 0.46; early number concepts: 0.47 b) English: 0.22; math: 0.26	a) Good b) Good
EYTSEN	(3) Multilevel analyses	–	Good
EPPNI	(3) Multilevel analyses	Pre-reading: 0.38 Early number concepts: 0.47	Good
SOEP	(3) a) Binary probit models, b) Binary probit models	a) – b) –	a) Fair b) Good
PRIMA	(3) ANOVA; Nominal-metric correlation	Math: 0.04; language: 0.03	Fair
DPPS	(3) Means; ANOVA; Multiple regression analyses	IQ on RAKIT: 0.58 Verbal intelligence: 0.36 Fluid intelligence: 0.44	Good
CH	(2) T-tests	–	Limited
PANEL1997	(3) Logistic regressions	–	Fair

Table 4 – continued: Statistical methods, effect sizes, and quality of the studies

Project	Statistical methods	Effect sizes	Quality of design
CLS	(3) a) Probit, linear, and negative binomial regressions (3) b) and c) Probit and negative binomial regressions	a) – b) – c) –	a), b), c) Good
ECLS-K	(3) a) Ordinary least squares regressions (3) b) Hierarchical linear models	a) Mean cognitive outcomes: ≈ 0.15 b) Reading: in Head Start: -0.12, in Non-Head Start: 0.10 Literacy: in Head Start: –, in Non-Head Start: 0.25 Math: in Head Start: -0.23, in Non-Head Start: 0.13 Science: in Head Start: -0.27, in Non-Head Start: 0.06	a) Good b) Good
Carolina	(3) T-tests; PROC mixed models; Longitudinal growth models	–	Good

Table 4 – continued: Statistical methods, effect sizes, and quality of the studies

Project	Statistical methods	Effect sizes	Quality of design
FACES	(2) a) Percentages (2) b) T-tests	a) – b) Vocabulary: 0.26; letter-word-identification: 0.05; early writing: 0.13; early math: 0.08; book knowledge: 0.67; color naming: 0.60	a) Limited b) Fair
H.S. Impact	(3) Means; Ordinary least squares models; Logistic regressions	Range of effect sizes for various measures: in pre-reading: 0.19 - 0.24; in pre-writing: n.s. - 0.16; in vocabulary: n.s. - 0.12; in oral comprehension: n.s.; in early math: n.s.	Good
Albuquerque	(3) Percentages; Logistic regressions	–	Fair
ABC	(3) Regression-discontinuity analysis	–	Good
Oklahoma	(3) Regression-discontinuity analysis	Letter-word-identification: a) 0.79, b) 0.985 Spelling: a) 0.64, b) 0.743 Applied problems: a) 0.38, b) 0.355	a) Good b) Good

Table 4 – continued: Statistical methods, effect sizes, and quality of the studies

Project	Statistical methods	Effect sizes	Quality of design
Georgia	(1) Means; (3) Hierarchical linear models	–	Fair
Delaware	(2) Percentages; T-tests	–	Limited
Miami	(3) Repeated measures MANOVA; ANCOVA	Cognitive skills: 0.33 - 0.55 Language skills: 0.52 - 0.55	Good
Vietnam	(3) Means, PROC GLM (least-squares means for different interventions)	–	Good
NCDS	(3) a), b) Ordinary least squares regressions	–	Fair
BCS	(3) a) Multiple regressions b) Instrumental variables estimates	a) – b) –	a) Fair b) Fair
NLSCY	(3) Percentages; Ordered response logistic regressions	–	Fair

Note – Further information on the classification of the statistical methods is given in the text. A dash (–) indicates that effect sizes were not indicated. Other research questions in the same studies might have been treated with other statistical methods; this table only displays the statistical analyses adopted to deal with the effects of early childhood education and care on cognitive development.

6.1.1 Cognitive achievement outcomes

With regard to *cognitive achievement outcomes*, the associations between preschool attendance and cognitive outcomes or educational attainment were mostly positive in 22 out of 32 studies (see table 2; the following conclusions are based on the results of the studies reported in this table; table 2 also indicates statistical significance of results). The sample sizes of these 22 studies ranged from $N = 311$ in the Vietnam study to $N = 4,667$ in the Head Start Impact study. In one study (on the PRIMA project), no effects of preschool attendance were identified. In another eight studies (concerning five projects), mixed results were found, notably in the ECLS-K, Albuquerque, ABC, NCDS, and BCS70 studies. In the Panel 1997, an earlier beginning was found to be particularly beneficial for cognitive development even after a variety of variables had been controlled, namely sex, position among brothers and sisters, nationality, birth trimester, socio-professional category and educational diploma of parents, employment of the mother, family size and structure (single parent vs. couple), care experience before enrollment to the "école maternelle," and several factors pertaining to characteristics of the institutions. As regards the presentation of the results, table 2 is self-explanatory for the most part. It indicates (1) the age at which the children were examined, (2) whether the treatment groups outperformed the comparison groups, (3) the domain in which achievement was measured, and (4) the institution for which the results are valid.

The findings of the studies about FACES and those about the Georgia study and the NLSCY require additional comment: The results of the study about FACES indicate the proportion of the gap between four-year-old program attendees and national norms which was closed between fall and spring of the Head Start year in three separate cohorts with regard to early reading competencies and vocabulary. With the exception of the early reading skills in cohort 1, the gaps in all the cohorts were closed considerably (i.e. up to 28%). A comparison between children's test outcomes and national norms was also made in the Georgia study. Its results are indicated as age-standardized mean scores of children when they entered (1) pre-kindergarten, (2) Head Start, and (3) private programs at the age of four years and these results were compared to the outcomes at seven years of age, that is, two years after the end of the program. When the results at age seven exceeded those at age four relative to national norms, the programs were considered to benefit the children.

As shown in table 2, program attendees made sizeable gains in terms of relative standing compared to national norms. Another important finding of the Georgia study was that Head Start children's achievement test scores were con-

Effects of early childhood care and education on cognitive development 93

sistently below those of pre-K, no preschool program, and - especially - private program children. Although this suggests that program features have a marked influence on the learning progress of children, this difference can be attributed more plausibly to differences in home learning environment or socio-economic status. These might have been worse for Head Start children since they faced more risk factors than their counterparts in the other programs. Moreover, the majority of children enrolled in Head Start were African-American, while the majority of children in private programs were White (Henry et al., 2004). Hence Head Start children could not catch up with their more favored peers (see also Henry et al., 2003). The NLSCY compared achievement outcomes of children (1) who attended early childhood education and care programs, with outcomes of children (2) who were cared for by a person other than the mother at two and three years of age, and with outcomes of children (3) who were cared for in the family environment by a parent at two and three years. This survey ascertained that children in early education and care had slightly better cognitive outcomes than their counterparts who were cared for by a person other than the mother, and they performed significantly better than children who were exclusively cared for in the family.

6.1.2 Special education

With regard to *special education* rates, two out of six studies (concerning the EYTSEN and the CLS projects) reduced the proportion of children who later needed special education or were at risk of special education needs. Two other studies (concerning the ECLS-K and the NCDS projects) found mixed results depending on the programs children attended. In the Albuquerque and in the Dutch Preschool studies, it was not possible to draw conclusions about the effectiveness of the preschool programs in preventing special education needs, as there was no control group without preschool experience (see tables 2 and 3).

6.1.3 Grade retention

The third major category of outcomes examined in several studies was *grade retention*. As shown in table 3, in the studies on the CLS and the Delaware projects, the number of children who were retained in grade was smaller for children who attended preschools than for those who did not attend preschool. The ECLS-K studies provided mixed results depending on the program types, and three other studies unfortunately could not secure a control group of matched children who did not attend preschool, notably the studies on the Panel 1997, the Albuquerque, and the Georgia projects.

6.1.4   School graduation

Finally, the *school graduation rates* and/or the *years of school attendance* were interpreted as an additional indicator of cognitive development. Four studies (concerning two projects, notably the NCDS and the CLS) allowed for a clear conclusion about the effectiveness of preschool in terms of fostering school graduation: In the NCDS project, no clear advantage of early education and care for the attainment of higher education degrees was found. However, the studies about the CLS project showed a clear advantage for preschool children as opposed to children without preschool attendance (see table 3).

Although this review suggests that preschool benefits children in most of the cognitive domains examined in the different studies, it also indicates that the extent to which preschool is capable of reducing grade retention and special education rates is more difficult to determine. The number of studies that have investigated retention and special education rates is too small to allow any clear conclusion. Cognitive achievement and scholastic success, however, are undoubtedly affected positively in the vast majority of cases.

6.2   Evidence of compensatory effects

A more detailed analysis can now provide evidence of whether the effects vary with the population served, that is, whether some groups of children derive a greater advantage from the programs than others. Socio-economic status variables are taken into account in order to answer the second research question of this review: Can preschool programs help to overcome inequalities among children from different social backgrounds? Theoretically, three patterns of results may emerge in studies of the differential effectiveness of early education and care programs: (a) children from families with a low socio-economic status gain more than their more advantaged peers, (b) these children gain less, or (c) children from families with a low socio-economic status and families with a high socio-economic status both benefit from early interventions. Two of these three patterns were identified here. Table 3 shows that of 26 studies that took account of families' socio-economic status, seven documented a particular benefit for disadvantaged children whereas ten documented a benefit for both disadvantaged and privileged children, that is, the programs did not all compensate for social disadvantage (see below). Only one study (concerning the EPPNI project) revealed that in some domains disadvantaged children made fewer improvements than their more privileged counterparts. Five projects specifically targeted socio-economically disadvantaged children. According to the eight studies on these five projects, they all benefited the attendees, thus it can be assumed that they have a compensatory effect. However, since they only addressed one particular group of children, a compensatory effect cannot be unambiguously attributed. In table 3, this is indicated in brackets ("targeted intervention"). In the following, the key findings of the studies are briefly summarized so that the dimensions used to indicate socio-economic status can be identified.

6.2.1 Projects benefiting mainly disadvantaged children

Four projects benefited mainly the disadvantaged children: the SOEP, the NCDS, the BCS, and the North Carolina project. The respective studies illustrate that socio-economic disadvantage was compensated for by attendance of the interventions. In table 3, these projects were reported as having had a compensatory effect: Using information from the German SOEP, Spiess et al. (2003) found no significant correlation between kindergarten attendance of German children and their later school placement, but they identified a significant positive correlation for children from immigrant families of Italian, Greek, Turkish, Spanish, and formerly Yugoslavian origin. These children were found to perform on average more poorly at school (Alba, Handl, & Müller, 1994). Children from immigrant families attended schools with restricted academic requirements ("Hauptschule") as opposed to schools with greater academic requirements ("Realschule," "Gymnasium") less often when they had attended kindergarten. In the NCDS, children from disadvantaged backgrounds did not gain more in absolute terms from pre-compulsory or preschool education than those from privileged backgrounds. If anything, taking into account that they tended to start from a lower base of attainment, their improvements were found to exceed those of their more advantaged peers in relative terms (see also Feinstein et al., 1999, for further details). In the BCS, socially disadvantaged children gained slightly more from their preschool experience than more advantaged children. The North Carolina project also benefited the disadvantaged children to a particular extent. In the according study by Peisner-Feinberg and Schaaf

(2008), children were categorized in different risk groups based on poverty level, special needs, English proficiency, and chronic health condition. Although initially children in high-risk groups scored lower than other children in language, literacy, math, and general knowledge tests, and entered pre-K at a deficit, they gained at a similar or even greater rate, and for some measures (e.g., letter knowledge, color knowledge) they even caught up with lower risk groups in kindergarten.

6.2.2 Projects benefiting privileged and disadvantaged children

As opposed to the projects that mainly benefited disadvantaged children, the projects mentioned hereafter yielded benefits for both advantaged and disadvantaged children: there appears to be no consistent advantage from preschool accruing to lower social class children as compared to their more advantaged peers. These are examples of projects that did not effectively compensate for social inequalities but brought about general cognitive progress for all the children involved to about the same extent. In table 3, these projects are reported as having compensated "partially" for socio-economic disadvantage.

This form of partial compensatory effect was observed in the following projects: In the EPPE project, the level of parental qualification, family socio-economic status, and the early years home learning environment were among the strongest predictors of academic attainment and progress, and there was only little evidence of differential effects of preschool according to the social status of the parents, although children with low early years home learning environment showed a benefit from attending a preschool as opposed to attending no preschool particularly if the preschool provision was of high quality and highly effective (EPPE, 2008a). The EPPNI (2004), on the other hand, had mixed results. As opposed to children with parents of a high socio-economic status (where parents were non-manual professionals), children from lower socio-economic status groups generally made less progress in numeracy and children from unemployed parents made less progress in literacy over the first four years of primary school. According to the Panel 1997, the French kindergarten did not effectively compensate for social disparities (Caille, 2001). In Albuquerque, the cognitive progress of children was associated with the economic status of the children's families. The most disadvantaged children were eligible to attend the free lunch programs and the most privileged children attended no support programs, while ACDC programs and reduced price lunch programs fell in between. As expected, on average, children who attended free lunch programs ranked below children from the other programs. They were followed by children from ACDC programs and reduced price lunch support programs (Boyle, 2007; Boyle & Roberts, 2003). In the Georgia study, children from wealthier families started with better cognitive skills, and their school readiness at the end of the program remained higher than the school readiness of children from poorer families; hence disadvantaged children could not catch up with privileged children during the intervention (Henry et al., 2003, 2004). Oklahoma's universal pre-kindergarten was shown to benefit children from diverse income brackets equally in absolute terms (Gormley et al., 2005; Gormley et al., 2008). And while important links between school readiness and several aspects of the home environment were identified in the NLSCY, no consistent effects of social disadvantage on learning progress were found (Lipps & Yiptong-Avila, 1999).

6.2.3 Projects that did not assess differential effects

In the remaining projects, the differential effects of preschool on subgroups of disadvantaged and privileged children were either not analyzed in the studies (PRIMA, ABC, Vietnam project) or the intervention was specifically targeted at socio-economically disadvantaged children so that a comparison with privileged children was not feasible (DPPS, Miami, CLS, FACES, H. S. Impact projects), or the sample size was not large enough to allow reliable separate conclusions on the development of different subgroups (Delaware study). It has to be noted, however, that all of the targeted interventions had, for the most part, positive effects on disadvantaged children. Theoretically, comparing treatment children in targeted programs with an age norm corresponds to comparing disadvantaged children at risk with, on average, typically developing children, so that gains point to compensatory effects. Or the following could be argued at least: provided that privileged children are not fostered in other programs at the same time, targeted interventions can compensate for socio-economic disadvantage. In the studies on the Miami, CLS, FACES, DPPS, and Head Start Impact projects, the differential influence of socio-economic status on the development was not investigated because all children were socio-economically disadvantaged. Although the ECLS-K did not measure socio-economic status, it investigated the influence of language backgrounds. Small effects of language background on special education and grade retention rates were identified. The language achievement of children from language minority backgrounds was lower than the achievement of children from families where English was the dominant language (Rumberger & Tran, 2006). Finally, although designed to investigate the development of disadvantaged children only, the evaluation of the study on the Miami School Readiness Project suggests that early care and education can help to overcome social differences if it specifically addresses economically disadvantaged children. Norm-referenced achievement test scores showed that poor children made significant gains in cognitive and language skills, so that by the end of the year, they were performing on average at or around the national average although they had started from well below the average (Winsler et al., 2008).

6.3 Age at entry, intensity, duration, and quality of programs

A number of additional aspects should be highlighted here, including age at entry and the intensity, duration, and quality of early education programs. Studies such as EPPE, PRIMA, CLS, Head Start Impact, and the Panel 1997 took into account the effects of age at entry and the duration of program attendance. Although other studies ascertained that an earlier beginning and a longer duration afford greater benefits to the participants (Bos et al., 2007; Gull & Burton, 1992; Ramey & Ramey, 1998), the present review is not conclusive. Longer preschool interventions do not necessarily result in better cognitive competencies (EPPE, 2008a; Driessen, 2004) although an early age at entry is associated with a more positive educational development in some instances (e.g., Caille, 2001; U.S. Department of Health and Human Services, 2005). However, the CLS provides evidence that an extended program can exceed a restricted program in terms of effectiveness. Children who received school-age services in first to third grades - in addition to preschool and kindergarten - up to nine years of age showed higher levels of cognitive achievement until 23 years of age (Reynolds et al., 2001).

The effects of intensity were analyzed in some studies. However, the empirical evidence in this review is too scarce for conclusions about the ideal intensity. While some other studies have established that more intensive interventions produce larger positive effects (Ramey & Ramey, 1998), results from a study based on the SOEP did not support this finding (Landvoigt et al., 2007), and the NICHD Study of Early Child Care (Belsky, 2006) highlighted that lots of time spent in any form of care - irrespective of its quality - can be related to problematic social development in subsequent years (although the effects on cognitive outcome measures were shown to be positive), which corroborated a finding of Vandell and Corasaniti (1990). For this reason, it seems reasonable to conclude that the quality of the programs including the early home learning environments (Foster, Lambert, Abbott-Shim, McCarty, & Franze, 2005) and family literacy environments (Christian, Morrison, & Bryant, 1998; Payne, Whitehurst, & Angell, 1994) also rank among the very important factors for a beneficial cognitive development (ECCE, 1999; Hodgen, 2007; Peisner-Feinberg et al., 2001). Hence whether or not children will be successful at school depends to a large extent on the overall quality of their experiences in early childhood.

According to the results of the EPPE (2008a), for instance, the early home learning environment is one of the most powerful predictors of cognitive attainment. In this project, the home environment measure was based on the frequency of parent-child interactions such as teaching the child the alphabet, playing with letters and numbers, visiting libraries, reading to the child, and teaching the child songs or nursery rhymes. Accordingly, these interactions can be regarded as essentials in the promotion of cognitive development. It should be noted, however, that the influence of a family compared to early center-based education may also reflect the potential effect of genetic differences, that is, genotype-based correlations between the childrearing environment parents provide and the cognitive achievement of their offspring. Furthermore, as highlighted above, exclusively family-based early education can be unfavorable in particular for children from families that do not provide their children with the opportunities for informal learning at home (e.g., Leseman, 2002). In sum, the present review suggests that high-quality early childhood experiences may play a more pivotal role for favorable cognitive development than age at entry, intensity, and duration of any intervention program.

7 Conclusion

The present paper reports on the effects of early childhood education and care on cognitive development and the extent to which preschool programs can establish equality of educational opportunity for children from different social backgrounds. As outlined, early education and care programs typically aim to enhance those intellectual and social abilities of children which are the basis for their subsequent development. They aim to provide children with a favorable start at school and to prevent adverse developments such as school failure, grade retention, or special education needs. Since early development of basic competencies is assumed to have the potential to affect children's longer-term attainment, early education and care interventions attempt to foster these competencies by providing an environment that stimulates beneficial development. Moreover, the programs usually strive to establish equality of educational opportunity for children from different social backgrounds because children growing up in environments with little cognitive stimulation do not have the same chance to develop their abilities as children from more privileged families. Apart from the general effects of early education and care on cognitive development, this paper has analyzed the extent to which early interventions diminish social inequalities due to differences in socio-economic status. The favorable effects of model interventions being well-established and uncontested among early childhood analysts, this review has focused on studies based on larger-scale projects that reflect how early childhood education and care can work in a real-world setting.

7.1 General effects

Drawing overall conclusions on the basis of a set of different studies is risky. Yet any review attempts to aggregate results of somewhat heterogeneous studies into some concluding statements. This is done in the following; the conclusions need to be read as an interpretation of the evidence: The majority of studies find that preschool experience gives children a more favorable start at school and there is evidence of persistent effects during the subsequent school years. In many instances, short-term effects exceed longer-term effects on cognitive development. Overall, these findings seem to be independent of study design quality as they applied to a variety of studies with heterogeneous methodological characteristics and quality. Hence we cannot assume any clear relation between the quality of studies and the cognitive outcomes of children. The results reviewed range from no effects on some or all cognitive outcome measures in a few studies to more sizable effects on several measures in, again, a few studies. However, many studies identified moderate effects in various domains. One can therefore conclude that preschool can endow children with a number of capacities that help them to master challenges at school more easily.

Early learning opportunities appear to enhance children's capacity to learn which might improve their later elementary school performance. By providing social and cognitive experiences, preschool programs supplement the home environments of children. They create a familiarity with (pre-) school institutions and procedures which might facilitate the formal schooling later on. The evidence in support of positive effects on special education and grade retention rates is less conclusive than might be expected. And the lack of information on these outcomes in many studies makes any general conclusions unwarranted. The evidence of positive effects on cognitive development, as measured by academic achievement tests, educational attainment, or years of school attendance can be ascertained with less ambiguity. The majority of the programs yielded positive effects. These findings corroborate the results of other studies which have established that preschool programs usually have significant positive short-term and moderate longer-term effects on the cognitive development of children (Anderson et al., 2003; Barnett, 1995, 2008; Currie, 2001; Nelson, Westhues, & MacLeod, 2003; Reynolds et al., 1997), and they contradict the assumption that the programs generally do not yield practically relevant benefits (Dollase, 2007). According to Magnuson et al. (2007), the advantages bestowed by early education and care will diminish by the second or third grade of formal schooling as children who did not attend any program start to catch up. The authors therefore conclude that formal schooling experiences are crucially important for the extent to which the effects persist. However, the few longer-term studies analyzed in this review indicate that positive effects can be maintained in some instances through adolescence and even into adulthood regardless of later experiences in school. No clear advantage of programs with parent support and parent involvement as opposed to those without these components was identified.

7.2 Compensatory effects

Along with the general effects of early education and care, this review has analyzed the potential of preschool programs to compensate for social inequalities. A number of studies show that the main beneficiaries of preschool interventions are children whose families are at lower levels of socio-economic status. However, other studies do not consistently report larger gains for these children. Instead, these studies illustrate that most children can benefit in equal measure regardless of their social backgrounds. In either case, research has demonstrated the value of providing preschool interventions for both socioeconomically disadvantaged and more privileged children. The present overview of studies suggests that the developmental progress of disadvantaged and more privileged children in preschool programs either proceeds in equal measure in absolute terms or offers larger gains in relative terms to disadvantaged children. This implies that children's cognitive development can be fostered by the programs. In addition, since children from disadvantaged families usually start off with less developed skills, they lag behind in their development when compared to more privileged children. The interventions obviously cannot make up completely for the developmental delay they started with. Hence this review is only partly in line with those studies that have identified the most striking benefits for disadvantaged children (e.g., Barnett, 1995; Büchel, Spiess, & Wagner, 1997; Dhuey, 2007; Peisner-Feinberg et al., 2001).

7.3 Policy and research recommendations

In addition to these effects of preschool programs, some important policy questions can be reviewed and research recommendations can be given on the basis of the present survey. In general, practical policy-related conclusions are to be drawn by policy makers rather than by scientists because policy inference is usually shaped not only by empirical evidence, but also by specific social values and economic conditions (e.g., Belsky, 2001). However, policy makers need to know whether particular types of programs are more productive than others according to the findings of current research. In this regard, some implications can be derived from the current review.

Interventions that have produced relatively distinct effects have adopted a broad, versatile approach by providing parent services and requiring parent involvement along with the center-based provision. Moreover, the quality of the early home learning environment has been shown to be an important predictor of subsequent cognitive attainment along with the center-based intervention. Strategies which support or encourage intense parental engagement in home learning activities could therefore enhance the benefits of center-based preschool attendance. Furthermore, it seems that the findings considered here do not allow conceiving of early education and care of children-especially of children from socio-economically disadvantaged families that provide only poor learning conditions as a purely private matter. In countries where attitudes towards early childhood and family policy have traditionally been underpinned by an ideology that places a high value on individual responsibility and by a philosophy of limiting government interventions in matters related to family (see for instance, Allen, 1988, for an analysis concerning the U.S.), policy makers should consider encouraging tax policies that allow families to make use of preschool arrangements which might otherwise remain inaccessible to them for economic reasons. Besides, preschool policies should strive to foster the establishment of equal educational opportunities. In many cases, early interventions have been implemented especially for socio-economically disadvantaged children; in other cases, both disadvantaged and privileged children have been targeted in early childhood programs. However, in any case, the development of children at risk due to adverse learning environments needs to be supported to a particular extent and most carefully in early intervention programs because it is only by improving these children's competencies that equality of educational opportunity can be established for children at the start of their life.

In early childhood education and care research, many studies have focused on the influence of preschool programs on child development and educational success up to now. However, research often has not attempted to disentangle potentially distinctive effects of diverse aspects of preschool experience. For this reason, the effects of quality of institutions and pedagogical curricula as well as the effects of age at entry, duration, and intensity of attendance should be taken into account jointly in further studies. By this means, conclusions from research would not remain limited exclusively to the effects of particular features of preschool, and the extent to which different aspects of early care and education are related to children's skill development or educational outcomes could be determined. This would necessitate thoroughly conducted large-scale - preferably longitudinal - studies with pre-test measures that are held constant when program effects are tested. However, paying attention more carefully to the specific effects of different early childhood education and care variables is worthwhile only if the sample of a study is reliable until the end of the study phase. Loss of participants over time, for instance, is unavoidable in social science research. However, selective drop-out of participants minimizes confidence in the quality and in the results of a study and it questions its validity. Hence if early childhood research ultimately aims to improve the lives of children, it can do so solely if it is carried out appropriately and in accordance with the latest and - above all - highest standards of scientific research.

Do effects of center-based care and education on vocabulary and mathematical skills vary with children's sociocultural background? Disparities in the use of and effects of early childhood services[6]

Abstract: Using data from a survey on cognitive proficiency levels of first graders in Switzerland (N = 1.830), this study analyzes (1) who has access to institutional childcare, (2) whether institutional childcare affects cognitive skills of children who differ in terms of socioeconomic status, home literacy, native country, and home language, and (3) how duration and intensity of childcare affect children's skills. The findings indicate sociocultural disparities in access to childcare. Multiple hierarchical regression analyses suggest that childcare experience did not enhance children's outcomes when social and cultural background characteristics were held constant. For childcare attendees, however, a longer duration of attendance had a positive effect on vocabulary and a higher intensity was related negatively to vocabulary. Children who did not speak German at home benefitted more from childcare in terms of vocabulary skills than German-speaking children. Social background was a significant predictor of vocabulary and math skills. Cultural background additionally impacted on vocabulary skills when social background was controlled for. Implications for policy are discussed.

1 Introduction

This study analyzes three major questions: First, does access to early childhood care and education services vary with children's sociocultural background? Second, do early care and education services affect cognitive skills of children from different backgrounds in primary school? Third, how do duration and intensity of attendance in such services affect the skills of children? The study

---

[6] Reprinted from *International Research in Early Childhood Education* with permission from Monash University. Citation details: Burger, K. (2012). Do effects of center-based care and education on vocabulary and mathematical skills vary with children's sociocultural background? Disparities in the use of and effects of early childhood services. *International Research in Early Childhood Education, 3*(1), 17-40.

relies on data from a survey on children's proficiency in various cognitive domains. It uses statistical estimation models (such as regression analyses) to account for the relationships between children's experience in center-based care and education and their vocabulary and mathematical skills in primary school.

Research suggests that early center-based care and education can improve children's development. In many instances, children—particularly those from socioeconomically disadvantaged backgrounds—who attended early childhood facilities enter school more ready to learn, with domain-specific language, literacy and numeracy skills being further developed than those of their counterparts who were not exposed to any comparable facility (e.g. Barnett, 1995). A majority of studies into the effects of early childhood care and education have analyzed children who entered care and education facilities and programs at about four years of age (see Burger, 2010b). However, less is known about the effects of institutional care and education that is geared to children below that age although a few studies have been carried out (e.g. Belsky et al., 2007; McCartney, 2010; NICHD, 2002a, 2003, 2007). In addition, while the empirical evidence about benefits of early care and education can be generalized potentially to various populations, it may suffer from country-specific biases as most of the major research has been conducted in the U.S. and in the U.K. Yet country-specific differences exist with regard to auspices, access, provision and quality of services as well as with regard to context factors such as fertility rates, child poverty rates, and parental leave policies (OECD, 2006). Thus, it can be hypothesized that children's experiences in early childhood institutions vary across countries (cf. Tietze et al., 1996). To date, no study has analyzed the effects of early care and education on direct measures of children's vocabulary and mathematical skills in primary school in Switzerland. The present analysis attempts to overcome this shortcoming by estimating such effects—as well as effects of duration and intensity of exposure to care and education—on children from diverse sociocultural backgrounds in the first grade of primary schools.

Evidence supports the idea that early childhood care and education can help overcome social inequalities among children from different social backgrounds (e.g., Burger, 2010b; Schütz & Wössmann, 2005a; Spiess et al., 2003). It is therefore important to assess who has access to care and education provision and how exactly this provision as well as sociocultural background characteristics affect children's skills. Drawing on data from a survey of first graders' cognitive proficiency carried out by Moser et al. (2005), the current study addresses these questions. It uses a cross-sectional design, retrospectively assessing effects of care and education in nurseries on children's competencies.

In Switzerland, nurseries target children before the age of kindergarten (i.e., from birth to about four years). The term nursery refers to a center-based care and education service as distinguished from parental care and informal care by relatives, nannies, or babysitters in private homes. Insofar, this term can be used interchangeably with the terms early childhood care and education, early childhood program, or childcare facility for children from birth to four years of age in related studies.

2 Previous research

2.1 Access to early childhood care and education programs

Children who are most at risk of adverse development are often the least likely to participate in early care and education programs (Hofferth et al., 1994; Zigler et al., 2006). Children's access to programs varies with factors such as ethnicity, parents' education and employment, socioeconomic status, and choice processes of a family (e.g., Jamieson et al., 1999; Kagan, 2006, Leseman, 2002; Shin, 2005). In Germany, for instance, children whose parents have higher degrees in education tend to be more likely to attend early childhood institutions (Konsortium, 2006; Meier, 2008) while children from migrant families and less wealthy parents often have lower rates of use of early childhood facilities (Becker & Tremel, 2006). Moreover, access to quality institutions is related to family resources across many countries, with low-income children being under-enrolled (Eurydice, 2009; Zigler et al., 2006) and centers serving predominantly higher-income families providing higher-quality care and education than centers serving less advantaged populations (Phillips et al., 1994). Given the shortage of early care and education spaces in Switzerland as well as the high costs that parents have to pay for these spaces as compared to other European countries (Flitner, 2009), it can be assumed that disparities in access to early care and education facilities exist in Switzerland as well.

2.2 Effects of early childhood care and education on child development

Apart from access to programs, researchers have investigated effects of programs on child development. A number of longitudinal studies in different national contexts provided evidence for positive effects on outcomes such as class repetition rates, special education placement, school achievement, educational attainment in adulthood, health, psychiatric symptoms, delinquency, employment ratio, and occupational status (Barnett, 1995, 2008; Büchel et al., 1997; Caughy et al., 1994; Kagitcibasi et al., 2009). Other studies, however, revealed only minor or no beneficial effects (Becker & Tremel, 2006; Dollase, 2007; Driessen, 2004) or a fading out of effects after the end of a program (Magnuson et al., 2007a; Zigler & Styfco, 1994).

A number of studies evaluated the effects of duration and intensity of programs on cognitive skills, as indexed mostly by variables like number of years and months (for duration) and days per week as well as hours per day (for intensity). Thorough analyses thereby took account of family background variables such as socioeconomic status or country of origin.

2.2.1 Effects of duration on cognitive skills

Several analyses suggest that a longer duration of early care and education yields better academic readiness in kindergarten (Gullo & Burton, 1992) as well as greater educational attainment (Büchner & Spiess, 2007; Caille, 2001) and more developed reading skills in subsequent school years (Bos et al., 2007). The Effective Preschool and Primary Education project found that the number of months a child attended an early childhood institution was related positively to cognitive attainment at the beginning of primary school over and above the effects of family socioeconomic status, income, mothers' qualification levels, and ethnic as well as language background until the start of primary school (Sammons et al., 2004). According to the Chicago Longitudinal Study, children who were exposed to an extended care and education service up to nine years in addition to preschool and kindergarten displayed higher cognitive achievement levels until 23 years of age (Reynolds et al., 2001). However, some studies found that longer lasting programs do not necessarily bring about more beneficial cognitive development (Driessen, 2004; EPPE, 2008a) whereas others yielded findings that varied with academic domains (NICHD, 2007) or established that an ideal length of time should not be exceeded in order to produce the greatest academic benefits for children (Loeb et al., 2007).

Effects of center-based care and education on children's skills 109

2.2.2 Effects of intensity on cognitive skills

Drawing on data from the Early Childhood Longitudinal Study, Loeb et al. (2007) found that the intensity of exposure to a preschool center—as measured by the number of hours per day—was associated with greater intellectual gains for children. This effect depended on family income and race. Higher intensity exposure was associated with better reading and math skills for low-income children, but not for children from high-income families, and English-proficient Hispanic children benefitted more than white or black children. According to a study based on the Socio-Economic Panel in Germany, higher-intensity childcare in the preschool years was related to a decreasing likelihood of attending the highest secondary school track as of twelve years of age, irrespective of the duration of childcare (Landvoigt et al., 2007). But intensity is not related systematically to cognitive outcomes (e.g., NICHD, 2000). Love et al. (2003) point out that quality may be a moderator between the amount of time spent in childcare services and child outcomes. That is, the quality of childcare may affect the strength of the association between the intensity of childcare and child outcomes. However, since numerous studies into the effects of intensity on academic achievement have focused on children in kindergartens (Cryan et al., 1992; Plucker et al., 2004; Votruba-Drzal et al., 2008), it is difficult to determine clear patterns of results for children below kindergarten age.

In sum, the studies into the effects of duration and intensity of early care and education have yielded somewhat ambiguous findings. The inconsistency in the evidence might be attributable to differences in the quality of program evaluations (Allen, 2008). Alternatively, contradictory results may be explained by the fact that family risk factors and child characteristics can moderate the association between childcare and child outcomes. For instance, non-maternal childcare can have opposite effects on child development as a function of family risk background (Côté et al., 2008). However, such moderating effects of family background (i.e., effects of family risk factors on the relationship between childcare and child development) have not been analyzed sufficiently yet. Finally, differing findings might be a result of different social and policy contexts or of the fact that the programs analyzed in various studies differ in respect of their quality. Small-scale, high-quality (model) programs with favorable staff-to-child ratios and various additional services such as health care and nutritional interventions typically produce greater and longer-term effects than large-scale public programs (Barnett & Belfield, 2006). Various studies into the effects of programs of outstanding quality exist (Barnett, 1995). However, the results of well-designed larger-scale analyses are more generalizable than those of studies focusing on such high-quality programs. The current study therefore draws on a large data set in order to assess cognitive effects that can be generalized to a larger population of children.

3 Nursery provision in Switzerland

Outcomes of care and education may vary with context and regulatory systems (Love et al., 2003). Policy and legal context as well as characteristics of care and education that may act as determinants of child development therefore need to be elucidated. Differences between nurseries and kindergartens in Switzerland must be taken into account.

In Switzerland, kindergarten pertains to the administrative system of education (ISCED 0). Although kindergarten is not compulsory in every canton, the vast majority of children attend kindergarten, the mean duration of attendance being somewhat below two years (EDK, 2010). Kindergarten curricula emphasize the advancement of socio-emotional, psychomotor, and cognitive development (CIIP, 1992). Nurseries, on the other hand, offer collective care and education to children prior to kindergarten age.

3.1 Guidelines of the federal association of nurseries

According to the guidelines of the Swiss association of nurseries, the pedagogical approach in nurseries includes care, fostering of early skills, integration, and education (KiTaS, 2008). The guidelines stipulate minimum standards. While they do not specify criteria pertaining to process quality such as the quality of teacher-child interactions, they focus on structural quality determinants.

3.2 Structural quality standards

The guidelines of the Swiss association of nurseries specify a benchmark of ten to twelve children of varying age per group. At least two educators have to be present per group. A one-to-one ratio between educators with a federally accredited diploma and educators without official training is requested. The resulting quota approximately corresponds to the staff-to-child ratios recommended by the European Commission Network on Childcare (1996) and by the Committee on Early Childhood, Adoption, and Dependent Care of the American

Academy of Pediatrics (2005). The guidelines of the Swiss association further stipulate that the professional staff is federally accredited as infant educators. 43% of the staff in nurseries does not have an official degree (BSV, 2010). As compared to the standards of the European Commission Network on Childcare (1996), the standards in Switzerland are relatively rigorous. However, the extent to which these standards are adopted in practice has not been assessed empirically.

3.3 Federal investments in nurseries

Federal investments in the early childhood care and education sector amount to 0.2% of the gross domestic product (Wolter et al., 2007). Thus, Switzerland invests less than most other European countries where investments vary between 0.3% (Poland) and 2.0% (Denmark) or the United States where investments add up to 0.4% (OECD, 2006). As a consequence, the demand for nurseries exceeds the supply. In the canton of Zurich, only 4.1 nurseries exist per 1.000 children at the age before compulsory schooling (Wolter et al., 2007).

3.4 Use of nurseries

In 2007, 32.5% of two-parent families used nurseries for their 0-to-6-year-old children (Stamm et al., 2009). 27.0% of children aged three and four years were enrolled in early care and education facilities including nurseries in Switzerland whereas 71.2% were enrolled in the OECD countries on average (OECD, 2009). Out of the families who use nurseries for their children, about 20% use a nursery for one day, about 33% for two days, and about 20% for three days per week. 64% of the children spend the whole day in a nursery whereas 33% spend half a day in a nursery (BSV, 2010).

4 Objectives of the study and its contribution to research

This study attempts to identify the influence of sociocultural background and nursery experience on vocabulary and mathematical proficiency of children at the beginning of the first grade, thereby analyzing whether effects of nursery experience differ as a function family backgrounds. A number of studies into the effects of early-years provisions have been completed in the United States (for reviews see Burger, 2010b; Currie, 2001; Karoly et al., 1998; Karoly et al., 2005; Shonkoff & Meisels, 2006; Waldfogel, 2002; Yoshikawa, 1995) as well as in other national contexts (UNESCO, 2007). In Switzerland, however, only one study into the effects of nurseries was conducted (Lanfranchi, 2002). It established that children who had been in extra-familial care and education settings experienced fewer problems on entry to primary school. Yet while Lanfranchi's study used teacher-reported proficiency levels, the present study evaluates direct measures of children's skills.

Mere exposure to a nursery is not the sole factor responsible for improvements in children's skills. Various child and family background factors— including socio-economic status, immigration background, and language spoken at home—contribute to child development (Bridges et al., 2004; Esser, 2006; Jung & Stone, 2008; Karoly et al., 1998; Melhuish & Petrogiannis, 2006; NCES, 2003; Siraj-Blatchford, 2009). In addition, the early home learning environment is an important predictor of child outcomes. Home literacy is one aspect of the home learning environment.[7] A summary of research suggests that there are associations between home literacy and socioeconomic background although there is wide variability in home literacy across different families (Phillips & Lonigan, 2009). A number of analyses further indicate relationships between home literacy and children's development of literacy skills and vocabulary (Huttenlocher et al., 1991; Sénéchal, 2006; Tabors et al., 2001). Consequently, it is important to assess empirically not only how participation in a nursery affects children's competencies, but also to what extent social and cultural background factors play a role in the acquisition of competencies. The current study addresses these questions. In addition, it makes a new contribution to the research literature by evaluating whether effects of nursery as well as duration and intensity of attendance in a nursery vary for children who differ in terms of socioeconomic status, home literacy, native country, and home language in Switzerland.

5   Research questions

Three major questions are addressed: (1) Do nursery attendees differ from non-attendees in respect of social and cultural background characteristics? (2) Do

---

7   Home literacy has been operationalized as a measure of frequency or exposure to literacy experiences, ranging from the mere counting of the number of books in a family's household to more sophisticated attempts to estimate the amount of time spent on literacy events such as shared book reading (Leseman & De Jong, 1998).

effects of nursery experience vary with children's socioeconomic status, home literacy, native country, and home language? And (3) how do duration and intensity of nursery attendance affect children's proficiency levels?

6 Method

6.1 Study design

Data were derived from a survey on cognitive proficiency levels of children which had been conducted in the Swiss canton of Zurich (Moser et al., 2005). Children's skills were assessed immediately after the beginning of the first grade of primary school. During one-on-one testing sessions, two cognitive dimensions—vocabulary and mathematics—were explored. At the same time, a parent questionnaire was distributed to collect retrospective data on children's nursery attendance and to assess social and cultural background characteristics of each child's family. The study adopts a cross-sectional design. Correlations between nursery attendance, family variables, and children's skills are carried out. In addition, multiple linear regression analyses are performed as they allow controls for intervening (background) factors.

6.2 Sample

In the summer of 2003, 11.118 children entered the first grade of primary school in the canton of Zurich. The sample included 120 school classes, containing 1.830 children with a mean age of 7.00 years. That corresponds to 16.5% of all children who entered the first grade. 49.5% of the children in the sample were female.

6.2.1 Languages spoken at home

Children who always spoke either Swiss German or High German at home constituted 73.3% of the sample. The remaining 26.7% never or only sometimes spoke German at home. German is the official language in the canton of Zurich. While Swiss German is the spoken language and High German is the written language of Swiss residents, High German is both the spoken and the written language of the residents of Germany. As Swiss German and High

German are similar languages, they are grouped together and distinguished from any other, foreign language.

6.2.2 Native country

Within the sample, 86.7% of children had lived in Switzerland since birth while 55.9% of mothers and 55.1% of fathers had lived in Switzerland since birth. The proportion of parents who had not lived in Switzerland since birth exceeded the 22.7% of the resident population (from 15 years upwards) who were not born in Switzerland (BfS, 2002).

6.2.3 Parental education

The educational background of the parents in the sample tended to be lower than the educational background of the (25- to 64-year-old) resident population of Switzerland in 2003 (BfS, 2009). Within the sample, 28.1% of fathers and 38.1% of mothers had completed only nine years of compulsory schooling. This compares with figures of 11.0% for men and 19.9% for women in Switzerland overall. Moreover, while 22.5% of men and 12.4% of women resident in Switzerland hold university degrees, none of the parents in the sample had obtained a university degree.

6.2.4 Housing conditions

Apart from educational background, the number of rooms per person in a household can be interpreted with caution as a rough indicator of a family's socioeconomic background (Galobardes et al., 2006). The families in the present sample had an average of 1.14 rooms per person at home (SD = 0.35).

6.2.5 Use of nursery and nursery attendance patterns

Of the 1.830 children in the sample, 472 attended a nursery before entering kindergarten (25.8%). For 408 children information about the duration of attendance was given: 218 children (53.4%) attended a nursery for one to two years whereas 190 children (46.6%) attended a nursery for over two years. For

Effects of center-based care and education on children's skills 115

411 children information about the intensity of nursery attendance was provided: 288 children (68.1%) had been in a nursery for one to three days a week and 123 children (29.1%) had been in a nursery for more than three days a week. Duration and intensity of nursery attendance were interrelated. Relative to children who attended a nursery for one to two years, children who attended nursery for more than two years were significantly more likely to be enrolled for more than three days a week, $\chi^2(1) = 8.574, p = .003$.

6.3   Measures and variables

6.3.1   Cognitive skill measures

A test of cognitive skills developed by Moser et al. (2003) was used. This test measures a child's vocabulary, that is, the ability to name objects and activities as well as comprehension of mathematical concepts including quantities, series, numbers, addition, and subtraction. The items assessing vocabulary are presented as pictures showing objects such as a cable car or activities such as a boy peeling an apple. The items evaluating mathematics are presented both as pictures and in a written form. For instance, pictorial items show a number of objects and five different numerals. The task for the child consists in determining the numeral (among the five alternatives) which correctly denotes the number of objects shown in the picture.

This cognitive test shares important features with measures used in related studies. As the British Ability Scales II (Elliott et al., 1997; Hill, 2005), it is composed of specific subscales. Both tests assess vocabulary and number skills. The subscale assessing vocabulary is modeled upon the Peabody Picture Vocabulary Test (Dunn & Dunn, 1997). However, in the Peabody test the examinee selects a picture that best illustrates a spoken word's meaning, whereas in the test by Moser et al. (2003) the examinee names objects and activities illustrated in pictures.

The scale measuring vocabulary consists of 20 items and the scale measuring mathematics consists of 46 items. Children's answers were rated (and coded) as wrong (0) when objects and activities were named incorrectly or mathematical concepts were not properly understood. They were rated as correct (1) when children's responses were accurate. The raw scores of the sum of the ratings of all items of a scale were standardized. Cronbach's α internal consistency reliability of the two scales amounted to .913 and .912, respectively. A confirmatory factor analysis established the loadings of each individual item on the scales. These loadings ranged between .444 and .749 on the vocabulary scale and between .210 and .670 on the mathematics scale. The Pearson intercorrelation between the vocabulary and the mathematics scales amounted to .280*** ($n = 1.592$).

6.3.2 Sociocultural background and nursery variables

A parent questionnaire assessed social and cultural background characteristics of each child's family and thus provided information used to create seven predictors for the regression analyses: (1) socioeconomic status (SES), an aggregate metric measure consisting of the number of years of mother's and fathers' education and the number of rooms per person in a family's household; (2) home literacy, operationalized as the number of books at home (0-200 vs. >200);[8] (3) native country, that is, whether a child had lived in Switzerland 'since birth' as opposed to 'not since birth,' and (4) home language German, that is, whether a child 'always' spoke Swiss or High German at home as opposed to 'sometimes or never.'[9] Finally, three variables relating to nursery experience were used: (5) nursery attendance, that is, whether a child attended a nursery or not; (6) duration of nursery experience (1-2 years vs. >2 years) and (7) intensity of nursery experience (1-3days/week vs. >3 days/week).

6.3.3 Interaction terms

A number of interaction terms are added to the regression models to determine whether the effects of nursery experience differ for diverse groups of children. Specifically, product terms are analyzed between each of the four background variables (1 to 4) and the three nursery-related variables (5 to 7).

---

[8] The cut off score of 200 books was chosen because it divided the sample best into two groups of children: 65.7% of children had 0-200 books and 34.3% of children had more than 200 books.

[9] These background measures must not be interpreted as direct indicators of the quality of an early family learning environment. The empirical evidence concerning the associations between sociocultural background and child development (see studies cited above) merely justifies the assumption that such background variables can be understood as approximate estimates of the preconditions for children's learning processes.

6.3.4 Data analytic approach

Aside from correlations, multiple linear regression models are performed as they allow for the inclusion of potential intervening variables as covariates. By controlling for SES, home literacy, language spoken at home and native country, background factors known to be associated with educational aspirations and use of early care and education provision for the offspring are held constant (Becker & Lauterbach, 2007; Bridges et al., 2004; Magnuson et al., 2004; NCES, 2003). Controlling statistically for factors which might affect skill development increases the likelihood of excluding parental selection effects. Furthermore, the influence of kindergarten in the years following nursery attendance is held constant.[10] Families who indicated that they had not used nursery may have used informal care by relatives or babysitters, for instance, but were assumed to have used no center-based care comparable to a nursery for their children.

The study adopts a quasi-experimental research strategy. Children who attended a nursery are contrasted with children lacking this experience. Sequential regressions are performed to estimate the association between children's exposure to nursery and children's skills in the first grade. Two models are analyzed for both outcome variables. The basic equations summarize the conceptual approach:

Model 1: $Y_i = \beta_0 + \beta_1 SB + \beta_2 CB + \beta_3 NA + \beta_4 NAxSCB + \varepsilon$
Model 2: $Y_i = \beta_0 + \beta_1 SB + \beta_2 CB + \beta_3 DA + \beta_4 IA + \varepsilon$

In model 1, the outcome (Y) of child (i) is a function of social background (SB) and cultural background (CB) of the child's family, nursery attendance (NA), interaction effects between nursery attendance and sociocultural background variables (NA x SCB), and a random and normally distributed error term (ε).

---

10   Out of 472 children with nursery experience, 423 children attended kindergarten for two years (89.9%). As this was the overwhelming majority, the analyses were carried out on data for these children only so that the duration of kindergarten attendance could not function as an intervening variable. In the resulting sample (n = 1.623), all children had two years of kindergarten experience. In Switzerland, kindergarten is a government-run institution and its pedagogical approaches as well as opening hours are relatively homogeneous in most institutions. It can therefore be assumed that the kindergarten experience was comparable with regards to curricula, educational aims, and intensity for all the children in the present sample. In 2003, the mean duration of kindergarten attendance was slightly less than two years in Switzerland (Wolter et al., 2007) suggesting that the sample can be considered as representative in this respect.

Model 2 focuses exclusively on children who attended a nursery, not on the total sample of children. It attempts to answer the research question about the extent to which duration and intensity of nursery attendance affect skill levels of children by including the predictors 'duration of attendance' (DA) and 'intensity of attendance' (IA) in a nursery instead of the predictor nursery attendance (NA). Thus a two-stage approach to regression analyses was chosen with model 1 focusing on the whole sample and model 2 focusing on the subsample of children with nursery experience.

The sequential regressions are calculated with increasing numbers of predictors: model 1 consists of four consecutive steps. The first step entails the analysis solely of the effect of social background on children's proficiency levels. In the second step, the effects of cultural background variables are added. Step three additionally includes the effects of nursery attendance and step four includes the effects of the interaction terms. Model 2 consists of three steps: social background (step 1), cultural background (step 2), and duration as well as intensity of nursery attendance (step 3).[11] This sequence corresponds to the natural order of influences on child development as sociocultural background variables impact on children prior to nursery experience. The increase in the variance explained (ΔR^2) will be the crucial test to evaluate the effect of nursery experience. The different blocks of predictors are entered according to the entrance criteria PIN = .05 and POUT = .10.

7 Results

7.1 Sociocultural differences between nursery attendees and non-attendees

As shown in table 1, children with nursery experience differed from comparison group children with regard to a number of background factors. Relative to the comparison group, nursery attendees' mothers and fathers had completed significantly more years of formal schooling (12.52 and 13.27 years vs. 10.85 and 12.46 years) and they had more rooms per person in the household on average (1.24 vs. 1.13). Thus the socioeconomic status was higher for children in the nursery group. A significantly greater percentage of nursery attendees lived in households with more than 200 books as opposed to fewer than 200 books (44% vs. 30.6%). Nursery attendees were less likely than non-attendees to al-

---

11   Interaction terms were not included in order to avoid multicollinearity.

ways speak Swiss German or High German at home (69.3% vs. 75.9%). The nursery group and the comparison group did not differ significantly in regard to sex and native country.

Table 1: Selected sample characteristics and differences between children with nursery experience and children without nursery experience (comparison group)

Variable	Nursery group (n = 423)		Comparison group (n = 1200)		Test statistics			
	M	SD	M	SD	t		df	p
Years of maternal education	12.52	3.70	10.85	3.53	-7.990		685.917	.000
Years of paternal education	13.27	3.99	12.46	4.04	-3.391		1528	.001
Number of rooms per person	1.238	0.41	1.126	0.32	-5.054		599.411	.000
Socioeconomic status	0.349	1.01	-.0603	0.37	-6.909		600.400	.000
	n	%	n	%	χ^2		df	
Sex					0.004		1	.951
Female	209	49.4	595	49.6				
Male	214	50.6	605	50.4				
Number of books at home					24.956		1	.000
0-200	234	56.0	825	69.4				
>200	184	44.0	363	30.6				
Native country					0.007		1	.934
In Switzerland since birth	378	91.7	1071	91.6				
In Switzerland not since birth	34	8.3	98	8.4				
Home language German					6.437		1	.011
Always spoken	269	69.3	831	75.9				
Never or sometimes spoken	119	30.7	264	24.1				

Note – All the children investigated attended kindergarten for two years. When counts do not add up to the total number of children, the respective missing numbers correspond to the proportion of missing values in the according variables. Percentages are presented for a column total of 100%. T-Tests for independent samples were calculated for metric variables, Pearson χ^2-tests were computed for categorical variables.

Effects of center-based care and education on children's skills   121

7.2   Correlations

Pearson correlations were calculated to determine bivariate associations between the metric predictor SES and the metric outcome variables. Point-biserial correlations established the relations between the dichotomous predictors and the metric outcomes. This section highlights the most important results: Nursery attendance did not correlate significantly with the vocabulary and mathematics outcomes. Duration of nursery attendance correlated positively with vocabulary ($r = .284^{***}$), but not with mathematics. Intensity of nursery attendance correlated negatively with the vocabulary measure ($r = -.303^{***}$). The vast majority of the social and cultural background variables correlated significantly with both outcome variables. Overall, the significant correlations ranged from $r = .110^{***}$ (between German as home language and mathematical skills) to $r = .627^{***}$ (between German as home language and vocabulary).

7.3   Effects of sociocultural background and nursery experience on children's skills

Tables 2 and 3 display coefficients from hierarchical multiple regressions of children's cognitive and social proficiency on social background, cultural background, nursery experience, and interactions. They present the standardized regression coefficients (β) and the change in the explained variance (ΔR^2), the intercept (constant) of the complete model with all four blocks of predictors entered, the coefficient of determination R^2, the F-value, the adjusted R^2, and the number of cases analyzed in each step of the regression.

Table 2: Hierarchical regressions predicting vocabulary in the first grade from social background, cultural background, nursery experience, and interactions

Predictor	Model 1 ΔR²	β	Model 2 ΔR²	β
Social background	.249***		.288***	
SES		.230***		.270***
Home literacy		.121***		.099*
Cultural background	.255***		.195***	
Native country		.109***		.084*
Home language German		.545***		.413***
Nursery experience	.000		.022**	
Attendance in a nursery		.099*		
Duration of attendance				.145***
Intensity of attendance				-.100*
Interactions	.005*			
Nursery x SES		.023		
Duration of attendance x SES				
Intensity of attendance x SES				
Nursery x Home literacy		.001		
Duration of attendance x Home literacy				
Intensity of attendance x Home literacy				
Nursery x Native country		.004		

Table 2 – Hierarchical regressions predicting vocabulary in the first grade from social background, cultural background, nursery experience, and interactions

Predictor	Model 1 ΔR²	β	Model 2 ΔR²	β
Duration of attendance x Native country				
Intensity of attendance x Native country		-.139**		
Nursery x German				
Duration of attendance x German				
Intensity of attendance x German				
(Constant)	.435		.502	
Total R²	.508		.505	
F	156.681***		58.159***	
Adjusted R²	.505		.496	
Number of cases for steps 1, 2, 3, (4)	1372, 1370, 1369, 1365		346, 344, 342	

Note – All children attended kindergarten for two years. Missing values were excluded pairwise. ΔR²: change in amount of variance explained (R²), β: standardized coefficients; + $p < .10$, * $p < .05$, ** $p < .01$, *** $p < .001$. Constant and standardized coefficients β are reported for the complete model with all predictors entered.

7.3.1 Vocabulary skills

Table 2 summarizes the findings of regression models predicting vocabulary. Model 1 suggests that all social and cultural background variables were significant predictors of children's vocabulary scores. Social background (SES and home literacy) explained 24.9% and cultural background (native country and home language) additionally explained 25.5% of variance in the vocabulary scores. There was no significant R^2 increase when the variable 'nursery attendance' was entered additionally into the model. However, the interaction between 'nursery attendance' and German as home language was significant. A split file regression analysis showed that the regression model for children who always spoke German at home accounted for 16.5% of variance ($F = 31.997$, $p = .000$, adjusted $R^2 = .160$, $N = 977$) in children's vocabulary scores whereas the regression model for children who never or only sometimes spoke German at home accounted for 23.4% of variance ($F = 16.226$, $p = .000$, adjusted $R^2 = .220$, $N = 324$). The overall model accounted for an adjusted variance of 50.5%.

Model 2 analyzes the effects of social and cultural background as well as of duration and intensity of nursery attendance in the subsample of children with nursery experience. A higher SES, greater home literacy, Switzerland as native country, and German as home language predicted significantly higher vocabulary scores. With social and cultural background variables held constant, a longer duration of nursery experience predicted higher scores whereas a higher intensity predicted lower scores in vocabulary. Model 2 accounted for 49.6% of adjusted variance in the outcome. The high determination coefficients R^2 might be a sign of multicollinearity among the predictors. However, the lowest tolerance value in model 1 was found for the interaction term Nursery x German (.219). That suggests that this interaction term correlates most strongly with all the other predictors and is therefore the least independent among the predictors. Nevertheless, the value does not fall below the critical threshold of .10 (Urban & Mayerl, 2006). In model 2, the lowest tolerance value was identified for SES (.659) and was thus not critical either.

7.3.2 Mathematical skills

Table 3 combines the results of regressions of mathematical competency on social and cultural background, nursery experience, and interaction variables. Model 1 suggests that mathematical competency is affected significantly by social background but not by cultural background, nursery attendance, or interactions. Model 2 indicates that among children with nursery experience, the block of social background variables explains a significant amount of variance in mathematical skills whereas cultural background has no significant effect. Duration and intensity of nursery attendance and interactions prove unrelated to mathematical competencies when social and cultural background variables are held constant. Altogether, the predictors in the two models account for only a small proportion of adjusted variance (2.5% and 3.2%) which suggests that various other factors influence mathematical competencies apart from the ones included in the analysis.

Table 3: Hierarchical regressions predicting mathematical skills in the first grade from social background, cultural background, nursery experience, and interactions

Predictor	Model 1 ΔR²	β	Model 2 ΔR²	β
Social background	.026***		.038**	
SES		.082*		.120+
Home literacy		.085*		.064
Cultural background	.002		.009	
Native country		-.011		.084
Home language German		.048		.043
Nursery experience	.001		.002	
Attendance in a nursery		-.007		
Duration of attendance				-.024
Intensity of attendance				-.028
Interactions	.002			
Nursery x SES		.023		
Duration of attendance x SES				
Intensity of attendance x SES				
Nursery x Home literacy		-.014		

Table 3 – continued: Hierarchical regressions predicting mathematical skills in the first grade from social background, cultural background, nursery experience, and interactions

Predictor	Model 1 ΔR^2	β	Model 2 ΔR^2	β
Duration of attendance x Home literacy				
Intensity of attendance x Home literacy		-.048		
Nursery x Native country				
Duration of attendance x Native country				
Intensity of attendance x Native country		-.003		
Nursery x German				
Duration of attendance x German				
Intensity of attendance x German				
(Constant)	.503		.444	
R^2	.031		.048	
F	4.926***		2.888**	
Adjusted R^2	.025		.032	
Number of cases for steps 1, 2, 3, (4)	1372, 1370, 1369, 1365		346, 344, 342	

Note – All children attended kindergarten for two years. Missing values were excluded pairwise. ΔR^2: change in amount of variance explained (R^2), β: standardized coefficients; $^+ p < .10$, $^* p < .05$, $^{**} p < .01$, $^{***} p < .001$. Constant and standardized coefficients β are reported for the complete model with all predictors entered.

8   Discussion

This study addressed three main questions: first, whether social and cultural differences exist between nursery attendees and non-attendees; second, whether effects of nursery experience vary with children's sociocultural backgrounds; and third, how duration and intensity of nursery attendance affect children's skills.

8.1   Differences between attendees and non-attendees

Social disparities in children's access to nurseries were identified. On average nursery attendees came from socially more privileged families than did non-attendees, as indicated by differences in socioeconomic status and home literacy. This finding is in line with the evidence of other studies (Jamieson et al., 1999; Kagan, 2006; Meier, 2008; PACE, 2002; Shin, 2005) and may encourage policy makers to take measures that facilitate the access to early childhood education and care provisions for socially disadvantaged children growing up in impoverished environments.

8.2   Do effects of nursery experience vary with children's sociocultural backgrounds?

In order to scrutinize differential effects of nursery on children from varying backgrounds, a more general question needs to be addressed first: did sociocultural background affect the skills of children in the present sample?

8.2.1   Effects of sociocultural background on children's skills

Regression analysis—a statistical technique used to examine the relationship between children's sociocultural background and their cognitive proficiency in primary school—indicated that children from socially more privileged families began their lives with higher skills than their more disadvantaged peers. Specifically, a higher SES and greater home literacy impacted positively on children's mathematical and vocabulary skills. With social background characteristics held constant (in order to rule out spurious relationships between variables), cultural background influenced vocabulary. Children who always spoke German at home and children whose native country was Switzerland attained higher vocabulary scores than children who only sometimes or never spoke German at home and children with a different native country.

Although the regression models predicting vocabulary might be to some extent tautological—as some of the predictors and the outcome vocabulary are relatively closely related to each other—the result concerning the influence of cultural background on vocabulary is consistent with findings that established adverse effects of various family background variables on children's emergent skills and achievement (Barnett & Belfield, 2006; Karoly et al., 1998; Ramey & Ramey, 2004). The findings support the idea that social disadvantage can have a detrimental impact on children's competencies (Duncan et al., 1994; Lee & Burkam, 2002; Niles et al., 2008). According to previous studies, low socioeconomic status can be harmful mainly when it is coupled with unfavorable home learning experiences (Melhuish et al., 2008) and other social risk factors such as exposure to violence since these factors can mediate the association between socioeconomic status and children's cognitive functioning and social well-being (Foster et al., 2005), that is, socioeconomic status can influence social risk factors which in turn can affect child outcomes.

Familiarity with a society's cultural background appears to be of importance for skill development. The results of the present study corroborate evidence of associations between a child's command of a society's language and the child's school achievement and educational success (Esser, 2006). Children from immigrant families often perform poorer than their native peers on a wide range of standardized measures of competencies (Dubowy et al., 2008) although the 'depth of immigration' may have an influence on such measures (Hakuta & D'Andrea, 1992). Policies that encourage the acquisition of a country's official language might help children with a migration background to develop capacities required to be competitive in achievement-oriented knowledge societies.

8.2.2   Effects of nursery and effects of duration and intensity of nursery attendance

This study identified a number of effects of nursery experience including an important differential effect on children from diverse linguistic backgrounds.

8.2.2.1 Nursery attendance

Neither vocabulary nor mathematical skills were enhanced by exposure to a nursery when social and cultural background was controlled for. However, it has to be noted that children who attended a nursery came from better educated and assumedly better earning families within the sample. As children from lower educated and less earning families might benefit more from attending childcare, the present result must not be interpreted as a general rule. Moreover, the insufficient supply of nurseries in the canton of Zurich might have lowered the overall quality of care and education in nurseries. Thus, in theory, the results might also be a consequence of a low quality of nurseries.

Although nursery attendance proved to have no significant effects on children's vocabulary and mathematical skills when background variables were held constant, the analysis of interactions (which determine whether the effects of nursery experience differ for different groups of children) revealed an interesting result: the impact of nursery on vocabulary was smaller for children who always spoke German at home than for children who never or only sometimes spoke German at home.

8.2.2.2 Duration of attendance

The assumption that duration of exposure to a nursery influences child development was confirmed only for the vocabulary outcome. A longer duration was more likely to be associated with higher scores, suggesting that the number of years children spend in early childhood services contribute to the development of their active knowledge of words and nouns.

8.2.2.3 Intensity of attendance

A higher intensity of nursery attendance was related negatively to vocabulary scores. This finding is consistent with some previous studies showing that risks are associated with intensity of childcare although these studies primarily point to risks related to parent-child relationships, social adjustment, levels of aggression, and distress during separations from the mother (Bates et al., 1994; Belsky, 2006; Loeb et al., 2007; NICHD, 1997).

8.3 Limitations of the study

The original study was carried out meticulously and it provided a wide range of information including careful one-on-one assessments of children's abilities. However, it did not collect data about the quality of nursery and family learning environments and it sourced information about nursery experience retrospectively. Thus, instead of a treatment effect, a selection effect might be found.[12] For this reason, important sociocultural background variables were held constant in the present regression analyses. They can be understood as indicators of the quality of a family learning environment since they were found to be linked with informal learning in the family and were hypothesized to be to a large extent responsible for children's developmental progress (Gauvain, 1998; Hoff, 2006; Hoff & Tian, 2005; Lee & Burkam, 2002; Leseman, 2002). This procedure and the estimation models used are consistent with the method and estimation models of important related studies (e.g., Loeb et al., 2007; Spiess et al., 2003). Note also that the children in the present sample were grouped in different primary school classes when their cognitive skills were tested. Individual test results might thus be related to particular characteristics of school classes. Intraclass correlations were performed and suggest that multilevel models could be conducted. Yet as the data set did not provide information about the characteristics of individual school classes, the present study refrained from using multilevel modeling (a technique frequently used to deal with data of children who are grouped together in classes).

8.4 Contextualizing the findings in research and implications for policy

In accordance with previous studies (Jordan et al., 1992; Magnuson et al., 2004; 2007b), the present study highlights that mathematical skills vary to a lesser degree with family environment variables than language skills. However, the current study yielded smaller effects of background variables and early intervention on mathematical skills than two previous analyses that were based on similar study designs (Magnuson et al., 2004, 2007b). The main reason for this dis-

---

12 A selection effect means that parents who decide to use a nursery for their child might hypothetically be those who care more about the conditions in which the child can acquire important competencies. Consequently, a superior test performance of children with nursery experience might be due to more extensive parent support—which would represent a selection effect—rather than to nursery attendance itself (see Spiess et al., 2003).

crepancy might be the fact that the previous regression models which accounted for greater variance included a larger set of measures of child and family characteristics including income-to-needs ratio, family structure and size, race and ethnicity, birth weight and weight at the time of measurement, home learning environment, and quality of the child's neighborhood and school environment (ibid.).

In view of different recent studies, the evidence about the effects of participation in early care and education services on cognitive skills ultimately remains inconsistent. In this study, nursery attendance did not explain any significant unique variance in vocabulary or mathematical skills over and above social and cultural background variables. This finding is in line with the result of a study from Turkey—based on a sample of families with low socioeconomic standing in terms of parental income, education levels, and housing conditions—which found no effects of early intervention on mathematics skills as measured at age seven (Kagitcibasi et al., 2001). However, the finding contradicts evidence from the Effective Preschool and Primary Education study (conducted in the UK) whereby preschool attendance impacted positively on mathematics skills of children from diverse social and ethnic backgrounds in primary school (EPPE, 2008a). It must be noted that the size of the impact of preschool in the EPPE study depended on the quality of the center. This suggests that differences in the results can be traced to variations in the quality of early childhood services (cf. Burchinal et al., 2000; Early et al., 2007; ECCE, 1999; NICHD, 2002a). In addition, further predictors of child outcomes have been described and might account for differing results, notably curriculum (Guimarães & McSherry, 2002; Schweinhart & Weikart, 1998; Siraj-Blatchford & Sylva, 2004; Stipek et al., 1995) and timing, breadth, and flexibility of programs (Bos et al., 2007; Gullo & Burton, 1992; Ramey & Ramey, 1998). So far, no study has taken into account all of the potentially significant explaining variables simultaneously.

8.5 Establishing equal educational opportunity

Early care and education programs frequently aim to establish equal educational opportunity for children by compensating for disadvantage and vulnerability resulting from factors such as poverty, ethnicity, gender, minority status, or religion (UNESCO, 2007). However, as long as discrepancies persist in access to early childhood services for children from different social backgrounds, these goals will remain purely theoretical. Where basic early childhood care and education is not accessible, educational attainment is likely to remain associated with the family backgrounds of children (e.g., Schütz & Wössmann, 2005b). Evidence of disparities in access might stimulate policymakers to facilitate the access of children from socially disadvantaged backgrounds to early childhood institutions. Although political measures supporting underprivileged children will be unlikely to destroy social inequality entirely, they might prevent social, cultural, and economic background—which now contribute considerably to inequality and disadvantage (e.g., McLoyd, 1998; Votruba-Drzal, 2003)—from determining children's development to the same distinct extent as nowadays.

A social history of ideas pertaining to childcare in France and in the United States[13]

Abstract: The historical trajectories of childcare institutions and of ideas pertaining to childcare show parallels in France and in the United States. Yet, these countries differ considerably in respect to their approaches to childcare and the use of childcare services. Relative to the French, American traditions of and attitudes towards childcare have been underpinned by an ideology of domesticity, that is, a high value placed on individual responsibility and a philosophy of limited government interventions in matters related to child-rearing and the family. In view of this discrepancy, this study traces the history of social, cultural, and political contexts within which childcare services have developed. It also examines the evolution of ideas and beliefs concerning institutional childcare in both countries. By comparing discourses about childcare, it aims to shed light on the causes of disparities in the standing of two important, corresponding, childcare facilities in the two societies – the French crèche and the American day nursery. By considering historical milestones and discursive paradigms about these facilities since their inception, the study contributes to the understanding of current approaches to institutional childcare in each society. The comparative-historical analysis suggests that Americans have assigned the responsibility of childcare and child-rearing to a greater degree to families, notably to mothers, whereas the French have tended to share responsibilities between the family and some structure of society. Conclusions as to how this affects childcare today are drawn.

Childcare institutions have developed within social, cultural, and political contexts. Their historical trajectories are linked with nation-specific societal and political discourses. Thereby, prevailing ideas about childcare and child-rearing are underpinned by theories and beliefs about parenting, the role of women in raising children, and the duties and functions of families and the nation state.

---

13 Reprinted from *Journal of Social History* with permission from Oxford University Press. Citation details: Burger, K. (2012). A social history of ideas pertaining to childcare in France and in the United States. *Journal of Social History*, 45(4), 1005-1025. doi:10.1093/jsh/shr144

Although the developments of institutional childcare and ideas pertaining thereto in France and the United States show remarkable parallels, the two countries differ in respect to their childcare approaches. Today, different rates of enrollment in childcare facilities suggest that historically institutional childcare might have been embedded more deeply in the French than in the American society. Currently, 43 percent of children less than three years old are enrolled in France whereas 31 percent are enrolled in the United States (OECD, 2010d). Moreover, while parents in France cover 27 percent of the costs of institutional childcare for children up to three years, parents in the United States pay 60 percent of these costs on average (OECD, 2006). In view of this discrepancy in the use and funding of institutional childcare, it is important to study both the societal conditions within which childcare facilities have developed and the evolution of theoretical concepts underlying childcare in both countries.

This study outlines relationships between societal contexts and major historical developments in two corresponding daycare facilities, the French crèche and the American day nursery, summarizing paramount processes in the evolution of these facilities and accompanying conceptual ideas that substantiated their existence. By enlightening discursive paradigms about childcare since the inception of the first formal daycare facilities, the study seeks to contribute to the understanding of current approaches in and societal attitudes toward institutional childcare in France and in the United States.

The analysis draws on a comparative-historical approach (Mahoney, 2004). It reviews primary sources of founders of childcare institutions, educational theorists, and administrative authorities as well as secondary sources from historical and social science research. The historic-pedagogical investigation thereby contrasts discursive and political frameworks within which French and American childcare institutions have been shaped.

1 A brief comparison of France and the U.S. today

Today, both France and the U.S. are industrial states with a high gross domestic product per capita in international comparison ($27,200 and $36,700, respectively), a relatively comparable fertility rate (1.89 and 2.07, respectively), and a similar labor force participation (63.7% in France, 23.6% of whom are in part-time employment; and 69.8% in the U.S., 18.8% of whom in part-time employment). The labor force participation of women with at least one child under six amounts to 65 percent in France and 58 percent in the U.S. However, the two countries differ in respect to traditions and policies relating to childcare. In France, mothers are entitled to 16 weeks of paid maternity leave for the first child and 26 weeks for subsequent children whereas in the United States no entitlement to paid maternity leave exists. Furthermore, French parents assume a smaller fraction of the costs of childcare than American parents (27% vs. 60%) (OECD, 2006). Considering the aforementioned resemblance of both countries, it is worth studying the origins of the latter differences.

2   *The beginnings of institutional childcare*

2.1   The French crèche

Although there were more ancient childcare facilities (Granier, 1891, p. 133), the first daycare center in the modern history of France arose in the 19th century from a philanthropic and religious concern for neglected children. At that time, in various areas of France, the industrialization brought about far-reaching changes in society which eventually resulted in a deterioration of the socioeconomic situation of a considerable proportion of the laboring classes and the poor (La Berge, 1991). Industrialization led to the employment of women and children as cheap labor in industry and to accompanying changes in family patterns and child-rearing. Between 1816 and 1844, child abandonment to public welfare was a serious problem, concerning about 18 percent of live births on average in Paris (Fuchs, 1984, p. 72). Against this background, Jean Baptiste Firmin Marbeau, adjunct to the mayor of the 1st arrondissement of Paris, noticed a lack of infrastructure to aid poor working mothers to care for their children aged less than two years. Marbeau belonged to the Social Catholic movement which aimed to combine Christian charity with the struggle against the exuberance of the economic liberalism that spread at that time to the social and economic detriment of the working classes (Bouve, 2001, p. 35f.). Working-class life gradually emerged as a concern of bourgeois social thinking and action during the early periods of industrialization (Lynch, 1988). In this context, Marbeau intended to help the poor and their children by establishing a childcare facility. On November 14, 1844, his endeavors led to the creation of the very first crèche in Paris, a daycare center designed to enable indigent mothers behaving morally to work without being compelled to abandon their children. The aid offered to these 'worthy poor' originated from traditional charity impulses. On behalf of Christianity and humanity, Marbeau appealed to the obligation of charity to offer help to the children of those overburdened mothers whose misery arose through no fault of their own: "L'humanité, la religion, l'intérêt public demandent qu'on vienne au secours de ces pauvres mères, au secours de ces pauvres enfants. Il importe au bien public que la Société, seconde mère des citoyens, veille sur tous les malheureux" (Marbeau, 1845, p. 61).

There was, however, an ulterior motive to the benevolent undertaking. According to Marbeau, out of one million inhabitants in Paris, 65,000 were enlisted in the *bureau de bienfaisance*, a welfare office designed to assist the indigent (ibid., p. 117). By fighting pauperism and making the lot of the indigent easier to bear, Marbeau aspired to inculcate bourgeois morality into the lower classes, to instill them respect and recognition of the social order, and to demonstrate that the rich took steps to combat the hardship of the poor. In addition, Marbeau emphasized the importance of the crèche as a site of improving public health and reducing infant mortality to guarantee a strong future manpower for France. He fervently campaigned for the propagation of the crèche, publishing a book entitled *Des Crèches* in 1845 and describing the whole array of practical purposes of the facility: increasing and improving the population; refining the morals of the destitute; encouraging cleanliness and resignation, and giving the poor classes the means to work; instilling recognition of and respect for the country's institutions and laws; forcing the poor, through good deeds, not to hate the rich; giving the latter an opportunity to efficiently rescue the unfortunate, and inculcating the feeling of pity and charity in their children; reducing misery and infant mortality; and preventing delinquency including infanticide, theft, and other crimes (Marbeau, 1845, p. 122f., 1994).

2.2   The American day nursery

Patterned on the French model of daily group infant care for the children of working mothers, day nurseries became the American counterparts to the French crèches (Lascarides & Hinitz, 2000, p. 360). They evolved similarly to crèches as part of a philanthropic movement that sought to help poor mothers to work and thus prevent them from becoming dependent on charity or welfare or turning to prostitution (Michel, 1999, p. 31). As in France, the early day nurseries were a result of the ongoing industrialization which called for women's labor in factories. The spread of the industrial labor system triggered rapid growth in city populations, altered societal patterns, and led to increased neglect of children. Many children of working parents were either locked up at home or allowed to wander the streets, left to fend for themselves during the day (Downs et al., 2004, p. 61).

However, day nurseries were also a response to extensive immigration: more than five million foreign families migrated to the United States between 1815 and 1860 (Clarke-Stewart, 1993, p. 30f.). Day nurseries thus offered protective, custodial care of neglected children mostly of immigrant and working-class mothers to keep children out of orphanages (Michel, 1999, 2001, p. 149, 2004). The first actual descendant of the French crèche was the Nursery for the Children of Poor Women in New York City, which was founded in 1854 (Lossing, 1884) by a committee of wealthy charitable women under the direction of Mary DuBois who was concerned about mothers who worked as wet nurses and typically had to leave their own infants with siblings, neighbors, or on their own (Vinovskis, 1993). While the term crèche, a loanword from the French language, had been used at first in the United States and denoted the genealogy of the institution, it was ousted in the course of time by the term day nursery (Mencken, 1990), even though the French crèche remained a reference point for certain founders and managers of day nurseries.

2.3 Early French influences on day nurseries

Efforts to introduce the French crèche in the United States were made among others by philanthropists such as Hanna Biddle, Maria Maltby Love, and Stephen Humphreys Gurteen who traced their inspiration for the establishment of a day nursery in Philadelphia (1863) and the Fitch Creche in Buffalo (1881) to tours of crèches in France (Prochner, 2003, p. 277f.; Rose, 1999). The nursery in Philadelphia, founded by Hanna Biddle, a member of an important Philadelphia family, was to become the first permanent day nursery and catered, at the time of its opening, for children of Civil War workers while their mothers cleaned the hospitals and manufactured clothing for soldiers (Rose, 1999, p. 18f.). Maria Maltby Love, a humanitarian visionary from an elite Buffalo family and adherent to the Social Gospel movement (Little, 1994), assisted Stephen Humphreys Gurteen, one of the most prominent figures in the crèche cause, a pioneer in American social welfare and founder of the first Charity Organization Society in the United States in 1877, in establishing the Fitch Creche in the city of Buffalo under the auspice of Gurteen's Society (Gurteen, 1881; State board of charities, 1894, p. 308). Gurteen was encouraged to visit a crèche in Paris by reports of its operation. He returned to Buffalo with plans for his newly founded Society, not only praising the French institutions but also devoting a great deal of effort to convincing Benjamin Fitch, a New York City philanthropist, to contribute the property that eventually made possible the Fitch Creche (Lewis, 1966).

3   Initial reception of institutional childcare

In France, Marbeau's crèche soon was endorsed widely. Encouraged from the very beginning by the press, by the administrative and religious authorities, and by the *Académie française* which offered Marbeau the Monthyon award for his book *Des Crèches*, the new institution began to propagate both in Paris and in municipalities outside the capital (Buisson, 1911). About twenty crèches were built in the capital and the largest towns in France were endowed with crèches before 1848 (Mozère, 1992, p. 44).

Unlike the crèche in France, the American day nursery provoked many negative reactions at first. One of the most frequent objections was that they harmed children. Opponents criticized the high mortality rates in day nurseries which were mainly due to the lack of biomedical remedies and infectious contagion among infants whose immune system was weakened by what later came to be termed hospitalism under institutional conditions (Michel, 2001, p. 149). Others simply considered the nurseries' setting as unsatisfactory and generally voiced concern about custodial care. Overall, popular support for day nurseries as a suitable form of childcare continued to be marginal throughout history. Sadie Ginsberg, a leader of the Child Study Association of America, later expressed this reluctance toward custodial care when she described it as "herding children. Feeding one end and wiping the other [...] No trained staff. Little or no suitable equipment. A garage, a storage place for children" (as cited in Lascarides & Hinitz, 2000, p. 361). However, a number of proponents advocated day nurseries as fervently as critics opposed them. The divergences of opinion revealed a great deal about the ongoing struggle for childcare, displaying a pattern of views that characterized the dynamics of the childcare movement over time. An account of Julia Ames can be seen as typical of the attitudes of nursery advocates: "The good work rapidly growing in the Old World, was not long in crossing the ocean and finding place in the hearts of America's philanthropic women, and today the crèches supported by them are ... veritable oases to the tired working-women and the hitherto uncared for waifs" (1886, p. 737). Ames stressed the need for crèches by referring to the discovery of a missionary employed by the Central Union who visited mothers to comfort and aid the worthy and stated that "in the poorest districts of the city, only one in four of the children of proper age to attend school do so; but, in the school of the street, the rest are learning the lessons which will train them to fill our prisons to overflowing in years to come" (ibid., p. 739). Until today, child neglect is deemed to be a precursor to delinquency, and the logic of this argument is still taken up by supporters of early childcare services (cf., Schweinhart, 2005).

4 The evolution of institutional childcare

4.1 Children's vulnerability, infant mortality, and the public health approach in France

In France, industrialization was coupled both with an increased use of child labor (Hobbs, McKechnie, & Lavalette, 1999, p. 94) and, subsequently, with legal protection of children through child labor legislation (Weissbach, 1977). Child labor was increasingly regarded as a social evil in the 1820s and 1830s and it came to be condemned as simply another commodity on a market that is purely subject to the laws of supply and demand rather than to the moral principles of civilization (Heywood, 1981, p. 34). A struggle to enact and enforce factory legislation followed when the first French legislation on child labor in 1841 attempted to put an end to the prevailing laissez-faire ideology in the matter of child labor. Crèches thus arose against the background of a growing understanding of children's physical and moral vulnerability. Social reformers and physicians raised concerns over the health and wellbeing of babies and young children, becoming mindful of children's delicate medical condition and the high infant mortality rate (cf., Bourdelais, 2004; Szreter, 2003). An interest in hygiene or, as it was called later, in preventive medicine, arose (Ackerknecht, 1948) and crèches were increasingly created and run with a distinct focus on public health and the improvement of the living conditions of young children in urban areas (La Berge, 1991).

4.2 Crèches as a response to fear of class conflicts

A motive other than the concern with children's health instigated the zeal of French philanthropists to combat the deplorable state of neglected children, notably the fear of future riots, class conflicts, or uprisings of the laborers who were seen as dangerous, depraved, and savage classes. These fears were rooted in the French experience of the Revolution, the July Revolution, and the Lyonnais working class insurrections of 1834 (La Berge, 1991). Thus, benevolent motives were blurred by a desire for social control. Social Catholicism, for instance, embodied the clerical doctrine of alleviating the fate of the poor without disrupting the social, political and economic order (Bouve, 2001, p. 36f). Insofar, crèches responded to a middle-class belief in the necessity of governing society.

4.3   Progress in the development of crèches

After the Revolution of 1848, the report of Thiers reaffirmed the traditional welfare doctrine, contesting any right to public assistance in regard to matters that fell within the scope of a virtue (Thiers, 1850). Thus, few crèches were created. Even though numerous ministerial circular letters urged the prefects to back up local initiatives, the crèches were not accorded any official recognition before 1862 when first regulations were published (Mozère, 1992, p. 46). In 1869, a decree officially recognized the *Société des Crèches* – which aimed to establish, support, propagate and improve crèches – as an establishment of public utility (Buisson, 1911). Furthermore, the Roussel law of 1874, the first law of medical and administrative child protection concerning foster children, contributed to an expansion of crèches (Rollet, 2001). In the last quarter of the 19th century, when public health reformers took an interest in crèches as a means to promote scientific infant care (La Berge, 1991, p. 82), crèches propagated to the effect that by 1902, the number of facilities in France amounted to 408. Next to the 66 crèches in Paris, 39 existed in the capital's suburbs and 303 were dispersed in 186 cities and bigger towns throughout the country (Buisson, 1911).

4.4   Day nurseries prior to the formation of the National Federation of Day Nurseries

As in France, most day nurseries in the United States were founded originally as independent efforts and funded by private charity. Frequently, new institutions originated in local initiatives of prosperous women in urban areas (Joffe, 1977, p. 5f.; Prochner, 2003, p. 279f.). Nursery constitutors and managers, moved by sympathy for the poor and distressed, sought to lend aid to the vulnerable offspring of the poor. In the second half of the 19th century, day nurseries increased in number mostly as a consequence of endeavors to combat the adverse effects of industrialization, expansion of cities, poverty, and the resulting social dislocation experienced by working families on children (Lascarides & Hinitz,

2000, p. 361; Sparks, 1986). In addition, the Civil War, which drew men out of families' homes and left many women widowed, created a need for daycare and stimulated the spread of day nurseries (Beer, 1957). However, as American day nurseries were offered mostly to and used by families whose fathers were unemployed or whose parents were separated, sick, in debt, or deceased – that is, by families considered to be 'pathological' – they widely fell into disrepute as being for distressed families, a last resort for children who were not cared for properly at home. Around the turn of the century, the typical charitable day nursery was "a place to which no middle-class mother would consider sending her children" (Michel, 1999, p. 50f.). Yet criticisms against the new facilities were voiced on both sides of the ocean.

4.5   Criticisms of institutional childcare

In France, doubts about the crèches' utility in matters related to the improvement of children's medical conditions were raised when a study carried out in the 66 crèches of Paris in 1902 estimated that more than a fifth of the infants were rachitic (Braunberger, 1902). On the whole, the crèche was far from being endorsed by the French society at the turn of the century. The political left and progressive circles raised concerns on the invasion of private life, in particular of the poor, by institutional interference. Some early socialists rejected the crèche due to doubts they had entertained previously about the Jules Ferry laws on primary education, as sustaining and invigorating the capitalist state. Furthermore, anticlerical republicans distrusted charitable institutions tightly related to the church and informed by the tenets of religious orders (Reynolds, 1990, 1996). In the course of the 20th century, misgivings about the institution's usefulness as an instrument to promote public health would endure and opponents would continue to insist on the harm caused by crèches. Adversaries from different parts of French society, including mothers, physicians and social scientists, would express criticisms about the assembling of too large a number of infants under one roof, the disruption of the attachment between mother and child, the detachment of the child from its original milieu, the injurious effects on the formation of the character (Guedeney, Grasso, & Starakis, 2004), the high infant mortality (DeLuca & Rollet, 1999), and the transmission of respiratory infections and ear, nose, throat, and digestive pathologies (Delour et al., 2004). However, despite these criticisms, the crèche retained its importance for many families in France, particularly in urban regions.

In the U.S., day nurseries were criticized on the same grounds. In addition, however, criticisms of day nurseries were rooted in an attack on female labor participation, supporting a philosophy of domesticity which defined the mother as the primary agent responsible for the care of children (Taylor Allen, 1988). The 'moral mother' was identified with the non-economic sphere of society and expected to raise her children in the family. Opponents of the economic system argued that day nurseries affirmed the exploitation of women under capitalism (Durst, 2005, p. 142). But critique also came from within the movement as some day nursery leaders reproached institutions for indiscriminate admission of children and thus for a lack of investigation of the parents' character (Rose, 1999, p. 89).

4.6 The day nursery movement during the Progressive era

The formation of the National Federation of Day Nurseries in 1898 marked a new period in the history of philanthropy (Michel, 1999, p. 53f.). Along with numerous Catholic charities as well as the National Association of Colored Women (which supported the creation of nurseries for African Americans), the National Federation of Day Nurseries contributed to a growth in institutional childcare. The number of day nurseries increased from fewer than 100 in 1892 to 250 in 1902 and to 618 in 1914 (Durst, 2005, p. 141). In Chicago, for instance, 31 day nurseries were established between 1891 and 1916, becoming a part of the city's social services (McDermott, 2009, p. 34f.). Josephine Jewell Dodge presided over the National Federation. Her conservative, class- and gender-based maternalism, which insisted that mothers care for their children at home, defined the childcare movement while she was in the office, virtually for the next thirty years. To the detriment of day nurseries, the Federation never made efforts to win governmental subsidies for childcare programs or to correct social problems, one of its main principles being that day nurseries remain in the hands of private charities run by upper-class volunteers. In combination with the Federation's reluctance to professionalize, this tenet soon paralyzed the day nursery movement.

As the nursery movement lost ground, the idea of mothers' pensions emerged. The White House Conference on Dependent Children in 1909 was the beginning of the mothers' pension campaign that sought to introduce government payments to mothers who lacked other means of support to remain at home and care for their children. This pension had the potential to break with the stigmatization that had characterized the treatment of needy mothers hitherto. However, funding levels were usually insufficient to cover all applicants. As poor mothers were prioritized, the pension remained a form of charity, albeit state-sponsored. Nevertheless, by the end of the Progressive Era, mothers' pensions were supported by federal, state, and local welfare officials, while day nurseries were left behind in the hands of private charities (Michel, 1999, p. 89).

The development of day nurseries had not only been impeded by the fact that day nurseries remained under the aegis of an outdated federation. A number of other reasons also hampered their progress. At the beginning of the 20th century, only very few states licensed day nurseries as the health standards were unsatisfactory in many instances (Lascarides & Hinitz, 2000, p. 362). At the same time, advocates of the early childhood education movement began to professionalize, promoting kindergartens (for children as of five years of age) and nursery schools (for children mostly between three and five years) that followed their own distinct trajectories. As kindergartens were incorporated into the public school system and nursery schools were increasingly used by the American middle- and upper-class families, the day nursery's reputation continued to deteriorate (Levy & Michel, 2002). Worried about the danger of undernourishment, poor hygiene, spreading infections, and the lack of proper medical inspections, day nursery board members began to regulate medical inspection and supervision in day nurseries (Lascarides & Hinitz, 2000, p. 362). However, that was not enough to put day nurseries back on the map. After World War I, day nurseries became identified once more with a population with particular deficiencies, that is, with parents in dire economic straits or parents who were a threat to their children (O'Connor, 1990). This was caused, among others, by the increasing influence of the mothers' pension policies, which enticed many working mothers to return home to take charge of their children, and by the professional development of social work which resulted in a more central role of social workers within day nurseries. The nurseries' clientele thus shifted to illegitimate children whose mothers were ineligible for pensions. Mothers could no longer enroll their children in a day nursery simply because they were employed; eventually, the day nurseries' focus changed to offer 'casework' services for particularly deficient families (Durst, 2005, p. 152; Joffe, 1977, p. 6). Thus in particular during the early post-war period, day nurseries became marginal institutions for marginal families again, poorly accepted and stigmatized as "necessary evils" (O'Connor, 1990, p. 138).

5 Institutional childcare prior to the Great Depression

The introduction of mothers' pensions in the U.S. coincided with the adoption of two important legal texts in France. On the eve of World War I, two laws were enacted under the influence of Senator Paul Strauss who presided over the League to Combat Infantile Mortality: a law concerning maternity leave and a law concerning government subsidies for poor families with multiple children (Contrepois, 2006, p. 41). After war had been declared, a bonus was disbursed to nursing mothers, draconian hygienic rules were put in force in crèches, and attempts were made to maintain and extend pre-war legislation on maternity leave. Yet, as opposed to the mothers' pensions in the United States which devaluated day nurseries, the new laws in France did not hamper the development of crèches.

During World War I, factory and work-place crèches gained attention in France as factories producing war weaponry recruited women workers in large numbers. However, as the demand for employees in munitions factories decreased after the end of the war, women were discarded and factory crèches were closed gradually. But women continued to constitute a considerable share of the French workforce in other sectors. The 1920s thus saw an expansion of existing workplace crèches. In addition, municipal crèche projects were launched and allowances were paid to women civil servants when nursing facilities could not be provided at work (Reynolds, 1990, p. 183).

In the years after the creation of the communist party in 1920, a reorientation of attitudes toward the crèche and childcare on the Soviet pattern might have been expected in France as in Bolshevik theory the key to women's liberation lay in bringing women into unmitigated participation in economic, social, and political life (Smith, 2002, p. 137f.). Interestingly, however, neither the socialists nor the communists addressed the crèches as a political priority to release women into the sphere of wage work or to substitute collectivist for traditional values. Left-wing councils that established crèches regarded them mainly as a means to improve child health in the working class, rather than as a means to collectivize society or to liberate women. Pronatalists, committed to raising the birthrate, deliberately attempted to prevent mothers from using childcare facilities by campaigning for family allowances and other benefits, opposing the crèche as being a pernicious prompt for mothers to take on paid work. Women's organizations of the inter-war period did not seek to increase the ratio of women in the labor market. And the groups officially classified as feminist typically consisted of socially conservative middle-class or upper-class women who spoke up for a strengthening of the family rather than for its remake where mothers would be employed in the job market (Reynolds, 1990).

6 Institutional childcare during the Depression and World War II

The Great Depression led to a decline in subsidies for crèches in the urban Paris region (Mozère, 1992, p. 48). As the Depression had its repercussions in most areas of the society, no more than 360 crèches existed in the urban regions of France by 1940, providing care to about 12,000 children (Reynolds, 1990, p. 188).

In the U.S., by contrast, the Depression improved the day nursery's standing as providing daycare was primarily conceived of as a jobs program. An expansion of childcare institutions took place as President Franklin D. Roosevelt initiated the National Industrial Recovery Act, a statute to assist the nation's economic recovery, as well as the Works Progress Administration, a New Deal agency that established relief measures for the unemployed. Thereby, Roosevelt provided funds for the establishment and propagation of Emergency Nursery Schools and he supplied work for jobless teachers, nurses, cooks, and other professionals. Sources vary, yet by 1937 the federal funds had rendered possible the creation of about 1,900 institutions that cared for approximately 40,000 children (Clarke-Stewart, 1993, p. 32). Until 1942, however, many institutions were forced to close down as teachers increasingly took up better-paying work in defense plants. But, like previous national crises, World War II increased the demands for childcare in the U.S. as women were mobilized into the defense industry. The Lanham Act, signed into law by President Roosevelt, made federal funds available for childcare to communities impacted by war as of 1942 (Michel, 2001, p. 152). However, most facilities closed when the Lanham funds were suspended after World War II. By terminating the Lanham Act, Congress put an end to the only national daycare policy ever enacted in the United States to that point (Zylan, 2000).

In France, on the other hand, World War II did not boost the development of crèches. While women were initially recruited into war work, they were laid off soon after the defeat of 1940 to Germany. Concerns about the falling birth rate were voiced (Bouve, 2001) and politicians adopted measures to counteract the superannuation of the French population (Norvez, 1990, p. 24) by encouraging women to stay at home instead of taking up employment. At the time, the family was elevated to a national symbol (Reynolds, 1990) and crèches were progressively closed down.

7 Institutional childcare after World War II

7.1 Childcare policies in post-war France

In France, the post-war years saw a flowering of important social measures including social security and family allowances. The generous family benefits which had been set up in the 1930s, increased in the 1940s, and extended after World War II – including benefits for housewives as well as a tax code that gave fiscal advantages to mothers at home – were driven by a concern about the nation's demographic balance and by pronatalist zeal (Morgan, 2003, p. 263). Against this background, the 1940s and 1950s became the 'golden age of familialism' (Prost, 1984, p. 8f.). An edict of November 2, 1945, instituted the *Protection Maternelle et Infantile*, a public health agency within the national health ministry designed to combat the demographic decline, and the crèches were brought under its purview. The post-World War II period through the 1970s became a period of expansion of childcare institutions. The implementation of the *Protection Maternelle et Infantile* in 1945 thereby constituted the definite passage from charity to a national responsibility and a turning away from the notion of social assistance to the notion of protection, regardless of the socioeconomic status and nationality of the recipients (Norvez, 1990, p. 84). Between 1961 and 1971, the number of children crèches could serve almost doubled (OCDE, 2003, p. 12). By 1971, there were 652 crèches, keeping 29,720 children, about half of which were located in Paris and its suburbs (David & Lézine, 1974, p. 71). As labor shortages arose during the 1970s, politicians across the political spectrum began devoting more resources to public crèches in order to increase the participation of women in the labor force (Morgan, 2003, p. 283) since the number of women in the labor force had constantly been below its peak of 48 percent in 1911 (Buisson, 1978, p. 6; Costa, 2000). At the time, an increasing number of middle-class families began to use crèches for their children while lower-class families increasingly drew on non-official services (Rayna, 1992, p. 347).

In the 1970s, the family benefits system began to play an additional role in funding and developing public daycare. The National Family Allowance Fund created two types of contracts, the *contrats-crèches* in 1983 and the *contrats-enfance* in 1988, which encouraged municipalities to develop their childcare facilities and to define a policy of universal access on their territories (OCDE, 2003, p. 13). Throughout the 1980s and 1990s, both conservative and socialist administrations continued to make public daycare more accessible, establishing an increasingly comprehensive state's responsibility for daycare (Morgan, 2003,

History of childcare in France and in the United States 149

p. 282f.). The 'childhood contracts' were altered in 1994 to include financial subsidies for investments in crèches and in 1999 to cover 66 percent of the expenses for the operation of crèches (OCDE, 2003, p. 13).
In 2004, about 220,000 children under three years (i.e., 10% of the children in this age bracket) were enrolled in crèches that were licensed and supervised by the *Protection Maternelle et Infantile* and 255,000 two-year-olds (i.e., 34.7%) were enrolled in the *école maternelle*, overseen by the national education inspector. 415,000 children under age three (20%) were cared for by *assistantes maternelles* (i.e., family daycare providers who care for one to three children in the provider's home on a regular basis) and 31,000 children (1.5%) were cared for by *garde à domicile* (home care giving) which is not subject to any regulations or licensing (OECD, 2004, p. 14f.). The most recent expansion in formal out-of-home care was initiated in 2009 when a convention was signed with the National Family Allowance Fund to create 200,000 additional childcare spaces by 2012 (Ministère du Travail de l'Emploi et de la Santé, 2010).

7.2   Childcare policies in post-war America

In the United States, major official agencies had competing interests as to the purpose and scope of a new daycare system after World War II. The primary adversaries grappling with daycare policy were the U.S. Children's Bureau, the U.S. Women's Bureau and the Office of Education. The U.S. Children's Bureau – a national agency established in 1912 within the Department of Commerce and Labor designed to investigate and report on the needs of children and youth (Lindenmeyer, 2001, p. 208) – sought to establish a childcare program directed to child welfare needs, whereas the U.S. Women's Bureau – an agency established in 1920 within the United States Department of Labor to promote the welfare of wage-earning women – viewed daycare through the lens of women's employment and aimed to address the needs of women workers. The Federal Office of Education, finally, tended to oppose nation-wide policies and argued for a more locally administered after-school and nursery school care instead. The differing positions of these official bodies undermined the enactment of a comprehensive childcare policy in the United States (Zylan, 2000, p. 625) and financial support from states and federal funding were thus piecemeal (Cohen, 1996).
From the 1960s until today, most childcare policies have been framed as a targeted poverty issue. Broad policies to support universal childcare have consistently been left off of the national agenda (Palley, 2010, p. 161). In 1967, the

Social Security Act was amended to provide money for daycare mainly for women receiving public welfare. Childcare became situated within child welfare services and programmatically aligned with Aid to Families with Dependent Children (AFDC) (Zylan, 2000, p. 625). In the late 1970s and 1980s, public subsidies of childcare were cut repeatedly (Kelly, 2003, p. 607f.). The Reagan administration diminished expenditures for childcare for the benefit of poor families but almost doubled federal funding for childcare for middle- and upper-class families in the 1980s (Michel, 2001, p. 154). The Family Support Act of 1988 provided AFDC recipients with an entitlement to vouchers for the care of their children up to age thirteen (Witte & Trowbridge, 2005, p. 15f.). The Childcare Development Act, passed in 1990, made additional funds available for childcare programming primarily for children in poverty (Palley, 2010, p. 160f.). In 1995, the federally funded community-based Early Head Start program for low-income families with infants and toddlers and pregnant women was established (U.S. Department of Health & Human Services, 2009). Some ten years later, during 2004, Early Head Start served 80,094 children. Thereby, 60,403 slots were funded by the Administration on Children and Families while the remaining slots were funded by other sources (Hamm & Ewen, 2006, p. 2f.). This remained a relatively small provision in view of the almost 20 million children under age five in the United States at that time (U.S. Census Bureau, 2004) and given that around the turn of the millennium, almost 80 percent of children under five with employed mothers were cared for in childcare centers, in family childcare homes, by relatives, or by nannies for at least some time each week, many of them even in full-time care of more than 35 hours a week (Capizzano & Adams, 2000). Since 1996, when the Temporary Assistance for Needy Families (TANF) was passed, women receiving TANF became eligible for poverty-based childcare for their children. In 2000, however, only about 14 percent of the eligible children benefited from this fund for childcare (Mezey, Greenberg, & Schumacher, 2002) although federal subsidies had increased since the 1996 changes in welfare (Kelly, 2003, p. 617). The American Recovery and Reinvestment Act of 2009 which was intended to create jobs and promote investment and consumer spending during the financial crisis beginning in 2007 made available grants worth $1.1 billion for Early Head Start expansion, seeking to nearly double the number of Early Head Start participants (U.S. Department of Health & Human Services, 2009). However, today, while the U.S. Department of Health and Human Services manages most of the funding for social services including Head Start, policy and provision of child care for children from birth to three years are matters for each State and therefore subject to variation (OECD, 2006, p. 428).

7.3 A brief balance of periods of prosperity of institutional childcare

In contrast to the French crèches, the day nurseries' periods of prosperity were more closely related to major national crises, notably the Civil War, the Great Depression, and World War II. In these periods, the debate about the aptness of institutional childcare gave way to the conviction that daycare met national, social, and economic demands. However, in the absence of crisis, the presumed harm it would do to children and families has been "invariably used as justification for withholding support from daycare" (Day, 1983, p. 40). As a consequence, day nurseries in the United States have been framed more distinctly as temporary relief interventions compared to crèches in France. Most recently, this was apparent in 2009 when the latest political measures were taken to advance institutional childcare in the two countries. While the United States made federal grants available for Early Head Start as a response to the financial crisis through the American Recovery and Reinvestment Act which was primarily designed to create employment, France expaded institutional childcare without formulating it as a means of overcoming financial difficulties or of creating labor for the unemployed.

8 Conclusions

Crèches and day nurseries both emerged as of the 1840s. They constituted the beginning of institutional childcare and grew into a branch of private charity in favor of the children of poor working families: both were brought under the auspices of national federations in the 19th century; both had similar, although not identical, agendas; and both were subject to expansion and cutback due to varying local or national policies, changing societal conceptualizations of institutional childcare, and changing views of the role of mothers since their inception. Yet despite these similarities, institutional childcare has not had the same standing in the two societies. The primary historical causes of disparities in the use and funding of crèches and day nurseries identified in this analysis are related to societal perceptions, purposes, funding, and administration of institutional childcare.

8.1 Societal perceptions of childcare institutions and their clientele

Originally, the crèche and the day nursery both received children of poor and distressed families, but the social background of children who typically used the facilities changed over time. In the United States, the day nurseries' clientele has been considered as a 'pathological' population in many instances, even though there have been several shifts in the clientele. Notwithstanding that middle- and upper-class families increasingly began to use formal out-of-home childcare more recently (Mulligan, Brimhall, & West, 2005, p. 12f.; Weinraub, Hill, & Hirsh-Pasek, 2002), institutional childcare could not recover from its reputation and thus largely remained stigmatized as a (transitory) poverty relief measure. In France, a significant shift in the clientele began to take place during and after World War II as women in state employment and other white-collar workers began to see crèches, which were increasingly included within municipal socialism's welfare policies, as a beneficial service and thus started taking advantage of crèches for their children. Children from working-class families were gradually replaced by children from middle-class families in crèches for two main reasons. First, the overall proportion of working-class families in France diminished during the 20th century. Second, social contributions from the Family Allowance Fund might have incited women with low incomes to stay at home (Bouve, 2001, p. 80f.). During the last decades, institutional childcare was used more frequently by children from parents with a higher employment status than by children from employees or unemployed parents (Micheaux & Monso, 2007). Thus, institutional childcare was not branded as a pure poverty issue. In the long term, the attitudes toward institutional childcare have been more favorable and using childcare facilities in France, including for infants as of three months, has been considered normal practice (Plantenga, 2009).

8.2 Purposes and continuity of childcare institutions

While both crèches and day nurseries intended to aid destitute families in child-rearing and holding a gainful position, the scope of the French crèche exceeded the combat against pauperism and the aid to mothers who worked out of dire economic necessity. In the course of the 19th century, the French bourgeoisie feared riots of the working classes and thus had interest in instilling them bourgeois middle-class morality by supplying social services. Moreover, from the second half of the 19th century until World War I, the small fraction of the population in the active age group along with a high child mortality rate caused concerns to increase the population (David & Lézine, 1974). Crèches thus became sites to improve public health and combat infant mortality through medicalization of crèches and teaching mothers the principles of hygienic infant care (Mozère, 2003). American day nurseries, on the other hand, remained largely cut off from social reform at the time (Hunter, 1904; O'Connor, 1995). Over time, they more consistently supported poor working mothers albeit retaining the primacy of the nuclear family as an agent of childcare and early childhood socialization. To a large extent, institutional childcare thereby constituted an aid for the needy in times of acute crisis rather than on a regular basis. Hence in the long term, crèches in France might have tended to pursue a more varied but nonetheless more stable agenda than American day nurseries.

8.3 Funding and administration of institutions

Crèches and day nurseries both originated in private philanthropy. However, while crèches were increasingly subsidized by some structure of the state over time, day nurseries received funding primarily in response to national crises. National associations formed in the 19th century. But in contrast to the *Société des Crèches*, the National Federation of Day Nurseries did not help day nurseries to win public funding and thus preserved their private character. In France, women were likely to be encouraged to care for their children at home and the provision of institutional childcare tended to be disrupted in periods of national hardship. For instance, while the most extensive daycare policy in the United States, the Lanham Act, was implemented in response to wartime requirements during World War II and terminated in 1945, the most substantial progress in federal funding of institutional childcare in France was associated with the *Protection Maternelle et Infantile* which was not instituted until after World War II. Up to now, Americans have used voluntary or philanthropic non-profit organizations for purposes France has frequently assigned to the state. This has produced a liberal welfare state in the U.S. in which private market arrangements deal with childcare while public subsidies are mostly restricted to low-income families or families who have failed on their own even though private and public sectors have cooperated in some instances (Hammack, 1989; Morgan, 2005, p. 246; Roseman, 1999, p. 7). By contrast, the French considered family matters to a greater degree as a public concern (Koven & Michel, 1990, p. 1099) since children were regarded as both private and public goods (Rollet & Morel, 2000). Often, the activities of voluntary organizations in France were subsidized publicly and regulated by the central state's government officials, by individual departments, or by the church. Consequently, state intervention in family affairs was socially more legitimized than in the U.S. where authorities remained ambivalent about the extent to which the state should assist families in childcare.

In sum, examination of the historical trajectories of crèches and day nurseries and of the relationship between ideas and institutions within historical contexts leads to the broad conclusions that discursive consistencies pertaining to childcare can be identified in France and the United States as of the implementation of the first facilities. In both countries, advocates praised the utility of the institutions and called upon societal responsibility for overburdened families while opponents feared the physical or psychological harm to children or intrusion of society into a strictly private domain. However, relative to the French, American traditions stood in a more distinct contrast with institutional interference in matters deemed to be the duty of the nuclear family. Thus historically, Americans have tended to favor the assignment of the primary responsibility of child-rearing to the mother whereas the French have defined childcare as both a private and a public concern and therefore supported public funding for childcare to a greater extent than Americans.

8.4 Limitations of the study

A final remark pertains to the limitations of the analysis. First, it has to be noted that neither crèches nor day nurseries have been very widely disseminated in view of the number of children towards whom they are geared. Other forms of childcare including child minders and relative care have been used frequently. The history of both institutions merely revealed that, on the whole, French approaches and attitudes to childcare have differed in some important respects from American traditions. Second, as a review of the history of institutional childcare and ideas pertaining thereto, the study was inevitably selective. Contradictory information was weighed in selected instances. By drawing, amongst others, on secondary sources, the study relied in part on previous appraisals. Instead of portraying the evolution of specific institutions and discourses in specific regions of each country in minute detail, it put emphasis on the most important milestones since mid-19th century by synthesizing varying sources into more general statements. Yet there were local disparities in childcare provision, use, ideas, and policies. Thus, the analysis did not constitute an exhaustive inquiry into the societal and political discourses, dominant ideas, theories, and beliefs about institutional childcare over time. It did, however, join in debate over the explanations of current structures of childcare in each society, thereby illuminating important causes of national specificities in institutional childcare.

Begehren, Sprache und Bildung: Pädagogische Reflexionen über «Die gerettete Zunge» von Elias Canetti[14]

Abstract: Desire manifests itself as a consequence of a lack of a certain object or condition. The experience of a lack is coupled with a desire to appropriate to oneself what is considered to remedy the perceived deficiency. So far, there has not been much research analyzing relationships between desire for linguistic proficiency, language development, and educational processes. However, such associations can be uncovered in the first part of Elias Canetti's autobiography ‹The tongue set free›. The aim of the present study is to reveal relationships between desire as a primum mobile of human activity, linguistic enhancement, and education. The analysis thereby relies on a hermeneutic analytic framework, drawing on Lacan's psychoanalytic conception of desire as an expression of a shortcoming of the basic human condition as well as on Humboldt's theory linking language and educational processes. The analysis shows that by progressively increasing symbolic structures, humans can cross boundaries of comprehension and diminish the experience of alienation from the world. The field of consciousness is widened as the development of language is accompanied by a changing relationship with the unintelligible. Eventually, this process of increasing language in order to decrease the realm of the incomprehensible may alter the relation between the self and the world. Such an alteration reflects an educational process, emerging as an epiphenomenon of the quest for appropriation of alien experiences.

Wer begehrt, tut dies in Ermangelung eines begehrten Objekts oder Zustands. Das subjektive Erleben eines Mangels richtet somit das Tun des Menschen auf ein – vielfach vorläufiges und wiederholt changierendes – Ziel aus. Es ist verknüpft mit dem Wunsch nach Aneignung dessen, was den Mangel zu beheben verspricht, mit einem Begehren nach Vervollständigung des Subjekts. Dieses Begehren wird in der Regel nicht mit Bildung in Verbindung gebracht. Und

---

14 Reprinted from «*Vierteljahrsschrift für wissenschaftliche Pädagogik*», with permission from Ferdinand Schöningh publishers. Citation details: Burger, K. (2009). Begehren, Sprache und Bildung: Pädagogische Reflexionen über ›Die gerettete Zunge‹ von Elias Canetti. *Vierteljahrsschrift für wissenschaftliche Pädagogik, 86*(2), 163-183.

Bildung wird oft nicht explizit im Zusammenhang mit Sprache gedacht. Doch zwischen dem Begehren, der Sprache und Bildung können Zusammenhänge angenommen werden, denen im Folgenden nachgegangen werden soll. Es werden Beziehungen zwischen einem näher zu bestimmenden Begehren, sprachlicher Entfaltung und individuellen Bildungsprozessen zu skizzieren sein. Im Zentrum steht erstens die Annahme, wonach sich Bildungsprozesse weitgehend im Medium der Sprache vollziehen; und zweitens wird angenommen, dass der Mensch ein Begehren nach sprachlicher Entwicklung aufweist, da ihm die Sprache eine Möglichkeit bietet, Fremdes auf sich zu beziehen und dadurch den Grad seiner Fremdheit zu verringern. Die Sprache kann somit als ein Instrument verstanden werden, sich des Fremden intellektuell zu bemächtigen, das heisst dieses an die eigenen Bewusstseinsstrukturen anzupassen. Im Folgenden werden diese Annahmen auf der Grundlage des ersten Teils von Elias Canettis Autobiographie – *Die gerettete Zunge* – untersucht. Vorweg wird dabei die Frage zu klären sein, in welcher Hinsicht diese Autobiographie mit bildungstheoretischen Ansätzen in Verbindung zu bringen ist und inwiefern sie dabei als Quelle historisch-pädagogischer Bildungsforschung dienen kann.

1   Autobiographie als Bildungsbiographie

Bildung wurde in der fiktionalen Literatur mehrfach zum Gegenstand der Reflexion gemacht. Dabei kann Bildung inhaltlich in vielfältiger Weise verstanden werden. In der Romantheorie und in der Pädagogik beispielsweise ist sie bereits aufgefasst worden als individuelle oder gesellschaftliche Praxis, als Entwicklungsprozess, als Zustand nach dem Abschluss eines solchen Prozesses oder als Inbegriff der kulturellen Werte eines Einzelnen, einer sozialen Schicht oder eines Volkes, sowie als spezifische Form des Bewusstseins, als kulturell geprägtes Deutungsmuster oder als Verhältnis eines Individuums zu sich und dem historisch gegebenen, gesellschaftlichen und kulturellen Kontext, der Welt (bspw. Bollenbeck, 1996; Friebertshäuser, Rieger-Ladich, & Wigger, 2006; Gössling, 2008; Jacobs & Krause, 1989; Korte, 2004; Selbmann, 1988). Wo Bildung thematisch als strukturtragendes Moment eines literarischen Werks fungiert, kann sie das Genre begründen und das Werk damit inhaltlich einem Typ Literatur, dem Bildungsroman, zuordnen, der sich abgrenzt gegenüber Gattungen wie etwa der Utopie, dem psychologischen, dem Abenteuer-, dem Gesellschaftsroman und anderen. In Anbetracht der Schwierigkeit einer präzisen Gattungsdefinition und der Debatte darum, ob eine Gattung eher ausgehend von inhaltlichen oder formalen Gesichtspunkten zu bestimmen sei, lässt sich festhalten, dass jeder Gattungsbegriff eine gewisse Offenheit und Flexibilität behalten muss, wenn er die ihm zugedachte Funktion erfüllen will, sämtliche literarischen Werke, die sich durch bestimmte Gattungsgemeinsamkeiten auszeichnen, unter einem Begriff zu subsumieren. Eine weite Definition, die ohne Nivellierung von Unterschieden zwischen Einzelfällen nicht auskommt, bietet sich daher an. Einer solchen Definition zufolge werden im Bildungsroman »Bildungsgeschichten und Bildungsprobleme« (Jacobs & Krause, 1989, S. 19) verhandelt, womit angedeutet ist, dass in dem Genre Gegenstände erziehungswissenschaftlicher Forschung ins Zentrum des Interesses gerückt werden (May, 2006, S. 11). Dies tritt umso offensichtlicher zutage, wenn konkreter bestimmt wird, dass im Bildungsroman die Entwicklung eines Individuums in seinem Lebenslauf oder einem Teil seines Lebens erzählt und dabei als Prozess der inneren Bildung in der Verschränkung von Subjekt und Welt interpretiert wird (vgl. Jacobs & Krause, 1989; Schrader, 1975; Selbmann, 1984, 1988). Inhaltlich sind Bildungsromane meist am Bewusstsein von der unwiederholbaren Besonderheit individueller Lebensgeschichten orientiert. Eine Besonderheit des Narrativs einer Bildungsgeschichte ist daher dessen Nähe zum autobiographischen Erzählen (vgl. Treml, 2005), das heisst zu einer vom Prinzip linear fortschreitender, kohärenter Entwicklung getragenen, komplexen Schilderung des Lebensgangs eines Einzelnen, welcher sich zugleich durch zahlreiche Diskontinuitäten kennzeichnet und dadurch seine je einzigartige Unverwechselbarkeit erlangt. Ein Werk, das sich von der paradigmatischen Normalform eines Bildungsromans nahezu ausschliesslich durch die Selbstbezeichnung als Autobiographie abgrenzen lässt, ist Canettis erster Teil seiner dreibändigen literarisierten Autobiographie. Sie steht im Mittelpunkt dieser Untersuchung und soll unter Rückgriff auf bildungstheoretische Überlegungen näher analysiert werden, da sie, so die Ausgangshypothese, als Chronik einer frühen Bildungslaufbahn gelesen werden kann. Ziel der Studie ist es nicht, durch eine lückenlose Heranführung der Sekundärliteratur einen umfassenden aktuellen Forschungsstand zu erarbeiten – dies ist weder hinsichtlich Canettis Autobiographie noch in Bezug auf die bildungsphilosophischen Theorien beabsichtigt, auf die bei der Analyse der geschilderten Bildungsprozesse prinzipiell rekurriert werden könnte. Stattdessen sollen die bildungsrelevanten Bezugspunkte der *Geretteten Zunge* untersucht und dabei die Frage gestellt werden, nach welchem Prinzip und unter welchen Bedingungen Bildungsprozesse bei Canetti ausgelöst und aufrechterhalten werden. Dies erscheint vor dem Hintergrund der kontinuierlichen Wandlungen, ja der Unabschliessbarkeit des Bildungsbegriffs, sowie in Anbetracht dessen, dass Korrekturen am Bildungsbegriff (vgl. Mollenhauer, 1987) immer schon zur Pflicht der Erziehungswissenschaftler gehörten, vertretbar.

2 Methodische Vorüberlegungen zum Verhältnis von (autobiographischer) Literatur und Pädagogik

Die Akzentuierung der Einmaligkeit von Bildungsgeschichten wirft die methodologisch wichtige Frage auf, ob ein (notgedrungen) kasuistischer Zugang zu einem Werk überhaupt allgemeine Schlussfolgerungen über Bildungsprozesse zulässt, ob also idiographische Analysen (Windelband, 1900) Aussagen von grösserer Tragweite erlauben, welche über die Beschreibung des rein Individuellen hinausgehen. Es stellt sich, mit anderen Worten, die Frage, ob der literarische Text als Quelle historisch-pädagogischer Bildungsforschung sinnvoll verwendet werden kann. »Wenn Erziehungswissenschaftler versuchen, Prozesse der Bildung und Werke der Kunst in einem Atemzug zu thematisieren, geschieht dies leicht in instrumentalisierender Absicht« (Hellekamps, 1998, S. 103), instrumentalisierend insofern, als Werke der Kunst Erkenntnisse über etwas ausser ihnen Gegebenes vermitteln sollen und so zu Vehikeln der Aufklärung bestimmter Sachverhalte erklärt werden. Dennoch können literarische Texte für die Bildungsforschung zur »Herausforderung« (Oelkers, 1991, S. 140) werden. Literarische Werke verdichten subjektive Standpunkte (vgl. Oelkers, 1985, S. 6), sie sind in der modernen Gesellschaft zum Ort des individuellen Ausdrucks geworden und können somit auch als der »andere Ort« (Casale, 2005, S. 20) der pädagogischen Reflexion verstanden werden, insofern sie eine »andere Seite philosophischer Wahrheiten« (ebd., S. 20) darstellen. Als Produkte einer selbstreferentiellen Erkundung und literarischen Gestaltung lebensweltlicher Erfahrungen sind sie Einzelfälle, möglicherweise künstlerisch entfremdete Einzelfälle. Dennoch können sie, sieht man einmal von der Frage nach der Authentizität der Darstellung von Erfahrungen ab, zur Diskussion bildungstheoretischer Ansätze herangezogen und nutzbar gemacht werden, da sie »nicht nur illustrier[en], was ohnehin bekannt ist, nicht nur narrativ ausbreite[n], was man im szientistischen Wissensstand in kürzeren Formulierungen zur Hand hat, sondern darüber hinausgehende oder intern subtiler differenzierende Vorkommnisse fingier[en], in denen gleichsam heuristische Hypothesen eingehüllt sind« (Mollenhauer, 1998, S. 488). Dies gilt auch für die Autobiographie. Indem sie eine individuelle Geschichte in ihrem Verlauf darstellt, bietet sie eine zwar brüchige, weil möglicherweise fingierte, aber heuristisch doch illustrative Grundlage zur Formulierung von Hypothesen oder Zweifeln in mehr oder minder methodischer Absicht. Wenn auch die Schlussfolgerung verfehlt wäre, dass es sich beim Berührungspunkt zwischen erzählender Literatur oder Autobiographie und theoretischen Überlegungen um einen Umschlagplatz zwischen dem Einmaligen und dem Allgemeinen handelt, wo sich das Besondere auf das

Allgemeine hin öffnet und subjektive Positionen theoretisch formulierte Regelfälle bestätigen oder infrage stellen, so lässt sich doch vermuten, dass die erzählende und die autobiographische Literatur theoretische Mutmassungen und begriffliche Konzepte in ein anderes Licht rücken und dadurch vorab unbeachtete Schattierungen entdecken lassen. In diesem Sinne ist diese Arbeit gedacht.

Literatur und Autobiographie spiegeln zudem einen besonderen Zugang zu den Phänomenen wider. Alle Pädagogik muss so tun, als könne sie fortschreitend positiv von aussen auf das Innere einwirken. Sie denkt von aussen nach innen (vgl. dazu Oelkers, 1985, S. 11). Die fiktionale und die autobiographische Literatur hingegen denken in die entgegengesetzte Richtung. Sie thematisieren innere Vorgänge in der Auseinandersetzung mit der äusseren Welt. Die von aussen an ein Subjekt herangetragene Pädagogik kann somit nicht als monokausaler Faktor für die Bildung des Subjekts verantwortlich erklärt werden, wenn dessen Entwicklung nebst äusseren Einflüssen immer auch zahlreichen intrapsychischen Prozessen mit je charakteristischer Eigendynamik unterworfen ist. Und schliesslich ist der Erwachsene nie einzig der oder das, zu dem ihn eine Pädagogik von aussen geformt hat. Friedrich von Blanckenburg bestimmte bereits in seiner im Jahr 1774 erschienenen Poetik *Versuch über den Roman*, welche als erste deutsche Romantheorie gilt, die »Ausbildung und Formung, die ein Charakter durch seine mancherley Beggenisse erhalten kann, ... seine innere Geschichte« (1965, S. 392), und nicht die Darstellung äusserer Geschehnisse und Entwicklungen, als konstitutiv für den Roman. Exemplarisch wird das Innere eines Protagonisten in den Mittelpunkt der Betrachtung gestellt und der Vollzug seiner Selbstbildung in der Auseinandersetzung mit der Welt beschrieben. Diesem Umstand soll hier Rechnung getragen werden. Es werden daher im Folgenden insbesondere jene Prozesse in den Blick genommen, die – in aller konstitutiven Verschränkung mit äusseren Einflussgrössen – als zentrale innere Bedingungsfaktoren verantwortlich sind für die Bildungsprozesse des Erzählers der *Geretteten Zunge*, Elias Canetti.

3   *›Die gerettete Zunge‹ als Untersuchungsgegenstand pädagogischer Forschung*

Autobiographien können als Grundlage erziehungswissenschaftlicher Forschung dienen, sofern sie pädagogisch relevante Motive in den Blick nehmen. Inwiefern jedoch kann die *Gerettete Zunge* als Quelle einer Analyse über Bildungsprozesse aufgefasst werden? Canetti rekonstruiert in seiner »Geschichte einer Jugend«, wie die *Gerettete Zunge* im Untertitel heisst, die Ursprünge einer Bildungslaufbahn, die sich formal untergliedern lässt in fünf Teile, welche fünf

Orten zuzurechnen sind, an denen Canetti von seiner Geburt im Jahr 1905 bis zu seinem siebzehnten Lebensjahr, also bis 1921, jeweils lebte. Dies sind Rustschuk in Bulgarien, Manchester, Wien und zwei unterschiedliche Orte in Zürich. Das Werk kann in weiten Teilen als eine Reflexion über frühe Erfahrungen mit Kultur- und Bildungsgütern gelesen werden, welche als ein Fundament von Bildungsprozessen zu verstehen sind: Canettis Vater brachte seinem Sohn regelmässig Bücher und sprach mit ihm darüber; als »das unvergleichlich Wichtige« (GZ, S. 111)[15] und »das Herz unseres Daseins« (S. 173) bezeichnete Canetti die Leseerfahrungen und die Gespräche mit seiner Mutter, einer gebildeten Frau, »der die Literaturen der Kultursprachen, die sie beherrschte, zum eigentlichen Inhalt ihres Lebens wurden« (S. 12) und deren »Menschenkenntnis an den grossen Werken der Weltliteratur geschult [war], aber auch an den Erfahrungen des eigenen Lebens« (S. 13), sodass Canetti zeitweilig alles, was er erlebte, mit Büchern in Zusammenhang brachte (S. 69), seine Mutter mit Medea, die Realität mit den Sagen des klassischen Altertums verglich (S. 143) und schliesslich behauptete: »[...] wenn ich damals etwas wie Sorge um die Zukunft überhaupt kannte, so galt sie ausschliesslich dem Bücherbestand der Welt« (S. 194). Bisweilen gibt sich die *Gerettete Zunge* somit als ein Protokoll einer frühen Bildungsgeschichte zu lesen, welche eng mit dem Erwerb von Sprache als Ausgangspunkt von Bildung verbunden ist. Unter diesem Gesichtspunkt kann Canettis erster Teil der Autobiographie als Grundlage pädagogischer Reflexion über Bildungsprozesse herangezogen werden. Er thematisiert innere und äussere, psychologische ebenso wie soziale und kulturelle Bedingungen der Entstehung von Bildung weitgehend in der Manier eines Bildungsromans, wobei der Bildungsprozess des Erzählers in Wechselwirkung mit dessen sprachlicher Entfaltung sowie in Abhängigkeit von bedeutsamen Bezugspersonen erfolgt, die in der Lage sind, ein Verlangen zu stiften, das fortan als entscheidendes Movens zur Auseinandersetzung mit dem Selbst und der Welt im Medium der Sprache fungiert. Es ist jedoch zu fragen, wie Bildung in diesem Zusammenhang konzipiert wird. Der dieser Arbeit zugrundegelegte Bildungsbegriff bedarf daher vor dem Hintergrund des bildungstheoretischen Diskurses der Erziehungswissenschaft einer näheren Bestimmung.

---

15 Sämtliche Seitenangaben ohne Autoren- und Jahresangaben beziehen sich im Folgenden auf Canetti (2005).

4 Zum erziehungswissenschaftlichen Diskurs über Bildung

Bildung umfasst sowohl die Annahme der Formung des einzelnen Menschen wie auch die Idee eines universalen Zwecks menschlichen Daseins in der Welt, wobei nicht nur dieses doppelte Verhältnis der Bildung zum Partikularen und zum Universellen – zum Individuum und der Menschheit an sich – den Bildungsbegriff zu einem Begriff mit einer breiten Bedeutungsvarianz und zu einer idealen Plattform für heterogene Deutungsmuster macht (Andresen, 2009, S. 79f). Die Bildungsphilosophie verdeutlicht nebst dieser zweifachen Bestimmung der Bildung auch, dass es keine »überhistorisch-allgemeinverbindliche oder innerhistorisch-relativistische Antwort« (Benner & Brüggen, 2004, S. 174) auf die Frage nach der Bildung gibt. Bisweilen wird, was mit Bildung bezeichnet werden kann, als »bestimmt unbestimmt« (Ehrenspeck & Rustemeyer, 1996) umschrieben, oder es wird betont, dass Bildung im pädagogischen Diskurs äusserst ambivalent und widersprüchlich kommuniziert wird (vgl. Tenorth, 1997) und dass der Begriff der Bildung dabei infolge seines inflationären Gebrauchs und seiner mehrfachen semantischen Auflladung (und Überladung) inhaltlich zunehmend entleert wird. Ein derart befrachteter Diskurs um Bildung in seiner weitläufigen Semantik bedeutet zwar nicht notwendig die »zu Ende gehende [...] Epoche des Begriffs« (Nipkow, 1977, S. 205), doch er verweist auf die Notwendigkeit, den Bildungsbegriff im Einzelfall je nach Problemstellung – abermals vorläufig – adäquat zu bestimmen und gegenüber herkömmlichen und möglicherweise überholten Begriffen abzugrenzen. Sieht man sich dabei die Debatte um den Begriff der Bildung näher an, so lässt sich vereinfachend feststellen, dass sich trotz diskursiver Heterogenität insbesondere drei wesentliche Akzentsetzungen abzeichnen (vgl. Ricken, 2006, S. 21f). Bildung wird erstens meist problematisiert als ein Vorgang, der auf Wissen bezogen und mit einer prozessualen Entwicklung verbunden ist. Damit werden auch Ungenügen und Mangel thematisch relevant, wenn von Bildung gesprochen wird. Pleines spricht den Prozesscharakter von Bildung an, wenn er den Vorgang der Bildung beschreibt als eine »dynamische, stets konkrete und individuelle Bewegung, als ein ständiges Sich-überschreiten, das jeden vorgegebenen Zustand und Bestand hinter sich lässt« (1989, S. 22). Zweitens wird Bildung traditionell als Kategorie mit einem selbstreferentiellen Grundzug verstanden. »›Bildung‹ steht im pädagogischen Gebrauch nicht für ein natürliches Werden, das von sich her mal so und mal anders geschieht, sondern für ein Werden nach gedanklichen Massgaben« (Ruhloff, 2000, S. 119). In dieser Sichtweise ist mit Bildung also die Konzentration auf selbstbezügliche Individualität verknüpft, der es in Relation mit der Welt vorrangig um das eigene Selbst geht, so dass das im Bildungsprozess begriffene Individuum im Horizont des Allgemeinen ein spezifisches, sich selbst reflektierendes Selbst- und Welt-Verhältnis entwickelt. Eine derart konzipierte Subjekt-Welt-Relation wurde im bildungstheoretischen Diskurs bereits als das Grundthema von Bildungstheorien formuliert (Tenorth, 1997). In diesem Sinne kann Bildung verstanden werden als ein ›Dispositiv‹ (vgl. Foucault, 1978), das die Art, sich zu sich, anderen und der Welt in ein Verhältnis zu setzen, in eine spezifische Form bringt. Werden Bildungssubjekte als »sinndeutende Wesen« (Fink, 1970; zit. nach Reichenbach 2007, S. 128) und »self-interpreting animals« (Taylor, 1985, S. 45) verstanden, so kann Bildung charakterisiert werden als die Form, in der Menschen sich im Rahmen ihrer strukturellen Verfasstheit und im Wechselverhältnis mit der Welt zu verstehen und auszulegen versuchen. Bildung wird in diesem Sinne verstehbar als der »reflexive Modus des menschlichen In-der-Welt-Seins« (Marotzki, 2006, S. 60). Schliesslich lässt sich als dritter Akzent der Rede über den Bildungsbegriff meist ein moralisches, normatives Moment beobachten, das es nicht zulässt, jegliche Gestaltungs- und Transformationsprozesse des Selbst als Bildungsprozesse aufzufassen (vgl. Benner & Brüggen, 2004). Nebst diesen drei prominenten Schwerpunkten der bildungstheoretischen Diskussion – der Prozesshaftigkeit, der Selbstreferentialität und der moralischen Dimension von Bildung – ist schliesslich eine weitere Kategorie zentral bei Bildungsprozessen: es ist die Kategorie der Sprache.

5 *Sprache und Bildung*

Die Sprache wurde in vielen theoretischen Ansätzen nicht explizit mit Bildung in Zusammenhang gebracht oder aber lediglich implizit als Bestandteil von Bildung mitgedacht. Gelegentlich wurde sie jedoch einer eingehenderen bildungstheoretischen Reflexion unterzogen. Explizite sprachtheoretische Bezüge enthält insbesondere die Theorie Wilhelm von Humboldts, wonach sich der Bildungsprozess des Menschen in der Struktur einer freien Wechselwirkung zwischen Mensch und Welt vollzieht und auf das Ziel ihrer Verknüpfung hin ausgerichtet ist. Dieser Prozess lässt sich als Interaktion von Selbsttätigkeit und Empfänglichkeit verstehen. Da der Mensch immer schon in eine Sprache hineingeboren wird, die geschichtlich gewachsen und dem Menschen gegeben ist, sucht dieser seine Bestimmung im Rahmen seiner sprachlichen und geschichtlichen Verfasstheit zu finden (Humboldt, 2002c, S. 226), indem er Perspektiven einnimmt, die jedoch durch die Sprache immer schon von anderen Menschen durchwirkt sind. Der Mensch spiegelt auf individuelle und eigentümliche Art die Sprache wider, in die er hineinwächst und die er zwar nicht schafft, durch die jeweilige Aneignung aber immer auch selbstbezüglich verändert, denn Humboldt versteht die Sprache nicht als »ergon« (Werk), sondern als »energeia« (Tätigkeit). Sie ist demnach als Arbeit zu begreifen, wodurch der Schaffende seine Umgebung verwandelt. Diese Umgebung ist aber zugleich auch Bedingung seines Schaffens, sodass der Schaffende, indem er anderes schafft, immer auch sich selber schafft. Die Sprache erschafft dabei das, wovon die Rede ist, und gibt den Blick frei auf etwas, was in seiner Eigenheit nicht eindeutig, sondern immer nur in und als Sprache wahrgenommen werden kann (vgl. auch Ladenthin, 1991, S. 264ff). Bildung vollzieht sich in einer »offenen Dialektik von Welterfahrung und Weltentwurf. In dieser steht die Welt dem Menschen niemals nur als eine bekannte, sondern stets zugleich als unbekannte und fremde gegenüber« (Benner & Brüggen, 2004, S. 195). Der Sprache kommt nun gemäss Humboldt die Funktion zu, diese Fremdheit der Welt an die je eigenen Strukturen des Menschen anzupassen. »Das nun ist es, was ich die eigentliche Kraft der Sprache nennen möchte, ihre Fähigkeit, den Trieb und die Kraft zu erhöhen, immerfort – wie Sie es nennen wollen – mehr Welt mit sich zu verknüpfen, oder aus sich zu entwickeln« (Humboldt, 2002e, S. 196f). Humboldts Bildungsgedanke umfasst dabei die Idee, dass Sprache nicht einfach nur Welt repräsentiert und Kommunikation ermöglicht, sie ist vielmehr Bedingung und konstitutiver Bestandteil des Bildungsprozesses: »Sie ist [...], wenn nicht überhaupt, doch wenigstens sinnlich das Mittel, durch welches der Mensch zugleich sich selbst und die Welt bildet, oder vielmehr seiner dadurch bewusst wird, dass er eine Welt von sich abscheidet« (ebd., S. 196). Die Sprachlichkeit des Menschen wird bei Humboldt insofern zu einer bedeutsamen Kategorie von Bildung, als sie eine Wechselwirkung von Ich und Welt befördert, ohne dass der Mensch jedoch sich, die Sprache oder die Welt ganz zu erfassen imstande wäre. Die Welt stellt sich dem Menschen gemäss Humboldt verhüllt dar, als ein ›unsichtbares Gebiet‹, in das der Mensch mit sprachlichen Begriffen einzudringen hofft, sodass er dieses Unsichtbare erfassen und sich in ihm vertraut fühlen kann:

> Der Mensch denkt, fühlt und lebt allein in der Sprache, und muss erst durch sie gebildet werden [...] Aber er empfindet und weiss, dass sie ihm nur ein Mittel ist, dass es ein unsichtbares Gebiet ausser ihr giebt, in dem er nur durch sie einheimisch zu werden trachtet. Die alltäglichste Empfindung und das tiefsinnigste Denken klagen über die Unzulänglichkeit der Sprache, und sehen jenes Gebiet als ein fernes Land an, zu dem nur sie, und sie nie ganz führt (Humboldt, 1959, S. 85).

Die Sprache dient in dieser Perspektive der Verwandlung von Fremdem zum Eigenen. Durch die Bezeichnung des Unbekannten wird dieses dem Selbst angeeignet. Der Mensch »umgiebt sich mit einer Welt von Lauten, um die Welt von Gegenständen in sich aufzunehmen und zu bearbeiten [...] Der Mensch lebt mit den Gegenständen hauptsächlich, ja [...] sogar ausschliesslich so, wie die Sprache sie ihm zuführt« (Humboldt, 2002c, S. 434). Der Mensch kann die Welt nicht anders erfahren als in der Sprache und die Sprache zeugt im Sprechen das, wovon sie zugleich spricht. Nebst einer intersubjektiven Verständigungsfunktion (durch die zeitgleich miteinander lebende sowie frühere und künftige Generationen miteinander verbunden werden) hat die Sprache laut Humboldt daher auch eine weltvermittelnde Funktion. Sie ermöglicht dem Menschen eine sprachliche Anbindung an die Welt; in ihr sind Mensch und Welt miteinander verwoben. Über die Sprache wird Bildung vermittelt und durch sie ist eine reflexive Bezugnahme des Menschen auf sich selbst erst möglich.

6 *Sprache und Bildung bei Canetti*

Canetti rückt diese Funktion der Sprache als Form der Bezugnahme auf die Welt dezidiert in den Vordergrund der *Geretteten Zunge*. Dass auch er die Sprache gleichsam als ein Werkzeug versteht, mittels dessen wir Unbekanntes sprachlich auf uns beziehen und dadurch den Grad seiner Fremdheit reduzieren, wird im Folgenden zu zeigen sein. Im Anschluss an Humboldts Überlegungen zum Zusammenhang von Sprache und Bildung soll hier der Frage nachgegangen werden, in welcher Hinsicht bei Canetti von einem im Medium der Sprache sich vollziehenden Bildungsprozess die Rede sein kann. Dabei wird der Bildungsprozess in Übereinstimmung mit anderen Ansätzen aufgefasst als ein Prozess, in dem der Mensch in der Interaktion mit sich, anderen Menschen und der Welt im Rahmen seiner strukturellen Disposition selbstreflexiv eine individuelle Form entwickelt, in der er sich zu sich und der Welt verhält, wobei der Sprache in diesem Prozess eine erstrangige Funktion zukommt. Sie fungiert als Medium, das es erlaubt, das ursprünglich Fremde (des Selbst, der anderen und der Welt) in einer fortschreitenden Dynamik in Eigenes zu überführen. Das Verständnis der in der *Geretteten Zunge* dargestellten Bildungsprozesse erfordert bei dieser Betonung der Funktion der Sprache allerdings eine Klärung des Prinzips, wodurch bei Canetti die Bildung der Sprache in Gang gesetzt wird. Von Bedeutung ist dabei die Frage, nach welchem Mechanismus Canetti sich im Verlauf seiner Entwicklung in die sprachliche Ordnung einfügt. Diese Frage wird hier unter einem spezifischen Gesichtspunkt analysiert: Mit Rekurs auf die psychoanalytische Theorie Jacques Lacans wird die Funktion des Begehrens als treibende Kraft des menschlichen Seins im Prozess der individuellen Eingliederung in die sprachliche Ordnung herausgearbeitet. Der folgenden Untersuchung sei dabei erstens die These zugrunde gelegt, wonach Canettis Eifer, sich mit Bildungsgütern, mit denen er in Berührung kommt, auseinanderzusetzen, durch ein Begehren nach Aneignung von Sprache erklärt werden kann. Zweitens steht die Annahme im Zentrum, wonach die Sprache dazu dient, die Fremdheit der Welt einschliesslich des Selbst und anderer Menschen der sich fortlaufend verändernden strukturellen Disposition des Menschen einzupassen.

7 Canettis Bildungsprozess als Annäherung an das Fremde und das Begehren nach Sprache

Der erste Teil der Autobiographie hat seinen Ausgangspunkt in Canettis frühester Erinnerung – der Erinnerung an die Drohung des lächelnden jungen Mannes, er würde dem kleinen Canetti die Zunge abschneiden, jener Erinnerung also an den drohenden Verlust der Sprache – und steht danach im Zeichen nicht nur der Errettung der Sprache, sondern mehr noch einer unablässigen Suche nach ihrer Erweiterung. Die gerettete Zunge, das heisst die gerettete Sprache. Canetti sprach in seinen ersten Lebensjahren nur Spanisch, eine Sprache, in der ›Zunge‹ zugleich auch ›Sprache‹ bedeutet (vgl. Rabinovici, 1996). Nicht zufällig, sondern entwicklungslogisch zwingend beschreibt Canetti die Episode des befürchteten Sprachverlusts als symbolisch für den Beginn seiner Erinnerungsfähigkeit. In ihr wird andeutungsweise bereits der Stellenwert der Sprache im Prozess der Bildung manifest. Dieser wird weiter bestätigt, wenn Canetti später schreibt: »Aus den Sätzen, die sie [die Mutter] mir [...] sagte, bin ich entstanden« (S. 155), und somit unterstellt, seine Existenz sei massgeblich sprachlich begründet.

Das Streben nach Sprache lässt sich analysieren unter Rückgriff auf Lacans Konzept des Begehrens. Wenn Lacan schreibt, »man muss das Begehren buchstäblich nehmen« (1973, S. 210), so heisst dies, man muss das Begehren als ein Begehren nach Sprache verstehen. An der Sprache ist auch Canettis Begehren ausgerichtet. Es ist bei ihm das Begehren nach Sprache als Instrument, sich des Fremden zu bemächtigen. Dieses Fremde kann dabei, für sich alleine genommen, nicht definiert werden. Es kann nur relational gedacht werden: es ist keine Eigenschaft von Personen, Gegenständen oder Sachverhalten, sondern Ausdruck einer Beziehung zu ihnen und fremd vermittels eines nicht fremden Vergleichs- und Bezugspunkts. Eigen und fremd gelten somit als relationale Kategorien. Die Bestimmung des Eigenen und des Fremden durchdringen einander, wobei das eine mit Blick auf das andere definiert wird und umgekehrt (vgl. Scior, 2002, S. 10ff). Ausgehend von der Annahme, dass die Sprache als Werkzeug zur Aneignung des Fremden verstanden werden kann, wäre davon auszugehen, dass das Fremde und das Eigene über die Sprache aufeinander bezogen werden können. Die Konfrontation mit dem Fremden stellt dabei die Bedingung dar für die Möglichkeit der Herausbildung des Eigenen und die Reflexion über Fremdes kann ein vertieftes Bewusstsein des Eigenen ermöglichen. Wenn bei Canetti also ein Begehren nach Sprache zum Ausdruck kommt, so ist dieses Begehren auch als ein Begehren nach Einbeziehung von Fremdem in die eigene Sprache zu verstehen.

Der erste Auslöser für Canettis Begehren nach Sprache ist in dessen Erfahrung zu sehen, dass seine Eltern mit ihm Spanisch, miteinander jedoch Deutsch redeten, wovon Canetti nichts verstehen durfte. Die Eltern hatten »eine eigene Sprache unter sich« (S. 33). Canetti konnte sie nicht deuten; er war dadurch aus deren Kommunikationsraum ausgeschlossen, der Zugang zur Sprache der Eltern blieb ihm verwehrt. Er fühlte sich, wenn seine Eltern miteinander Gespräche führten, jenseits ihrer sprachlichen Ordnung, und bettelte deshalb, sie möchten ihm die deutschen Worte erklären, denn er glaubte, »dass es sich um wunderbare Dinge handeln müsse, die man nur in dieser Sprache sagen könne« (S. 34). In diesem Verhältnis zum Symbolischen der Eltern, das kraft seiner Unentzifferbarkeit in der Sphäre des Imaginären verbleibt, deutet sich an, inwiefern dieses Symbolische für Canetti zum Ort des Begehrens wird. Canetti stösst vorerst ausschliesslich auf Signifikanten, noch entziehen sich ihm die Signifikate (vgl. auch Widmer, 1997). Die prägende Differenzerfahrung – die Trennung zwischen Canetti und der sprachlichen Ordnung der Eltern – lässt Canetti den sein Subjekt konstituierenden Mangel erkennen, was zur Folge hat, dass er die Sätze, die er von seinen Eltern gehört hatte, für sich nachbuchstabiert, »im genauen Tonfall, wie Zauberformeln« (S. 33), wodurch er anfängt, sie sich anzueignen, denn »unter den vielen heftigen Wünschen dieser Zeit blieb es für [ihn] der heftigste, [die] geheime Sprache zu verstehen« (S. 33), die seine Eltern untereinander reden. Canettis »unstillbare Sehnsucht nach Buchstaben« (S. 38) wurde zunächst bereits durch den Vater geweckt. Später, als Canetti der deutschen Sprache mächtig ist und deutsche Worte für ihn keine Zauberformeln mehr darstellen, verschiebt sich dieses Begehren, die Sprache zu entziffern, auf das Begehren, die Wissenschaften zu verstehen. Das »Zauberwort« (S. 236) ist dann das Attribut »wissenschaftlich« (S. 236). Die Wissenschaft als andere, noch nicht entschlüsselte Sprache wird für Canetti nunmehr zum Versprechen, sich befreien zu können von gewohnten Mustern des Denkens und abermals Unbekanntes an die bereits gebildeten, eigenen symbolischen Strukturen anzupassen. Canetti stellt sich in dieser Zeit neue, noch nicht existierende Schulfächer vor und er erfindet Namen für sie; diese bleiben jedoch leer, sodass sie sein Begehren nicht erfüllen können und er das, was er begehrt, in den Wissenschaften zu suchen beginnt. Hier glaubt er dieses fürs Erste zwar zu finden, doch auch die Wissenschaften werden sein Begehren nicht dauerhaft stillen. Canettis Mutter fasst den Mechanismus der Entstehung und des Erlöschens des Begehrens in Worte, als sie ihm auf seine Bekundung, er werde immer lernen wollen, entgegnet, er werde in totem Wissen ersticken, sein Wissen sei nur deshalb noch nicht tot, weil er es zurzeit noch nicht besitze: »Erst wenn man's hat, wird es zu etwas Totem« (S. 325). Kaum erlischt das Begehren für das Eine, entsteht ein Begehren für anderes. Dieses Prinzip hält das Begehren aufrecht. Canettis Bildungsprozess, der eine Zielgerichtetheit grösstenteils vermissen lässt, vollzieht sich daher in einer rückhaltlosen Überantwortung Canettis an sämtliche ihm zugängliche Diskurse (vgl. Steussloff, 1994, S. 282). Bildung ist in diesem Sinne mit der Paradoxie verknüpft, durch andere erst zum Eigenen kommen, das heisst in der Abarbeitung am Fremden erst das Eigene hervorbringen zu können. Die Beschäftigung mit dem Fremden wird dabei begünstigt durch das Begehren, das durch eine permanente Unruhe gekennzeichnet ist. Es gibt sich mit keinem Objekt dauerhaft zufrieden (vgl. Widmer, 1997) und veranlasst Canetti auf diese Weise zur beständigen Fortführung seiner sprachlichen Selbstkultivierung. Es bewirkt somit eine andauernde Aneignung von Sprache. In den Bildungsprozess ist es insofern impliziert, als es das Subjekt der Bildung, Canetti, dazu bewegt, Fremdes in die innere Ordnung seines Denkens, Interpretierens, Urteilens und Wahrnehmens einzugliedern und damit die Form seiner Weltauffassung zu verändern. Canetti resümiert gegen Ende der *Geretteten Zunge*: »Mit der Erfahrung Kannitverstans, als die Eltern in einer mir unbekannten Sprache zueinander redeten, hatte mein Leben begonnen, und was sich im Unverständnis einzelner Gelegenheiten erhöhte [...] das hatte sich bei mir als Erhöhung einer ganzen Sprache ausgewirkt« (S. 285). In dieser Wendung umschreibt Canetti die genannte Differenzerfahrung zwischen ihm und der Sprache seiner Eltern emphatisch als den Ursprung seines Daseins; und er attestiert Situationen, die eine Irritation in Form von Unverständnis bewirken, die Kraft, die sprachliche Genese zu stimulieren und so zur Ausbildung und andauernden Fortentwicklung der Sprache beizutragen.

Von einer »räuberischen Unersättlichkeit« (Von Matt, 2007, S. 47) getrieben, macht sich Canetti zu Eigen, was andere ihm an Weltwissen aufbereitet haben. »Alle Ereignisse ausserhalb von Literatur-, Buch-, Kunst-Debatten werden mindestens auf ihre Bedeutung für ein künftiges Dasein als Dichter bewertet« (Hanuschek, 2005, S. 56), und das heisst für ein Dasein in und durch die Sprache. Vordergründig ist insbesondere ein Motiv für diesen Drang zu identifizieren, sich sämtlicher Versatzstücke zu bedienen und sie in den eigenen Erfahrungsschatz einzupassen. Dieses ist in der Kategorie einer »Erweiterung, Befreiung von Grenzen und Beschränkungen« (S. 236) zu verorten. Intellektuelle Erfahrungen empfindet Canetti seinen eigenen Angaben zufolge physisch, als ein Gefühl körperlicher Erweiterung. Die Entfaltung der Sprache entspricht in diesem Licht einer Entgrenzung, einer die Dimension des rein Sprachlichen transzendierenden Erfahrung, die Canetti in derselben Metaphorik umschreibt wie Humboldt, nämlich als das Eintreten in ein unbekanntes Gebiet, das einem durch dessen sprachliche Bezeichnung zunehmend vertrauter wird:

> Es gehörte dazu, dass man schon manches andere wusste, dass das Neue aber in keiner Weise damit zusammenhing. Etwas, das von allem Übrigen separiert war, siedelte sich dort an, wo vorher nichts war. Eine Türe ging plötzlich auf, wo man nichts vermutet hatte, und man fand sich in einer Landschaft mit eigenem Licht, wo alles neue Namen trug und sich weiter und weiter, bis ins Unendliche erstreckte. Da bewegte man sich nun staunend, dahin, dorthin, wie es einen gelüstete, und es war, als wäre man noch nie woanders gewesen (S. 236).

In dieser Denkfigur deutet Canetti ausserdem an, dass sich das uns Unbekannte prinzipiell nie erschöpft. Es wären daher endlos viele Bezeichnungen zu finden, um dieses uns Fremde an uns anzupassen, sodass das Begehren als unaufhörlicher Antrieb – hier nach Reduktion des Fremden durch sprachliche Benennung – nicht erlöschen wird. Mit der Ausbildung neuer symbolischer Strukturen ist bei Canetti die Illusion verbunden, er habe sich immer schon in diesen symbolischen Strukturen bewegt, »als wäre man noch nie woanders gewesen« (S. 236). Hier tritt eine als neu zu anerkennende Ordnung zutage, die mit ihrem Auftauchen eine veränderte Perspektive in die Vergangenheit eröffnet und den Eindruck erweckt, diese Ordnung habe nie nicht da sein können, sie müsse immer schon existiert haben. Ist diese symbolische Struktur erst einmal erfasst, so ist es im Licht der neuen Erfahrung unmöglich, über das, was ihr vorausging, anders zu reflektieren als mit Hilfe der Symbole, die jetzt angewandt werden können. Was an neuen Strukturen auftaucht, scheint bereits von jeher und ununterbrochen vorhanden gewesen zu sein. Zugleich wird durch die neue Struktur das, was uns fremd ist, nie erschöpfend erfasst, sodass stets eine Lücke bleiben muss, die zu füllen uns begehrenswert erscheint. Dieses Prinzip findet seinen Ausdruck in Canettis Aussage: »Was immer auf mich zukam, schlug feste Wurzeln [...]. Kaum war es in mir, bezog es sich auf anderes, verband sich damit, wuchs weiter [...] und rief nach Neuem« (S. 203). Die Frage ist daher angebracht, wie dieses Begehren im Einzelnen beschaffen ist, in Funktion tritt und die sprachliche Bildung in Gang setzt.

8 Das Begehren

Das Begehren steht in Jacques Lacans Theorie in einem unmittelbaren Verhältnis zum Imaginären. Es ist Ausdruck eines Mangels,[16] der das menschliche Sein konstituiert, und es präsentiert das, was in Wirklichkeit gerade nicht präsent ist. Das Begehren entstammt dem Mangel und es strebt nach phantasmagorischer Fülle, dem nicht zu gewinnenden Objekt des Begehrens (vgl. Möde, 1995, S. 54). Im Fall von Canetti und mit Blick auf die Frage nach der Bildung der Sprache lässt sich diese Konstellation beispielhaft als das Missverhältnis zwischen dem durch sprachliche Unvollständigkeit gekennzeichneten Kind und dem Phantasma der Vollkommenheit der Sprache der Eltern oder der Sprache überhaupt konturieren. Dies erscheint insofern gerechtfertigt, als Lacan das Subjekt konzipiert als ein der Sprache unterworfenes Subjekt, das erst als Subjekt gilt, sofern es spricht (1973, S. 227). Das Phantasma stellt dabei laut Lacan die Instanz dar, vermittels deren sich das Subjekt auf der Ebene seines Begehrens halten kann (ebd., S. 230). Begünstigt wird das Phantasma bei Canetti etwa durch den Umstand, dass man in dessen Geburtsort, Rustschuk, täglich sieben oder acht Sprachen hören konnte und auf diese Weise einer Vielfalt an sprachlichen Fremdheiten ausgesetzt war. Aus der Diskrepanz zwischen dem Mangel und der imaginären Erfüllung speist sich die Grunddynamik des psychischen Strebens. Das Begehren lässt sich nicht zufrieden stellen, es bleibt unbefriedigt und macht sich eben deswegen fortwährend von selbst bemerkbar. Dem begehrenden Subjekt genügt kein Objekt, und das Begehren lässt den Mangel in einer endlosen Bewegung immer dort neu entstehen, wo er eben überwunden schien (vgl. Pagel, 2007), weswegen Lacan auch vom »Paradox des Begehrens« (1973, S. 230) spricht. Bei Canetti richtet sich das Begehren nun unter anderem darauf, sprachlich das noch unbesiedelte ›Unendliche‹ zu benennen. Canetti versucht somit das zu vervollständigen, was gerade nicht oder noch nicht in seinen sprachlichen Strukturen repräsentiert ist. Sein Begehren manifestiert sich im Auseinanderklaffen, das heisst in der Lücke zwischen den noch nicht bezeichneten Aspekten der Welt und dem Wunsch nach deren Bezeichnung. Aus der Perspektive des Begehrens ist jedoch jedes vorläufige Objekt der Erfüllung das

---

16 Im französischen Original von Lacan auch als ›manque à être‹ bezeichnet, was vielfach als Seinsverfehlen oder Seinsverfehlung ins Deutsche übertragen wurde.

falsche, also noch nicht das Objekt der absoluten Erfüllung. Das Begehren verewigt sich daher selbst. Ihm geht es nicht um dessen eigene Erfüllung, das heisst um die Beseitigung des Mangels, sondern um das Hervorbringen von Begehren selbst in einer unabschliessbaren Bewegung. Nichts kann ihm je vollständig genügen, kein Objekt vermag ihm ganz zu entsprechen, es bleibt stets ein Rest an Unbefriedigtsein, der dem Ort des unstillbaren Begehrens entspricht. Dies kommt auch etwa zum Ausdruck, wenn Canetti seinen Drang nach ›Wissen‹ mit einem »Freiheitsdrang« (S. 254) in Verbindung bringt und erklärt, dass er in seinem Streben nach Erweiterung des Wissens »keinen Punkt im Auge [hat], den er erlangen will, eben über solche Punkte will er hinaus« (S. 254). Was er einmal erreicht hat, ist er sogleich bestrebt, hinter sich zu lassen, rastlos versucht er, seine eigenen Kenntnisse zu überschreiten. In Canettis Worten ist diese Betriebsamkeit motiviert durch eine »Sehnsucht nach Neuem« (S. 237). Dass er sich dauernd ruhelos hinter sich selbst zurücklassen will, liegt jedoch insbesondere auch in der Mangelerfahrung begründet, anderen gegenüber in bestimmter Hinsicht unterlegen zu sein. Selbst Kameraden, die sich durch kein besonderes Schulwissen auszeichneten, lassen Canetti seine »Ahnungslosigkeit auf vielen Gebieten« (S. 262) erkennen, wenn sie sich in ihren Gesprächen unterhalten und dabei ihre punktuelle Überlegenheit zum Vorschein kommt, und sie lösen in ihm eine Bewunderung für sie aus, die sein Begehren weiter nährt. Das Begehren ist stets das Begehren nach dem anderen, da man unmöglich etwas begehren kann, was man bereits hat. Auf diese Weise wird das Objekt des Begehrens fortgesetzt weiter hinausgeschoben (vgl. Evans, 2002). Canettis Formulierung – »da ich nach allem strebte, was mir nicht nahe war [...]« (S. 317) – fasst dieses Prinzip zusammen. Weil das Begehren immer auf den Mangel bezogen bleibt, genügen Canetti kein Fortschritt, keine Neuordnung seines Wissens, keine Erweiterung seiner sprachlichen Strukturen ganz, das Begehren findet letztlich immer wieder den Mangel, ja es begehrt den Mangel und gibt sich einem unablässigen Kreisen um ihn hin, denn das Begehren ist das Begehren nach dem Begehren, es ist das Begehren nach dem Mangel und nach Nicht-Befriedigung.

9   Die prägende Funktion des sozialen Rahmens

Dieses Begehren ist jedoch nicht die einzige Quelle des menschlichen Strebens. Entscheidende Impulse kommen auch aus der sozialen Umwelt, die im Falle Canettis die beharrliche Hingabe an die Literatur und die Erweiterung seiner Sprache mit nur wenigen unbedeutenden Ausnahmen fortlaufend neu entfacht.

Zwei ineinander laufende und sich gegenseitig ausbalancierende Prozesse regen somit die psychische Neigung an, nicht von der eigenen Selbstentfaltung abzulassen: einerseits das Begehren des Subjekts ungeachtet des sozialen Gefüges und dessen Erwartungen an und Wirkungen auf das Subjekt, andererseits die Beschäftigung des Subjekts mit seiner Zugehörigkeit zum sozialen Bezugssystem und dessen Rückwirkungen auf das Subjekt. Die prozesshafte Suche nach Vervollständigung des Subjekts erweist sich bildungstheoretisch als bedeutsam, da sich der in einer unabgeschlossenen und unabschliessbaren Bewegung angestrebte Zustand der Vollkommenheit nie als gesicherter Sachverhalt einstellt, als imaginärer Ort jedoch die aktive Abarbeitung des Subjekts am Selbst und an der Welt vorantreibt. Dem übergeordneten sozialen Rahmen kommt dabei für die Entfaltung des Subjekts eine erstrangige Bedeutung zu. So auch bei Canetti. Er ist in dieser sozialen Matrix verbunden mit den Eltern und über diese wiederum mit der Sprache, durch die er sich bildet. Der frühen Prägung durch dieses gesellschaftliche System ist hier näher nachzugehen.

Canetti wächst in einer gelehrten Familie mit einer langen Bildungstradition auf. Die Mutter stammt aus einer Kaufmannsfamilie, der Vater rechnet zu seinen Vorfahren Ärzte, Dichter und Philosophen. Beide Eltern interessieren sich für Literatur und ermöglichen ihrem Sohn den ständigen Umgang mit Büchern. Den gedanklichen Austausch mit der Mutter verabsolutiert Canetti als »das Wichtigste überhaupt« (S. 127) und in der Beziehung zu seiner Mutter hatten »alle geistigen Dinge [...] das Übergewicht« (S. 173), sodass Canetti später über seine Mutter sagen wird: »Ich war den Buchstaben und den Worten verfallen, und wenn das ein Hochmut war, so hatte sie mich beharrlich dazu erzogen« (S. 328). Die Mutter, eine dieser Persönlichkeiten, die als Eltern Lehrer sind, eine Eifernde für die europäische Hochkultur (vgl. Sontag, 1990), figuriert nebst dem früh verstorbenen Vater als Schlüsselfigur in der Prägung der Haltung ihres Sohns, sich mit allem zu konfrontieren, was seine Begriffe erweitern könnte. Sie eröffnet ihm die Sphären des Geistes und führt ihn ein in eine durch die Ubiquität von Büchern im Elternhaushalt sowie durch verschiedene bedeutsame Lehrpersonen in Schulen bestimmte Bildungswelt. Sie versucht nicht, ihn missionarisch für eine bestimmte Idee einzunehmen oder ihn, auf potentielle Zweckmäßigkeiten bedacht, in eine bestimmte Richtung zu drängen. Sie ermöglicht ihm die Beschäftigung mit der Sprache und mit den in der Literatur aufgeworfenen intellektuellen Fragen, gewährt ihm Freiheiten in der Wahl der Lektüre und verschont ihn weitgehend mit bürgerlichem Zweckdenken und utilitaristischen Bildungszielen.

Canettis Beziehung zu den grossen Werken der abendländischen Kultur wurde zuallererst bereits durch die Anstrengungen des Vaters begründet. Er hat dem Sohn Bücher zu lesen gegeben, die er wohlweislich für ihn ausgewählt hat: Tausendundeine Nacht, Grimms Märchen, Robinson Crusoe, Gullivers Travels, Tales von Shakespeare, Don Quijote, Dante, Wilhelm Tell. Anders die Mutter: sie lässt ihren Sohn frei wählen, womit er sich beschäftigen will, sie wird »zur Grossmut selbst [...] für alles, was dachte, fühlte und litt, wobei die Bewunderung für den leuchtenden Vorgang des Denkens, das jedem gegeben war, den Vorrang hatte« (S. 203). Unter ihrem Einfluss wird kaum ein Stoff für den Sohn im Voraus selektiert, kaum einer wird ihm vorenthalten. Nie muss er etwas aus bloss praktischen Gründen tun, und was er auch auffassen mag, es wird nahezu alles gleichermassen gebilligt. Die einzige, dafür aber rigorose Forderung an den Sohn ist die nach der Sorgfalt und der Ernsthaftigkeit im Umgang mit dem Ideengut anderer. »Genau und gründlich musste man sein und eine Meinung ohne Schwindeleien vertreten können, aber diese Gründlichkeit galt der Sache selbst und nicht irgendeinem Nutzen, den sie für einen haben könnte« (S. 203). In Übereinstimmung mit diesem Gebot tituliert die Mutter konsequenterweise all jene, die etwa einen Autor nur mangelhaft kennen und zu faul sind, »etwas von Grund auf zu erfahren« (S. 200), als Schwätzer und Wirrköpfe. Als »Halm im Wind« (S. 201) verspottet sie, wer sich vorschnell von einem einmal eingenommenen Standpunkt absetzt, und auch sie selber nimmt nichts ungeprüft hin, wodurch sich denn auch ihr Misstrauen vor eiligen Bekehrungen erklären lässt. Sie ist keine Systematikerin. Was ihre Auffassungen einander zuordnet, ist letzten Endes ein Prinzip: das der Achtung vor dem Denken anderer. In ihm ist System enthalten. Unter dem unausgesprochenen Diktat, dass mit allem, was auf dem Gebiet des Geistes zu verorten ist, exakt und gewissenhaft zu verfahren sei, lernt der Sohn »auf alle möglichen Weisen, ohne es jemals als Zwang oder Belastung zu empfinden« (S. 202f), wobei ihm jeder zukünftige Lesestoff als Verheissung erscheint – als Fremdes, das es einzuholen gilt. Steussloff erachtet es daher als »erstaunlich, dass das schreibende Ich die sich hier abzeichnende Tendenz der Diskontinuität, sprich die sich im Verlust, über seine Prägungen verfügen zu können, manifestierende dekonstruktivistische Ausrichtung seiner Ich-Bildung nicht als bedrohlich empfindet« (1994, S. 282). Immerhin, so ist entgegenzuhalten, wählt Canetti in der Schule seinen eigenen, durchaus exklusiven Kreis an Freunden. Unter den Gleichaltrigen, die zu seinen näheren Weggefährten werden, hebt er selbst in der Zürcher Zeit insbesondere zwei hervor: den Sohn eines Psychologieprofessors, Walter Wreschner, mit dem er eine literarische Freundschaft schliesst, und den Sohn eines österreichischen Parlamentariers, Hans Wehrli, mit dem er sich immer nur über ›wirkliche‹ Dinge, das heisst über alles, »was mit Wissen und Künsten und der weiteren Welt zusammenhängt« (S. 250), unterhält. Hinzu kommt andererseits freilich die Kultur der

Künstler und Dichter der Pension Yalta, die Canetti nicht selbst auswählt. Früh schon anerkennt Canetti den Status anderer in der Bildung seines Selbst: »Seit [...] meinem zehnten Lebensjahr [...] ist es eine Art Glaubenssatz von mir, dass ich aus vielen Personen bestehe, deren ich mir keineswegs bewusst bin. Ich denke, sie bestimmen, was mich an Menschen, denen ich begegne, anzieht oder abstösst. Sie waren das Brot und das Salz der frühen Jahre. Sie sind das eigentliche, das verborgene Leben meines Geistes« (S. 111f). Ein differenziertes soziales Geflecht strukturiert somit Canettis Entwicklung, im Verlauf derer er sich eine Sprache zunehmend nutzbar macht, um die Welt zu begreifen, indem er Wirklichkeit in Bezug auf sich sprachlich erzeugt. Ohne die provokative Anregung seiner sprachlichen Entwicklung durch andere und die fortwährende sprachliche Auseinandersetzung mit ihnen, ohne das herausfordernde Begehren dieser anderen wäre die sukzessive Ausweitung seiner eigenen sprachlichen Grenzen nicht denkbar. Es ist das Begehren seiner nächsten Bezugspersonen, dass sein Begehren nach Sprache aufrechterhalten wird, da er in erster Linie über die Sprache zu einem sozialen Wesen wird und dadurch fähig zur Selbsterkenntnis und zur Kommunikation, sodass auch in diesem Sinn zutrifft, dass »das Begehren des Menschen [...] das Begehren des Anderen« (Lacan, 1978, S. 105) ist.

10 *Literatur und Sprache*

Die Literatur hat in diesem Prozess der sprachlichen Entgrenzung einen herausragenden Stellenwert. Sie nimmt Canetti ein für die durch andere präformierten sprachlichen Darstellungen der Welt. Die geschriebene und in der Pension Yalta auch die gesprochene, vorgetragene Literatur, mit der er in Kontakt kommt, erarbeitet wie jede Literatur eine Sprache, die sprachbewusst ist und modellhaft ein Werkzeug bereitstellt, mit dem sich Wirklichkeit einnehmen lässt, indem sie Wirklichkeit in und als Sprache schafft. Nicht nur, dass alles, was Thema von Literatur ist, durch Sprache entsteht, die Literatur zeigt vielmehr auch den Vorgang der Versprachlichung von Themen auf. Ihre Geschichten mögen fingiert sein, die Form, in der sie in Sprache gefasst werden, ist jedoch real. Dabei kann die literarische Form der Versprachlichung zum Modell der sprachlichen Erfassung der Welt überhaupt werden. Die Literatur führt vor, wie sich Bedeutung sprachlich konstituiert. Ihre sinnstiftende Bezugskategorie kann dabei einzig die der Sprache sein (vgl. Ladenthin, 1991, S. 236ff), dieselbe Kategorie also, in der der Mensch einen Zugang zur Welt findet, und in der je nach Entwicklungsstand seiner Sprache ein mehr oder minder elaborierter oder restringierter Bezug zur Welt möglich wird. Die sprachliche Reflexion erschliesst dem Menschen die Welt. Das Arbeiten in der Sprache wird so zum »Weltgewinn« (vgl. Menze, 1965, S. 258), wobei das Erschliessen von Welt in Sprache inhaltlich durch das wachsende innere Lexikon und formal durch rhetorische Figuren wie Ironie, Parabel, Hyperbel und andere erweitert werden kann. Indem der Wortschatz ausgeweitet und Tropen in die Sprache aufgenommen werden, wird auch eine qualitativ andere Selbst- und Welterfahrung ermöglicht, zum Beispiel dadurch, dass neue Bezüge zur Welt durch deren Bezeichnung entstehen, oder dadurch, dass die Metaphorik der Sprache andere, bisher unbekannte Wirklichkeitsbereiche eröffnet. Die Literatur kann sich selber nicht anders denn als Sprache begreifen. Sie transportiert als Inhalt ein Medium – die Sprache – in dem der Mensch eine Form finden kann, sich zum Selbst und der Welt auf spezifische Weise zu verhalten. Das zunehmende Erschliessen von Sprache ist in diesem Sinn die Bedingung der Möglichkeit für das Erschliessen von Selbst und Welt (vgl. Ladenthin, 1991, S. 353), wobei die Sprache im Sinne Humboldts nicht isolierte Dinge oder Sachverhalte bezeichnet, sondern diese vielmehr unter den Bedingungen der Form der Sprache konstituieren. Die Literatur konfrontiert das Subjekt, Canetti, mit einer Versprachlichung von Welt, die über die Grenzen seines bisherigen Sprachgebrauchs hinausgeht und dadurch die Voraussetzung für das Begehren schafft, diese sprachlichen Limitierungen selber sukzessive zu überschreiten.

Das Begehren wird in der Folge die Entfaltung von Sprache mobilisieren und dadurch die Entfaltung des Selbst begünstigen. Dabei entsteht in dem Prozess der sprachlichen Aneignung von Fremdem an die Strukturen des Selbst eine charakteristische Form des Selbst- und Weltverhältnisses. Es wäre nicht von einem Bildungsprozess im genannten Sinn zu reden, wenn dieses Verhältnis sich nicht durch die Interaktion mit sich und der Welt verändern würde und der Gewinn an Sprache nicht einen Gewinn an Welterfahrung darstellen würde. Bei Canetti verändert sich das Selbst- und Weltverhältnis insbesondere durch eine zunehmend differenziertere, im Medium der Sprache sich vollziehende Selbstreflexion im Verlauf der sprachlichen Entwicklung. In diesem Sinn kann bei ihm von einem Bildungsprozess die Rede sein. Canettis Suche nach Sprache erschöpft sich unter diesem Gesichtspunkt nicht in der Akkumulation von Begriffen, sein Drang nach Wissen resultiert nicht allein in einer stets vorläufigen Summe von Wissensvorräten und die hinzugewonnene Virtuosität im Umgang mit Sprache ist nicht das eigentliche Kriterium für Bildungsprozesse. Vielmehr ist ein Bildungsprozess bei Canetti in einem Wandel der Beziehung zu seiner Mutter zu identifizieren. In seinen frühen Jahren war Canetti seiner Mutter intellektuell kategorisch unterworfen. Über die Gespräche mit ihr hält er

Begehren, Sprache und Bildung 177

fest: »Wenn es eine geistige Substanz gibt, die man in frühen Jahren empfängt, auf die man sich immer bezieht, von der man nie loskommt, so war es diese. Ich war von blindem Vertrauen zur Mutter erfüllt« (S. 111f). In der Mutter konzentrierte sich für Canetti »alle Autorität« (S. 269), nie zweifelte er an ihrer Glaubwürdigkeit, und wenn es um folgenreiche Angelegenheiten ging, so erwartete er »ihren Spruch wie andere den eines Gottes oder eines Propheten« (S. 269). Der geistige Einfluss der Mutter ging dabei bis zu dem Punkt, an dem die Mutter in ihm eine Feindschaft gegen einen seiner Schulkollegen schürte, indem sie bewusst dementierte, was dieser korrekt über die menschliche Fortpflanzung gesagt hatte, damit sie sich die sexuelle Aufklärung ihres Sohnes noch ersparen konnte. Canetti wird später feststellen, dass ihn die Worte seiner Mutter mit einem solchem Hass gegen seinen Schulkollegen erfüllt hatten, dass der unumschränkte Glaube an die Mutter als »blinde Anhängerschaft« (S. 133) verstanden werden musste. Später jedoch beginnt sich Canetti von seiner Mutter geistig zu emanzipieren, als er in der Zeit seines Aufenthalts in der Pension Yalta regelmässig Vorträge besucht und sich dadurch intensiver mit dem Denken anderer Personen auseinandersetzt. Über die Beziehung zu seiner Mutter hält er fest: »Damals entstanden die ersten Keime der späteren Entfremdung zwischen uns. Als die Wissbegier, die sie auf jede Weise gefördert hatte, eine Richtung nahm, die ihr fremd war, begann sie an meiner Wahrhaftigkeit und an meinem Charakter zu zweifeln« (S. 238). In dieser Verselbständigung Canettis zeigt sich beispielhaft, wie sich Veränderungen im Verhältnis zu sich und zur Mutter vollzogen haben. Diese Veränderungen wirken sich wiederum auf das Verhältnis der Mutter zu ihrem Sohn aus. Es kommt so weit, dass die Mutter – wenn auch unter dem Schock des Todes ihres Ehemanns – die Züricher Zeit beenden will und glaubt, ihr Sohn würde hier verblöden, sie fragt nach dem Recht ihres Sohnes auf die fortwährende Beschäftigung mit den grossen Denkern und nach dem Zusammenhang zwischen der Literatur und dem wahren Leben, der ›Wirklichkeit‹, sie hinterfragt die Idylle, in der ihr Sohn lebt, das Interesse, das er aufbringt für die Wissenschaften, seine Leidenschaft für Bücher, sein unablässiges Befasstsein mit der Theorie, wo sie zuvor noch die grösste Toleranz gegenüber verschiedenartigen Interessen aufbrachte und ihren Sohn lehrte, was »Weite ist [...] dass man Sovieles und Gegensätzliches in sich fassen kann, dass alles scheinbar Unvereinbare zugleich seine Gültigkeit hat« (S. 198). Dieser Wandel in der Beziehung markiert den Beginn einer »Entzweiung« (S. 322) zwischen ihr und ihrem Sohn, einer qualitativ veränderten Beziehung zu ihm.

11 Abschliessende Betrachtung

Die Untersuchung des Bildungsprozesses Canettis ging von zwei Kernannahmen aus. Erstens wurde ein Zusammenhang zwischen dem Begehren als dem psychischen Antrieb zur Beseitigung eines primordialen Mangels und dem Bildungsprozess als einem Prozess der sprachlich gestifteten, individuellen Formung eines selbstreflexiven Verhältnisses zu sich und der Welt postuliert. Zweitens wurde die Sprache aufgefasst als ein Vehikel des Menschen, sich des Fremden zunehmend (jedoch nie vollständig) zu bemächtigen. Das Subjekt befindet sich in der Logik dieser Argumentation in einer Bewegung zum Anderen hin, um dieses Andere als Eigenes aufzuheben. Durch die Überführung des Unbekannten in die Ordnung der Sprache wird demnach Fremdheit reduziert. Jeder Zuwachs an Sprache kann als eine Grenzüberschreitung aufgefasst werden, die sich in einer Veränderung der Bewusstseinsstruktur niederschlagen kann. Als auslösendes Moment eines derart verstandenen sprachlichen Bildungsprozesses wurde eine produktive Differenz zwischen den bereits gebildeten und den potentiell noch zu bildenden symbolischen Repräsentationen des Subjekts angenommen, welche dem Subjekt den eigenen Mangel fortwährend vergegenwärtigt. Das Begehren zielt darauf ab, diesen Mangel zu beheben. Da dieser jedoch nicht beseitigt werden kann und im Dauerzustand des Begehrens anhaltend fühlbar bleibt, kann auch das Begehren nie abschliessend befriedigt werden, sodass dieses nach einer kontinuierlichen Ausweitung der Sprache strebt. Im Vorgang der Aneignung des Fremden durch die Entfaltung der Sprache vollzieht sich ein Bildungsprozess, in dem sich dem Subjekt nicht nur eine Sprache zunehmend erschliesst, vielmehr bildet das Subjekt auch progressiv eine Form aus, in der es sich zu sich und der Welt in ein Verhältnis bringt.

Bildungsprozesse finden dabei in der Sprache den Ort der Reflexion. Da jeder reflexive Bezug des Menschen auf sich einzig sprachlich gelingt und das Begehren – indem es nach einer anhaltenden Erweiterung der Sprache ruft – auch eine kontinuierliche Entwicklung der Sprache anregt, verfeinert sich die Bezugnahme des Menschen zu sich im Prozess der Bildung. Zudem geht mit der Bildung der Sprache die Entwicklung der Bezugnahme auf Fremdes einher, woraus schliesslich ein qualitativ verändertes Verhältnis des Subjekts zu sich und der Welt resultieren kann, das den Vollzug eines Bildungsprozesses reflektiert. In diesem Sinne ist schliesslich auch Humboldts Aussage zu verstehen, der Mensch müsse durch die Sprache gebildet werden, um durch die Sprache in Gebieten einheimisch zu werden, die ihm zunächst unsichtbar sind und somit verborgen bleiben (vgl. Humboldt, 1959, S. 85).

Es ist abschliessend zu fragen, inwiefern die Berücksichtigung der psychoanalytischen Theorie Lacans im bildungstheoretischen Diskurs eine neue Perspektive auf bestehende theoretische Ansätze eröffnet. Müssen Bildungsprozesse auf der Folie der Überlegungen zum Begehren nach Sprache als Begehren nach Aneignung des Fremden theoretisch in eine neue Form gebracht werden? Bildung kann auch vor dem Hintergrund der Ausführungen zum Begehren übereinstimmend mit anderen Annäherungen an den Bildungsbegriff als ein reflexives Bezogensein auf das Selbst und die Welt einschliesslich des Fremden aufgefasst werden, wobei der Bildungsprozess als Prozess der dauerhaften Formung und Verfeinerung dieses Bezogenseins zu konzipieren ist. Der prozesshafte und unabschliessbare Charakter der Bildung tritt unter Berücksichtigung der Überlegungen zum Begehren ebenso deutlich zutage wie bei begrifflichen Bestimmungen der Bildung, welche die mit Bildung verbundene Dimension der individuellen (oder generell menschlichen) Entwicklung hervorheben. Von einem »Modus des menschlichen In-der-Welt-Seins« (Marotzki, 2006, S. 60) kann folglich nur insofern die Rede sein, als diesem Modus ein dynamischer und in die Zukunft gerichteter Charakter zugesprochen wird. Erweitert wird die Sicht auf die Bildung durch die Annahme, wonach sich Bildung zwingend in der Sprache verwirklicht. Als zentrales Element erscheint der Gestus der Bemächtigung von Fremdem durch die Einordnung in die eigenen Strukturen der Repräsentationen von Welt. Bezogen auf Canettis ersten Teil der Autobiographie bedeutet dies konkret, dass der Ausschluss aus dem Kommunikationsraum der Eltern als produktive Differenzerfahrung Canettis Verhalten strukturiert und Bemühungen auslöst, Fremdes zu verstehen und sich anzueignen. Diese Bemühungen werden später durch das Begehren erhalten, sich sprachlich zunehmend mehr Fremdes anzueignen, das heisst durch und in Sprache Eigenes zu erzeugen. Bildung ist in diesem Sinn als ein Epiphänomen des Strebens nach Aneignung des Fremden zu verstehen, wobei das Begehren diesen Aneignungsprozess aufrechterhält. Was sich in diesem Prozess langfristig sedimentiert, ist Bildung.

IV Synopsis

Early childhood care and education has become a subject of increasing public interest in a great number of countries and among several international organizations and foundations. The subject is on the agenda not only of many practitioners but also of economists, politicians and other stakeholders. In some countries, the heightened interest has converted into growing levels of services for young children. This interest has been spurred by a number of societal changes in economically more developed countries. They include the increase in female labor force participation, immigration, declining fertility rates, changing patterns of family organization, and a concern for the well-being of children from low-income and poor families. At the same time, research focusing on different aspects surrounding early childhood programs and services has expanded in particular in Western English-speaking countries as well as in parts of Europe. Yet some important questions had not been addressed in research so far. The present studies tackled some of these questions. They provide value-added insights by focusing on effects of early childhood care and education on children, the importance of family background for child development, the use of institutional services among different families, the history of such services in selected countries, and the way in which children acquire competences both within and outside early childhood care and education institutions.

This synthesis of research illustrates the chief findings and delineates the main conclusions that can be derived from the present studies. It summarizes the overarching ideas which link the four original studies, placing emphasis on the key research questions: whether early childhood care and education can establish equality of opportunity among children from various social backgrounds, how early childhood care and education as well as a variety of family characteristics can affect child development, how childcare has evolved historically, and how children can acquire skills in early childhood. Furthermore, implications of this research for practice are discussed and prospects for future research are presented.

1 Equal opportunities in the light of social disparities: a persistent challenge for early childhood care and education

Inequalities between children broadly reflect class, race, and gender divisions within societies. While such inequalities may be mitigated through early childhood services in some countries, they are intensified in others (e.g., where the provision of services is sparser). In most instances, societal structures penetrate and shape children's early care and education experiences. This may be one of the reasons why some children derive more benefit from such experiences than others. Inequities embedded in various dimensions of social structure such as family organization, socioeconomic status, gender, women's labor force participation, or availability of extra-familial care services affect children's schooling and opportunities. Relatively rigid social stratification takes place over the course of children's formal schooling, yet much of the social sorting begins earlier. For instance, racial segregation and socioeconomic polarization can lead to social isolation and decreasing life chances for some groups of people. Differences in family circumstances, cultural values, political economies, employment levels, fertility rates, and social norms can translate into beliefs and activities that support or hinder children's development. In addition, disparities in the availability, funding, administration, and features of formal early childhood services also create inequalities and help some children do better than others. In Switzerland, for instance, a legal entitlement to a free early childhood service – the kindergarten – exists for children as of five years in most cantons. The same legal entitlement exists in most of the United States. However, in France, children are entitled to a free early childhood service space as of three years, and in some communes, children have access from two years of age. In many countries, costs for private services may impose disproportionately high burdens on families with low incomes. But gaps in the use of private services are not only related to socioeconomic status, but also to ethnicity, minority status, location and other family characteristics. Typically, highly disadvantaged children are less likely than their more privileged counterparts to receive care and education in formal arrangements and more likely to receive informal care by relatives and friends. Such differentials may underpin existing socioeconomic inequalities by segregating some children in less formal types of services and prevent them from becoming as proficient in a set of social and intellectual skills as their peers who might be exposed to more stimulating learning environments.

In principle, school is the arena where children from various backgrounds meet and benefit legally from equal opportunities. Equality of opportunity exists where everyone is accorded the same chance to acquire his or her capacities and to be acknowledged for accomplishments irrespective of characteristics such as gender, religion, political stance, color of the skin, or social background, that is, characteristics which are not related to personal diligence and effort. In practice, however, equality of opportunity is not given consistently when children enter education systems as some children have had better opportunities than others for learning during their first years of life and have therefore acquired more competences which are necessary to perform well at school. While children's early care and education experiences are not the only, or even necessarily the most powerful influences on children's school careers, evidence is growing that such experiences do matter since they can complement informal learning at home beneficially in case they are of high quality. A good start in life can support learning and help children enter elementary school with competences, knowledge, and behaviors required for learning as well as for meeting teachers' expectations and social norms.

The history of early childhood care and education shows that the concern for equal opportunity for all children has been prominent in many countries, albeit not in equal measure at all times. For instance, while many childcare services in 19th-century America primarily aimed to help poor working mothers to earn a livelihood and to prevent mothers from abandoning their children to public welfare, the idea of supporting the development of socially disadvantaged children in order to bestow better life chances on the children was intensified most notably during the 1960s as president Lyndon B. Johnson launched his 'war on poverty' and implemented Head Start, the most widespread compensatory education program for underprivileged preschool children. Hence while the child's welfare and opportunities in life have been a major concern since the foundation of the first early childhood institutions, the principal focus of these institutions has shifted slightly over time. Notably, the main scopes have been subject to variations due to differing local or national policies, changing societal conceptualizations of services, and changing views of the role and duties of mothers, the family, and the nation state in childrearing. Yet in democratic societies, the establishment and longer-term maintenance of equality of opportunity at the start of a child's school career remains a political challenge that needs to be tackled carefully in the future.

2 How early childhood care and education can influence children's skills

The first years of life are not only a period of significant opportunity for growth but also for vulnerability to harm. The early developmental opportunities establish an important foundation for children's cognitive and behavioral skills later in life. Whether early childhood care and education programs have an impact on child development is therefore among the most frequently asked questions in this field. As shown in the present research, a number of important previous analyses have focused specifically on the effects on cognitive development of children from socioeconomically deprived milieus, the interest in these effects deriving from the belief that early childhood programs contribute to establish equality of educational opportunity among children from various backgrounds. Although cognitive development is only one of various indicators of a successful development (such as social skills, health status, attitudes, or motivation to achieve), acquisition of cognitive skills can carry over to school competence and educational attainment and may thus affect social development in the longer run. Insofar, analysis of cognitive development in the early years of life can be indicative of children's overall growth.

Most studies established that experiences in a formal early childhood setting prior to school enrollment enhances children's cognitive development and thus helps children have a more beneficial start at school. In addition, empirical evidence suggests that cognitive effects of early care and education persist during subsequent years. While a number of studies (including the empirical analysis of first graders' cognitive competence at hand) provide no cognitive effects, a large proportion of analyses identify at least moderate positive effects on various cognitive measures in the short- and medium-term. Some also provide evidence for long-term effects mostly when certain conditions are met including a high quality of early care and education experiences, appropriate developmental timing of interventions, suitable program intensity and duration, well-designed curricula, sufficient breadth and flexibility of programs and appropriate support measures in subsequent school years. On the basis of the present research, it can be concluded that institutional care and education in the preschool years which meets these criteria can endow children with important cognitive capabilities which are useful to cope with everyday challenges at school.

However, the review article and the study into the effects of center-based care and education in Switzerland showed that cognitive effects vary with children's family backgrounds, confirming previous findings that relative to more privileged children, those from socioeconomically disadvantaged backgrounds (with less opportunity for informal learning) tend to benefit to a particular extent from programs in terms of their development. Furthermore, children from immigrant families can derive more distinct benefit from exposure to care and education programs in terms of their language development, as demonstrated in the analysis of cognitive proficiency levels in the canton of Zurich. Yet early childhood care and education programs typically cannot be expected to balance out any kind of social inequalities. This finding remains a cause for concern and further action for policymakers who seek to provide socially more equitable systems of early care and education.

The analysis of interrelations between an individual's desire (i.e. a psychological driving force) and language development reveals that educational processes do not occur exclusively in institutional settings. Important educational processes are triggered by factors other than the didactic and instructional activities of professional staff or specific learning materials and environments in early childhood centers. For instance, a desire for language enhancement can manifest itself as a consequence of a lack of language comprehension. The experience of this cognitive lack is coupled with a desire to appropriate to oneself what is considered to remedy the perceived deficiency. That is, desire originates in a state of deprivation and aspires to remedy this deficit. It thereby governs concrete behaviors and directs individuals' goals including that of appropriating unintelligible experiences to the self and advancing language knowledge. As educational processes essentially take place in the medium of language, the development of language enhances the likelihood for educational processes to occur. Thereby, language is understood as a vehicle to integrate alien experiences into the realm of the intelligible in a continuous, albeit interminable process. Unintelligible experiences are transformed to and incorporated into the symbolic order of language whereby the degree of unintelligibility is reduced or eliminated. The perceived difference between the actual command of language and the potentiality of total command of language constitutes a source of desire for language enhancement. By progressively increasing symbolic structures, boundaries of comprehension are crossed, the experience of alienation is diminished, and conceptual understanding is widened as the development of language is accompanied by a changing relationship with the unintelligible. Eventually, this process of increasing language in order to decrease the domain of incomprehensible experiences may alter the relation between the self and the world. Such an alteration reflects an educational process which emerges as an epiphenomenon of the quest for appropriation of alien experiences.

The present research also suggests that questions surrounding the development of children in formal settings have not come up only recently. Historically, the concern for safe and healthy institutions to support children's wellbeing and advance their skills emerged as early as the first childcare facilities in the 19th century. Thereby, ideas and experiences about care and education and assumptions about how institutions affect children circulated beyond national frontiers. As such assumptions changed over time and across geographical regions, the questions around child development as well as pertaining answers varied accordingly. However, one question has been raised consistently, notably whether exposure to an institutional setting aids or harms children. The answers to that question have not been homogeneous at all times. Instead, they partly depended on sociopolitical contexts and predominant societal discourses, on the types of studies that were conducted, on the choice of research methods, and on the rigor of the conclusions drawn on the basis of the evidence from these studies. This also implies that children may make individual experiences under different historical conditions and in different institutional settings and that they may react in their own ways to pedagogical measures. Hence historical research indicates that there are no atemporal, universally valid answers to questions surrounding child development in early childhood facilities and it suggests that specific analyses will be required to address specific questions revolving around the impact of various types of settings on children's skills.

3 Implications of the present research for practice

That research in early childhood care and education should be used to improve the lives of children is a truism. New findings from research may require us to modify, sharpen and improve practices in early childhood care and education. Not only do these findings spark the imagination, they add to our understanding about promises and pitfalls in early childhood care and education and help to improve practices to enhance children's development and decrease their vulnerability to deprivation and deficit. The contributions at hand have a number of implications for practice. They point ways toward effective decision-making in policy as well as toward more optimal environments through which to provide care and education for young children. However, as research findings need to be contested, debated and tested again before a consensus can be reached on recommendations for practice or policy, the implications of this research are presented not as the last word on new approaches but to spur dialogue about how to improve practice. As the basic goal of any research is theory

– that is, understanding, explaining and predicting phenomena and representing these phenomena by specifying relations between various variables and analytic concepts – the potential of research to impact on practice has been questioned. It is therefore important to be mindful of gaps between scientific studies and practice when implications of the present research for practice are discussed (see Carnine, 1997; Greenwood & Abbott, 2001).[17]

3.1 What type of early childhood care and education should we implement?

Early childhood programs can impact beneficially on cognitive development as measured through a number of different indicators such as cognitive achievement tests, school grades, grade retention, school achievement, or school dropout. Yet in order to maximize cognitive effects, a variety of criteria are to be met. Programs ought to adopt a broad, multipurpose approach including parent services and parent involvement along with center-based provision. They need to target particularly disadvantaged children to a greater extent in order to support the acquisition of skills of these children effectively and they should offer additional support measures during subsequent school years in order to sustain initial effects. Furthermore, programs should be more extensively publicly sub-

---

17 Eight hypotheses have been formulated to explain an alleged lack of relation between educational research and practice. First, research is not authoritative or persuasive enough. This can apply when the quality of studies is not high enough to provide compelling, unambiguous results to practitioners. Second, research is not sufficiently relevant for practice as it has not addressed practitioners' questions adequately. Third, research is not sufficiently accessible or findings have not been presented in intelligible ways. Fourth, education systems are too stable or too unstable and thus incapable of responding coherently to evidence from research as they are either inherently intractable or conversely overly susceptible to change and therefore incapable to engage in systematic change (Kennedy, 1997). Fifth, a gap between research and practice may be expected to arise when the theories of researchers do not articulate with the theories of practitioners (Robinson, 1998). Sixth, practitioners respond more positively to innovation when they can consider change in relation to their beliefs and assumptions about their profession. Yet researchers may fail to consider caregivers' and teachers' beliefs and values when recommending change. Seventh, the type of culture of care and education institutions may affect the degree to which research is implemented. While staff development activities frequently focus on the professional staff as responsible for improving practice, attention given to the cultural context of the institution is typically insufficient. Eighth, reform initiated by practitioners and institutions frequently fails as it lacks outside change agents who act as outside force prompt, guide, and structure (Fuchs & Fuchs, 2001).

sidized for those families who cannot afford them but would be most in need of their services. This holds true in particular for countries which stress individual responsibility in matters related to raising children in social and family policies. It should be noted that these implications apply where the establishment of equality of educational opportunity among children from various socioeconomic backgrounds is striven for. Thus they are based on a principle that ought to be characteristic of achievement-oriented societies, yet not necessarily for any type of society. For instance, in communities where cognitive skills are valued differently, the above-mentioned recommendations might not apply in equal measure.

3.2 For whom should we implement early childhood care and education?

This research suggests that children who grow up in socially more disadvantaged families have less access to center-based care and education programs. In the light of this evidence, policymakers should consider implementing services for these children wherever their home learning environments are impoverished. They should have a clear strategy whether or not to regulate the access to center-based care and education. Answering questions around regulation involves sociopolitical considerations. Although research cannot make suggestions based on societal values, the findings from the present studies inform decision-makers that social disparities including cognitive achievement gaps between different children cannot be eliminated where the access to centers is unregulated (as it is the case in Switzerland). A theoretical framework favoring social equity in society would therefore suggest that policymakers take measures to include in particular children from more deprived social backgrounds in early childhood care and education centers. Promoting the participation of disadvantaged children in centers would decrease inequalities in access and allow those children who are most in need to experience and benefit from center-based care and education.

3.3 Should early childhood care and education be regulated?

As the study into the history of childcare in France and the United States revealed, public regulation helps establish institutions in a more sustained manner. In addition, regulation may ensure more effective and higher-quality services. From this it follows that regulation of services is desirable. Effective regulation may include a national definition of program standards, adequate funding of programs so as to allow compliance with program standards, a participatory approach to standards definition, implementation and quality improvement, the provision of opportunities for professional development and of incentives to assist providers in advancing the quality agenda, and effective supervisory agencies. Any program and facility providing care and education to children should be regulated and regular teachers, caregivers and program administrators should be licensed. Licensing standards should be clear and reflect research findings relating to regulation. Regulations should be vigorously and equitably enforced. Incentive mechanisms need to encourage the achievement of high-quality services. Families should be informed about the importance of the early years and of ways to create environments promoting children's learning and development. Sufficient levels of resources should be invested to ensure that children's healthy development and learning are not harmed in early childhood services (cf., NAYEC, 1998). However, although sound regulations are a cornerstone of an effective system of early childhood services, further aspects need to be warranted for all programs in the market, including an all-encompassing approach to addressing the needs of children, an effective system of professional development to guarantee a well-qualified workforce, equitable financing to ensure access for all children to early care and education facilities, and active involvement of all stakeholders, including providers, practitioners, and parents in early childhood programs.

3.4   Why should practitioners be sensitive to social and cultural context characteristics?

Understanding children's development in early childhood care and education settings requires viewing every child within the context of that child's family, learning milieu, community, and the society at large. Social and cultural context characteristics can have a powerful influence on the developing child. In order to meet the needs of young children, practitioners therefore need to be sensitive to variations in children's (prior and current) social and cultural experiences, different home languages, and varying community backgrounds. Societies and cultures shape and interpret children's development and behavior in their own ways. Practitioners ought to be aware of the influence of such contexts on a child's developing capabilities as children may demonstrate their developmental achievements in a variety of forms. Each of these forms should be acknowledged appropriately. For practitioners, familiarity with their own and others' cultural perspectives is important as this helps realize that multiple perspectives must be taken into account in decisions about caregiving and teaching techniques. As children become members of a given society or culture, they have to learn to function comfortably within this context and respond meaningfully to its requirements. Early childhood care and education practitioners can facilitate the adaptation of children to this context where they acknowledge social and cultural differences wich impact on children's growing up.

3.5 What should parents know?

This research did not investigate parenting techniques or child-rearing practices. Nevertheless, its findings have a number of implications for parental beliefs and behaviors in matters related to raising young children. Notably, parents ought to be aware that there are historical variations in the way caregivers, educators, policy-makers and families thought about childcare practices, raised children and adapted to implicit or explicit societal expectations and conventions. Moreover, parents should know that ideas and experiences relating to early care and education have evolved under particular cultural and socio-political conditions and that, consequently, prevailing theoretical concepts need to be reexamined critically when they become normalizing concepts by virtue of mere tradition rather than on scientifically justified grounds. For instance, societal perceptions of the child as a primarily private good or else as a public good in society can be questioned and deciphered as socially constructed and historically contingent categories. Knowing about the malleability of concepts may help parents to identify and challenge certain (transitory) regimes of truth, that is, taken-for-granted, standardizing views of early care and education which tend to be the products of a historical vision of human activity. As a result, it should become apparent that children can experience different forms of childhoods and that the conception of 'normal' early childhood care and education is, to a certain degree, an adult construction that varies over time and space. For this reason, diverging viewpoints exist as to whether young children should be attended to primarily at home or else in an institutional setting. An ideological divide such as the conflict of opinion about the ideal form of care and education in the preschool years in Switzerland can appear in many countries. Frequently, lobbyists either call for a strengthening of the family in the upbringing of children and they criticize the invasion of the family through some sort of community or state intervention or else they argue that institutional early childhood services can improve children's lives and are therefore to be promoted for the sake of the well-being of children and families. However, while there is some degree of variability in what a childhood can look like, parents should also know that in order to thrive, children need a stimulating environment which provides them with a variety of learning opportunities. Thereby, developmentally appropriate social and intellectual experiences are important for a well-rounded child development. Children whose learning processes are not encouraged and supported adequately by sensitive parents and caregivers are less likely to acquire the competences which will help them to perform well at school later in life. That is, although some educational processes seem to occur independently of exterior influences and look like autonomous self-education, both social and intellectual learning essentially take place most effectively in social settings where they can be influenced positively by other human beings. For instance, when a child is exposed to an environment that evokes the child's desire for linguistic forms of expression, language development can take place more successfully. Insofar, child development and education are fuelled by other people with more advanced knowledge and skills rather than exclusively by some sort of inherent drives to learn and enhance capacities.

4 Prospects for future research

Some prospects for future research can be deduced from the present studies. These studies have contributed new insights into the effects and the use of early childhood care and education programs. Furthermore, historical trajectories of childcare institutions have been highlighted and societal as well as political discourses about childcare have been traced in selected countries over time. Finally, the study about the links between a desire to remove a primordial language-related deficit and educational processes pointed out those educational processes also take place outside of institutional settings. However, a number of challenges for future research persist as outlined in the following paragraphs.

4.1 *Ensuring multiple methodical approaches and disciplines in early childhood research*

Today, quantitative empirical research is predominant in the field of early childhood care and education. However, a wide research perspective using various focuses, disciplines and approaches is important. Disciplines such as anthropology, biology, health, history, psychology, education and sociology all have specific perspectives and methods to offer to the field. Using different paradigms helps contesting one-sided or traditional views from various angles. One reason why traditional views can be problematic or unjustified is that they may relate to a type of early childhood care and education that is viewed as universal for all children, yet this particular form of care and education may be historically contingent and context-dependent. Childhood is not fixed; rather it is mobile and shifting over time and across regions and countries. Children cannot be studied in isolation from society as a whole since children experience varied childhoods under different political, geographic, cultural and social circumstances. For this reason, it seems inappropriate to study children by using primarily one type of method, that is, by describing them principally by means of statistical averages although statistics can be a powerful means to depict human behavior and skills. Scientific knowledge about children and child development needs to be understood in terms of the historical, political, social and economic conditions under which this knowledge was produced. Using different disciplines and methods allows for insights into the social, cultural, economic, organizational, and policy environments of early childhood care and education. Frequently, research questions raised differ as a function of methods and disciplines. In order to ensure unbiased perspectives, a variety of disciplines need to be engaged with questions surrounding early childhood since these disciplines have developed multiple unique and alternative ways of approaching the study of children for a long time. In sum, views of children and human development in early care and education have changed and are changing over time. In sum, main factors impacting on children and their development are economic, demographic, cultural, social and political. By using different methodical approaches, more meticulous attention can be given to historical changes of thought, practice and attitudes relating to young children in early childhood care and education. Differing approaches allow for conclusions that may compete against each other and thereby stimulate paradigm development which is required for scientific evolution.

4.2 Avoiding ethnocentric description of children: technological challenges

Early childhood studies including the present analyses largely draw on concepts, theories, and findings from research stemming from Western countries. As a result, the technologies used to analyze and describe children have been developed to a large extent on the basis of assumptions that represent viewpoints characteristic of the according cultures. Yet these viewpoints cannot always do justice to the experiences of children who grow up in different cultural communities. In the future, the techniques and theoretical frameworks to study and portray children and their development therefore need to be culturally sensitive and open to variations in the conceptualization of key characteristics of human behavior and intellect. For instance, a study into the caregiving style in twelve countries concluded that caregiving practices in the United States are atypical in terms of the degree of mothers' sociability with their children and in the number of playful interactions in which children are treated as equals (Whiting & Edwards, 1992). However, this type of caregiving has become part of child development orthodoxy as the normal way for adults to interact with their offspring (Woodhead, 2005). In view of this finding, tools for assessing child development should not be restricted to aspects that are valued in one culture where children from different cultural backgrounds are compared. Such tools and the conceptual categories used in research should not neglect the global and thus varied contexts of child development. Dominant expectations of what normal child development is should not reflect features of a specific cultural niche which is considered as a standard for all. Although any particular account of children can never encompass all varieties of childhood in different contexts, research should attempt not to overlook the diversities in children's experiences, ways of learning, playing, and developing. That is, researchers need to avoid relying on normalized culture-bound images of standard development and human behavior and acknowledge a wider range of possible, healthy pathways through early childhood instead.

4.3 Challenges in comparative-historical research

It is understood in all disciplines that future endeavors rest on the lessons from the past. The study into the history of childcare highlights how the past is related to the present. Cross-national historical research enables us to recognize ideas and discourses in one country which challenge dominant common sense knowledge in another. However, in historical research on childcare, some questions remain to be answered. In particular, two major questions emerge from the comparative-historical study into childcare in France and in the United States. First, a specific theoretical issue requires further clarification, notably how societal conceptions of the role of mothers toward children have changed over time. Looking at France from the 17th to the 20th century, Elisabeth Badinter provided evidence that motherhood and maternal behavior have been subject to historical variation. She showed that no uniform, universal, or absolute behavior on the part of the mother existed by revealing the changing nature in maternal feelings and conduct as well as variations in maternal love and in the relationship between men and women in society. Historical contexts influenced mothers' emotions, ambitions, and actions in relation to their children and child-rearing practices (Badinter, 1980). By questioning the myth of the naturally self-sacrificing mother and the notion of maternal instinct, Badinter's book provoked controversies which the present historical account could not trace in detail. However, further studies should analyze in depth how perceptions of motherhood are socially and culturally constructed and how ways in which mothers raise children depend on societal contexts. A second question arising from the historical analysis concerns a methodical issue in historical research. Reviews of the history of institutional childcare and ideas pertaining thereto are inevitably selective. Contradictory information needs to be weighed in selected instances. By drawing, amongst others, on secondary sources, studies frequently rely on previous appraisals. Instead of portraying the evolution of specific institutions, practices and discourses in specific regions of a given country in minute detail, comparative studies frequently place emphasis on important milestones and general historical tendencies by synthesizing varying sources into more general statements in order to allow for conclusions concerning distinctive characteristics of different societies. Yet typically there are local disparities in childcare provision, use, ideas, and policies. The access to and enrollment of children in center-based care are related to a variety of factors including racial and ethnic backgrounds, economic status of the family, parents' education level and employment, and geographic area. Thus, comparative-historical studies focusing on phenomena in different countries usually cannot constitute exhaustive inquiries into any kind of societal and political discourses or all types of ideas and beliefs about institutional childcare over time. Although a number studies have contributed perspectives to debates over the reasons for particular structures of childcare in different societies, future studies should address the question of how historical cross-cultural research can come to conclusions regarding entire countries without disregarding local disparities in the supply, use, policies, regulatory frameworks and ideas relating to childcare. Comparative studies need to take into consideration inconsistent and heterogeneous positions and trends in different countries as any country's stance toward questions surrounding the structural organization of society is composed of a multitude of diverging opinions and beliefs and is therefore inevitably and intricately differentiated within itself. What may appear to be a distinct and characteristic illustration of attitudes to a given question might turn out to be more multifaceted when studied from different angles. For instance, local disparities in approaches to institutional childcare and differences in the availability of childcare might entail diverging views on questions at stake. Thus exemplary regional and small-scale specificities should be taken into account in more detail and societal discourses should be reflected in a fine-grained manner in future studies.

4.4   Equality of opportunity: Defining the scope of responsibilities of early childhood institutions

A great deal of research in early childhood care and education revolves around equality of educational opportunity. In general, equality of opportunity figures prominently in discussions about the nature of a just society and the assertion of some kind of equal opportunity is a professed policy goal in most Western democracies. Conceptions of the normative principle of equality of opportunity thereby range from the absence of discrimination based on gender, class, ethnicity, religion, or minority status to the elimination of the impact of socioeconomic background factors or biological disparities on the attainment of advantage of members of a society. In practice, many administrations seek to improve educational opportunities of children who lag behind in their development due to a variety of family characteristics or detrimental learning environments in early childhood. That is, they attempt to reduce inequality among children by offering services that compensate for disadvantage and vulnerability. Children at risk of educational failure are therefore the object of a variety of programs that seek to address the challenge through programs that aim to enhance children's development and improve their home and community environments. Links between socioeconomic background and educational achievement are reinforced, for instance, by the lack of access of children in poor neighborhoods to adequate early childhood care and education services. Even where access is provided, educational institutions do not necessarily reduce the gap between children from socially deprived backgrounds and those from more privileged backgrounds. Rather, they tend to accentuate the gap as children follow their curricula over time although some educational systems manage to a greater extent to compensate for socioeconomic disadvantage and ensure that children from deprived backgrounds do not fall irretrievably behind in academic achievement. However, future research should meet the scientific desideratum of defining more precisely how to consider not only the possibilities but also the limits of institutions to impact on children's opportunities. So far, theorists have reflected a great deal on why institutions should intervene in the lives of underprivileged children. However, they have tended to omit addressing the question regarding the confines of institutional duties and possibilities. A few exceptions exist. Lanfranchi (2010), for instance, attempted to define the educational mandate of extra-familial early childhood services and schools by drawing on Boudon's (1974) distinction between primary and secondary effects of social origin on educational inequalities. While primary effects refer to the influence of social origin on children's abilities or hereditary weaknesses, secondary effects operate over and above academic performance or mental deficiency through the choices that families make within the educational system in the course of children's educational careers. Secondary effects thus reflect the fact that school choices vary across social backgrounds. Inequalities based on secondary effects may represent discriminatory practices and barriers imposed on the child by parents. Boudon's distinction between primary and secondary effects lays out two basic mechanisms that produce inequality in educational attainment. According to Lanfranchi, early childhood services and schools are expected to prevent inequality that stems from primary effects of social origin, but they can barely meet the challenge of neutralizing secondary effects of origin. While Lanfranchi's reflections can be a starting point for a scholarly debate about the scopes of institutions, his theorization still seems too rudimentary to offer satisfactory answers. In particular, it is questionable whether educational institutions can and should eliminate inequality that derives from children's actual abilities. Thus more research is needed to clarify the duties and responsibilities of institutions as parts of societal systems. This research will have to take account of the value systems of societies and deal with normative and ethical questions. In order to define the scope of responsibilities of institutions in influencing children's lives, (interdisciplinary) research should be carried out which considers demographic, economic, social and political conditions and thereby draws on both statistical data and theoretical approaches. This research should inform policymakers and practitioners about concrete strategies relating to the organization of pedagogical interventions in institutions for young children.

4.5   Generalizability of findings from research on literary accounts

In this research, Elias Canetti's work «The tongue set free» was read as a record of educational experiences and used as a source of pedagogical reflection on educational processes in early childhood. As opposed to quantitative empirical investigations, literary works and autobiographies can adopt a less nomothetic, more idiosyncratic view on education which may be antithetical to certain mainstream visions of children and education. While it can be assumed that individual literary and autobiographical accounts can be generalized to a larger population, shortcomings may exist with respect to the larger representativeness of these accounts. Although large-scale surveys are not necessarily representative of a society as a whole, particular literary or autobiographical protagonists may represent specific types of character or singular peculiarities rather than general rules and principles about the workings of human beings. Specifically, the character in Elias Canetti's work can be considered as an ideal type of a child who grows into a member of the educated class within a social context that provides a multitude of opportunities for learning and development. Although desire, understood as the inherent psychological flipside of a human lack, can be interpreted as an anthropological fact, it remains questionable whether educational processes occur identically for other children whose endeavors to become literate and appropriate alien experiences to themselves are more limited. Future studies might therefore address the question of the generalizability of the educational experiences outlined in Elias Canetti's autobiographical work.

5 Concluding remarks

Children's early experiences create the basis for subsequent development and learning. Strong early childhood foundations and sound early care and education institutions can contribute to ensure a smooth transition to primary school, decrease the probability of dropping out of school, enhance the chances of completing more years of education, and break up the cycle of economic hardship and social disadvantage. From the earliest age, child development and learning are fostered through children's interactions and relationships with caring human beings in secure, nurturing and stimulating environments. Insofar, early childhood is both a time of great potential for human growth and a period of particular fragility. For this reason, early intervention is crucial to support child development as well as to contribute to the creation of more equitable societies where school success and life chances in general depend on socioeconomic background to a lesser extent than today.

The present research has thrown light on crucial questions in early childhood care and education, outlining a number of major areas and topics for consideration by researchers as well as by the main stakeholders in the field early childhood care and education including practitioners and policymakers. The axiomatic principle underlying any research in early childhood is that child well-being is to be enhanced. Child well-being is a multidimensional construct incorporating physical, psychological, cognitive, behavioral, social and economic domains. For this reason, ideal and comprehensive early childhood care and education has to attend to a multitude of requirements. Notably, it has to take account of social and cultural contexts of early childhood development; be mindful of the timing, duration and intensity of intervention as well as of the population that it targets; respect children's natural learning skills and development potentials; take care of children with diverse and special needs; attend to families' capacities to support children's development; encourage family involvement; provide a regulatory framework that ensures service quality as well as children's rights to care and education which protects them from harm and advances their health and development; reduce educational disadvantage and exclusion of deprived children and promote social inclusion of various children including those from minority populations; prepare children from diverse backgrounds for school; immerse children with foreign mother tongues in the country's official language in a manner that is respectful of children's origins and, where applicable, foreign customs and habits; and be responsive to demographic changes and challenges such as increasing population diversity, population decline, demographic ageing, immigration and other social, cultural and economic changes over time. For instance, immigrant populations may not have the same qualification levels and the same educational degrees, and children from minority groups may frequently fall behind in school. Education systems need to find methods to cope with such challenges. As student achievement gaps between socially privileged and disadvantaged children can be identified as early as at the beginning of elementary school, it is probable that early childhood services will be used increasingly to address some of these issues. Tackling disadvantage and setting strong foundations for beneficial development and learning thus begins in the earliest years of life. In sum, comprehensive early childhood care and education services will be expected to improve the lives and educational opportunities in particular of those children who are most vulnerable and deprived of favorable learning environments. A major onus will be placed on these services to adopt a holistic approach encompassing health, social and intellectual development and overall child well-being because well-designed services can be vital to offset different forms of socioeconomic inequality and resulting disparities in educational achievement.

The studies at hand have underlined the significance of the early years of children's lives in shaping the quality of their childhoods and future education and well-being. They have pointed out potentials and limits of institutional care and education in addressing the needs of children and in enhancing human capabilities, equality of educational opportunity, and social equity. Early childhood research and practice is a complex field. Despite the advances made in research and practice in recent years, challenges remain. Child poverty, social

IV Synopsis

disadvantage and exclusion, child health and well-being, the needs of diverse children in early care and education settings, the relationship between institutions and families and the assurance of educational opportunities and social equity are challenges that researchers, practitioners and policymakers must face when designing research projects or implementing and carrying out programs for young children. The present studies were conducted in the belief that research can provide insights to confront these challenges. It was hoped that the evidence would help to narrow achievement gaps between children from different socioeconomic backgrounds, lay the foundations to counteract social inequalities that derive from factors beyond the control of individuals such as ethnicity, gender, political stance, or minority status, and, eventually, improve the prospects of all children to thrive in future societies.

Acknowledgements

Entering unknown territory in social science has been a demanding and, consequently, gratifying undertaking. Whoever strives to develop scientific knowledge will have to follow Ralph Waldo Emerson's advice: "Do not go where the path may lead, go instead where there is no path and leave a trail." I embraced Emerson's maxim on my academic journey, yet it is understood that I did not build trails in complete isolation. This research would not have been possible without substantial support of many academic and non-academic colleagues and I am indebted to all whose help and cooperation aided in the completion of my work. First and foremost, I wish to thank my supervisor, Professor Dr. Margrit Stamm, for her scholarly advice, academic supervision, and interest in my research. I owe her gratitude not only for accompanying me through my travel but also for granting me the permission to use data from the survey of first graders conducted by Urs Moser, Margrit Stamm and Judith Hollenweger in the Canton of Zurich. I am grateful to the Swiss National Science Foundation which awarded me a scholarship for prospective researchers and, in doing so, granted me the liberty to focus meticulously on conducting my research. The University of Fribourg, the Sorbonne University Paris IV, and the University of Maryland College Park were vitalizing academic environments to advance my project and I would like to thank all those scholars whose perspectives opened up new avenues of thinking for me. I am much obliged to Professor Dr. Rita Casale who commented on a draft of the paper about desire, language, and education. Special thanks to the scholars who accommodated me at my host institutions, Professor Dr. Jean-Noël Luc and Professor Dr. Barbara Finkelstein. I felt honored by their interest in my work and appreciated any academic discussion. I also give my thanks to Sonya Michel at the Woodrow Wilson International Center for Scholars in Washington, D.C., who assisted me with useful information on the scholarly landscape of the history of early childhood care and education in the United States. Last but not least, I am grateful for any scholarly exchange as well as friendship with my academic colleagues at the University of Fribourg and beyond. Not only did they create an enabling environment and help me deviate from well-trodden paths, they might also have left traces in my work. I am aware that there are many more who contributed to the success of my work and I would like to express my gratitude to all of them.

References

Ackerknecht, E. H. (1948). Hygiene in France, 1815-1848. *Bulletin of the History of Medicine, XXII*(2), 117–155.

Adams, G., Tout, K., & Zaslow, M. (2007). *Early care and education for children in low-income families: patterns of use, quality, and potential policy implications* (Paper 4. Roundtable on Children in Low-Income Families). The Urban Institute. Retrieved May 13, 2011, from www.urban.org/UploadedPDF/411482_early_care.pdf.

Adema, W., & Whiteford, P. (2007). *Babies and bosses: Reconciling work and family life : a synthesis of findings for OECD countries*. Paris: OECD.

Ahn, N., & Mira, P. (2002). A note on the changing relationship between fertility and female employment rates in developed countries. *Journal of the Population Economics, 15*(4), 667–682.

Ahnert, L. (2010). *Wieviel Mutter braucht ein Kind?: Bindung-Bildung-Betreuung: öffentlich + privat*. Heidelberg, Neckar: Spektrum Akad. Verl.

Alba, R., Handl., J., & Müller, W. (1994). Ethnische Ungleichheit im deutschen Bildungssystem [Ethnical inequalities in the German education system]. *Kölner Zeitschrift für Soziologie und Sozialpsychologie, 46*, 209-223.

Allen, A. T. (1988). "Let us live with our children": Kindergarten movements in Germany and the United States, 1840-1914. *History of Education Quarterly, 28*(1), 23–48.

Allen, B. L. (2008). Evaluating Sure Start, Head Start, and Early Head Start: Finding their signals amidst methodological static. *NHSA Dialog, 11*(2), 110–132.

Ames, J. A. (1886). The crèche, or baby mission. *Lend a Hand, 1*(12), 736–739.

Ananian, S., & Robert-Bobée, I. (2009). *Modes de garde et d'accueil des enfants de moins de 6 ans en 2007* (études et résultats n° 678). Paris: Direction de la recherche, des études, de l'évaluation et des statistiques (DREES).

Anderson, L. M., Shinn, C., Fullilove, M. T., Scrimshaw, S. C., Fielding, J. E., Normand, J., et al. (2003). The effectiveness of early childhood development programs. *American Journal of Preventive Medicine, 24*, 32-46.

Andresen, S. (2009). Bildung. In S. Andresen, R. Casale, T. Gabriel, R. Horlacher, S. Larcher Klee & J. Oelkers (Hrsg.), *Handwörterbuch Erziehungswissenschaft* (pp. 76–90). Weinheim: Beltz.

Anger, C., Plünnecke, A., & Tröger, M. (2007). *Renditen der Bildung - Investitionen in den frühkindlichen Bereich* [Return of education – Investments in the preschool sector]. Köln: Institut der deutschen Wirtschaft.

American Academy of Pediatrics (2005). Quality early education and child care from birth to kindergarten. *Pediatrics, 115*(1), 187–191.
Anderson, L. M., Shinn, C., Fullilove, M., Scrimshaw, S., Fielding, J., Normand, J., et al. (2003). The effectiveness of early childhood development programs: A systematic review. *American Journal of Preventive Medicine, 24*(3S), 32–46.
Andersson, B. E. (1992). Effects of day-care on cognitive and socioemotional competence of thirteen-year-old Swedish schoolchildren. *Child Development, 63*(1), 20–36.
Anger, C., Plünnecke, A., & Tröger, M. (2007). *Renditen der Bildung - Investititionen in den frühkindlichen Bereich*. Köln: Institut der deutschen Wirtschaft Köln.
Arendt, H. (1961). *Between past and future: Six exercices in political thought*. New York: Viking Press.
Arneson, R. (2009). Equality of opportunity. In E. N. Zalta (Ed.), *The Stanford Encyclopedia of Philosophy*. Stanford, CA. Retrieved August 20, 2011, from: http://plato.stanford.edu.
Ary, D., Jacobs, L. C., Sorensen, C., & Razavieh, A. (2009). *Introduction to research in education* (8th ed.). Belmont, CA: Wadsworth.
Badinter, E. (1980). *L'amour en plus: Histoire de l'amour maternel (XVII-XX siècle)*. Paris: Flammarion.
Barnett, S. W. (1993). Benefit-cost analysis of preschool education: Findings from a 25-year follow-up. *American Journal of Orthopsychiatry, 36*, 500–508.
Barnett, S. W. (1995). Long-term effects of early childhood programs on cognitive and school outcomes. *The Future of Children, 5*(3), 25-50.
Barnett, S. W. (1998). Long-term cognitive and academic effects of early childhood education on children in poverty. *Preventive Medicine, 27*(2), 204–207.
Barnett, S. W. (2008). *Preschool education and its lasting effects: Research and policy implications* (EPRU Policy Brief). Boulder and Tempe: Education and the Public Interest Center & Education and Policy Research Unit.
Barnett, S. W. (2011). Effectiveness of early educational intervention. *Science, 333*(6045), 975–978.
Barnett, W. S., & Belfield, C. R. (2006). Early childhood development and social mobility. *The Future of Children, 16*(2), 73-98.
Barnett, W. S., Brown, K., & Shore, R. (2004). *The universal vs. targeted debate: Should the United States have preschool for all?* (Preschool Policy Matters NIEER Policy Briefs). New Brunswick, NJ: National Institute for Early Education Research. Retrieved May 12, 2008, from http://nieer.org/resources/policybriefs/6.pdf
Barnett, S. W., & Masse, L. N. (2007). Comparative benefit-cost analysis of the Abecedarian program and its policy implications. *Economics of Education Review, 26*, 113–125.
Bates, J. E., Marvinney, D., Kelly, T., Dodge K. A., Bennett, D. S., & Pettit, G. S. (1994). Child-care history and kindergarten adjustment. *Developmental Psychology, 30*(5), 690–700.

References

Baumert, J., Bos, W., Brockman, J., Gruehn, S., Klieme, E., Köller, O., et al. (2000). *TIMMS/III-Deutschland. Der Abschlussbericht. Zusammenfassung ausgewählter Ergebnisse der Dritten Internationalen Mathematik- und Naturwissenschaftlichen Bildung am Ende der Schullaufbahn.* Berlin: MPI, IPN, HUB.

Becker, N., & Becker, P. (2009). *Developing quality care for young children: How to turn early care settings into magical places.* Thousand Oaks, CA: Corwin Press.

Becker, R., & Lauterbach, W. (2007). Vom Nutzen vorschulischer Erziehung und Elementarbildung: Bessere Chancen für Arbeiterkinder? [On the benefit of preschool and elementary education: Better chances for working-class children?] In R. Becker & W. Lauterbach (Eds.), *Bildung als Privileg. Erklärungen und Befunde zu den Ursachen der Bildungsungleichheit* (2nd ed., pp. 125–156). Wiesbaden: VS Verlag für Sozialwissenschaften.

Becker, R., & Tremel, P. (2006). Auswirkungen vorschulischer Kinderbetreuung auf die Bildungschancen von Migrantenkindern [Effects of preschool care on educational opportunities of migrant children]. *Soziale Welt, 57,* 397–418.

Beer, E. S. (1957). *Working mothers and the day nursery.* New York: Whiteside and Morrow.

Belsky, J. (1988b). The "effects" of infant day care reconsidered. *Early Childhood Research Quarterly, 3,* 235–272.

Belsky, J. (2001). Emanuel Miller lecture: Developmental risks (still) associated with early child care. *Journal of Child Psychology and Psychiatry, 42*(7), 845–859.

Belsky, J. (2006). Early child care and early child development: Major findings of the NICHD Study of Early Child Care. *European Journal of Developmental Psychology, 3*(1), 95–110.

Belsky, J. (2009). *Early day care and infant-mother attachment security.* Centre of Excellence for Early Childhood Development: Encyclopedia on Early Childhood Development.

Belsky, J. (1988a). Infant day care and socioemotional development: The United States. *Journal of Child Psychology and Psychiatry, 29*(4), 397–406.

Belsky, J., Vandell, D. L., Burchinal, M., Clarke-Stewart, K. A., McCartney, K., & Owen, M. T. (2007). Are There Long-Term Effects of Early Child Care? *Child Development, 78*(2), 681–701.

Belsky, J., Bakermans-Kranenburg, M. J., & van IJzendoorn, M. H. (2007). For better and for worse: Differential susceptibility to environmental influences. *Current Directions in Psychological Science, 16*(6), 300–304.

Benner, D., & Brüggen, F. (2004). Bildsamkeit/Bildung. In D. Benner & J. Oelkers (Hrsg.), *Historisches Wörterbuch der Pädagogik* (S. 174-215). Weinheim, Basel: Beltz.

Bennett, K. K., Weigel, D. J., & Martin, S. S. (2002). Children's acquisition of early literacy skills: Examining family contributions. *Early Childhood Research Quarterly, 17*(3), 295–317.

Bertelsmann Stiftung (2011). *Soziale Gerechtigkeit in der OECD - Wo steht Deutschland? [Social equity in OECD countries - On what level does Germany rank?]* (Sustainable governance indicators 2011). Gütersloh: Berterlsmann Stiftung.

Bertrand, J. (2008). Preschool programs: Effective curriculum. Comments on Kagan and Kauerz and on Schweinhart. In R. E. Tremblay, R. Barr, & R. Peters (Eds.), *Encyclopedia on early childhood development* (pp. 1–7). Montréal: Centre of Excellence for Early Childhood Development.
BfS: Bundesamt für Statistik. (2002). *Bevölkerung* [Population] (Pressemitteilung Nr. 0350-0209-60). Neuchâtel: Bundesamt für Statistik. Retrieved July 29, 2010, from www.bfs.admin.ch/bfs/portal/de/index/themen/01/22/press.Document.24677.pdf.
BfS: Bundesamt für Statistik. (2009). *Bildungsstand der Wohnbevölkerung: Höchste abgeschlossene Ausbildung, 2003, 25-64-jährige Wohnbevölkerung* [Educational background of the resident population: Highest degree obtained, 2003, 25- to 64-year-olds]. Retrieved from www.bfs.admin.ch/bfs/portal/de/index/themen/15/02/key/ind5.indicator.51131.511.html?open=1#1
Bierman, K. L., Domitrovich, C. E., Nix, R. L., Gest, S. D., Welsh, J. A., Greenberg, M. T., et al. (2008). Promoting academic and socio-emotional school readiness: The Head Start REDI program. *Child Development, 79*(6), 1802–1817.
Bierman, K. L., Torres, M. M., Domitrovich C. E., Welsh, J. A., & Gest, S. D. (2009). Behavioral and cognitive readiness for school: Cross-domain associations for children attending Head Start. *Social Development, 18*(2), 305–323.
Blanckenburg, F. (1965). *Versuch über den Roman*. Faksimile der Originalausgabe von 1774. Stuttgart: Metzlersche Verlagsbuchhandlung. (Original erschienen 1774).
Blass, R. B. (2006). A psychoanalytic understanding of the desire for knowledge as reflected in Freud's Leonardo da Vinci and a memory of his childhood. *International Journal of Psychoanalysis, 87*, 1259–1276.
Bock-Famulla, K. (2002). *Volkswirtschaftlicher Ertrag von Kindertagesstätten* [Economic return of day-care facilities] (Gutachten im Auftrag der Max-Traeger-Stiftung der Gewerkschaft Erziehung und Wissenschaft). Bielefeld: Universität Bielefeld.
Bollenbeck, G. (1996). *Bildung und Kultur*. Glanz und Elend eines deutschen Deutungsmusters. Suhrkamp: Frankfurt am Main.
Boocock, S. S. (1995). Early chilhood programs in other nations: Goals and outcomes. *The Future of Children, 5*(3), 94–114.
Bos, W., Hornberg, S., Arnold, K.-H., Faust, G., Fried, L., Lankes, et al. (2007). *IGLU 2006. Lesekompetenzen von Grundschulkindern in Deutschland im internationalen Vergleich* [IGLU 2006. Reading skills of elementary school children in Germany in an international comparison]. Münster: Waxmann.
Boudon, R. (1974). *Education, opportunity, and social inequality: Changing prospects in Western society*. New York: Wiley.
Boulding, K. E. (1975). The pursuit of equality. In J. D. Smith (Ed.), *The personal distribution of income and wealth* (pp. 9–28). Massachusetts, MA: NBER.
Bourdelais, P. (2004). Improving public health in France. The local political mobilization in the nineteenth century. *Hygiea Internationalis, 4*(1, special issue), 229–254.

References

Bouve, C. (2001). *Les crèches collectives: Usagers et représentations sociales. Contribution à une sociologie de la petite enfance* [The collective crèches : Social users and representations. Contribution to a sociology of childhood]. Paris: L'Harmattan.

Bowlby, J. (1969). *Attachment and loss.* London: Hogarth Press and the Institute of Psycho-Analysis.

Bowman, B. T., Donovan, S., & Burns, M. S. (Eds.) (2001). *Eager to learn: Educating our preschoolers.* Washington, DC: National Academy Press.

Boyle, R. (2007). *Long-term follow-up of child development programs in Albuquerque: through 2006* (Report submitted to the city of Albuquerque). Albuquerque: The Institute for Social Research, University of New Mexico. Retrieved May 23, 2008, from www.isrunm.net/files/98861237314426reporttext.pdf

Boyle, R., & Roberts, A. (2003). *Long-term follow-up of child development programs in Albuquerque, phase II* (Report submitted to the city of Albuquerque). Albuquerque: The Institute for Social Research, University of New Mexico. Retrieved May 22, 2008, from http://abec.unm.edu/resources/gallery/text/child_dev_program_II.pdf

Bradley, R. (2002). Environment and parenting. In M. Bornstein (Ed.), *Handbook of parenting* (pp. 281–344). Hillsdale, N.: Lawrence Erlbaum.

Bradley, R. H., Corwyn, R. F., McAdoo, P. H., & Coll, C. G. (2001). The home environments of children in the United States part I: Variations by age, ethnicity, and poverty status. *Child Development, 72*(6), 1844–1867.

Braunberger, P. (1902). *Etude d'hygiène infantile. Rachitisme et crèches* [Study of infantile hygiene. Rachitis and crèches] (tome 6, no 114). Thèse de médicine, Paris.

Bravo, D., Sanhueza, C., & Urzua, S. (2008). *Ability, schooling choices and gender labor market discrimination: Evidence for Chile.* Washington, D.C: Inter-American Development Bank.

Bridges, M., Fuller, B., Rumberger, R., & Tran L. (2004). *Preschool for California's children: Promising benefits, unequal access* (Policy Brief 04-3). Santa Barbara: PACE and UC Linguistic Minority Research Institute.

Briss, P. A., Zaza, S., Pappaioanou, M., Fielding, J., Wright-De Agüero, L., Truman, B. I., et al. (2000). Developing an evidence-based guide to community preventive services - methods. *American Journal of Preventive Medicine, 18*(1S), 35-43.

Broberg, A. G., Wessels, H., Lamb, M. E., & Hwang, C. P. (1997). Effects of day care on the development of cognitive abilities in 8-year-olds: A longitudinal study. *Developmental Psychology, 33*(1), 62–69.

Brooks-Gunn, J. (2003). *Do you believe in magic? What we can expect from early childhood intervention programs* (Social Policy Report Vol. XVII No. 1). Ann Arbor, MI: Society for Research in Child Development.

Bryant, C. G. A. (1975). Kuhn, paradigms and sociology. *The British Journal of Sociology, 26*(3), 354–359.

Bryant, D. M., Burchinal, M., Lau, L. B., & Sparling, J. J. (1994). Family and classroom correlates of Head Start children's developmental outcomes. *Early Childhood Research Quarterly, 9*(289-309).

BSV. (2010). *Finanzhilfen für familienergänzende Kinderbetreuung: Bilanz nach sieben Jahren* [Financial subsidies for extra-familial child care: balance after seven years]. Bern: Bundesamt für Sozialversicherungen. Retrieved July 8, 2010, from www.bsv.admin.ch/praxis/kinderbetreuung/00112/index.html?lang=de

Buchmann, M., & Fend, H. (2002). *Halb drinnen – halb draussen. Analysen zur Arbeitsmarktintegration von Frauen.* Chur/Zürich: Rüegger.

Büchel, F., Spiess, K. C., & Wagner, G. (1997). Bildungseffekte vorschulischer Kinderbetreuung [Educational effects of preschool care]. *Kölner Zeitschrift für Soziologie und Sozialpsychologie, 49*(3), 528-539.

Büchner, C., & Spiess, C. K. (2007). *Die Dauer vorschulischer Betreuungs- und Bildungserfahrungen: Ergebnisse auf der Basis von Paneldaten* [The duration of preschool care and education experiences: Findings on the basis of panel data]. (Discussion papers 687). Berlin: DIW.

Buisson, F. (Ed.) (1911). *Nouveau dictionnaire de pédagogie et d'instruction primaire* [New dictionary of pedagogy and primary instruction]. Paris: Librairie Hachette et Cie.

Buisson, R. (1978). *Les crèches d'entreprise. Exemple: la crèche du groupe hospitalier Pellegrin-Tondu à Bordeaux.* Dissertation, Unités d'Enseignement et de Recherche des Sciences Médicales. Université de Bordeaux.

Burchinal, M. R., Roberts, J. E., Riggins, R., Zeisel, S., Neebe, E., & Bryant, D. (2000a). Relating quality of center-based child care to early cognitive and language development longitudinally. *Child Development, 71*(2), 339–357.

Burchinal, M. R., Peisner-Feinberg, E., Bryant, D. M., & Clifford, R. (2000). Children's social and cognitive development and child-care quality: Testing for differential associations related to poverty, gender, or ethnicity. *Applied Developmental Science, 4*(3), 149–165.

Burchinal, M. R., Roberts, J. E., Riggins, J., Zeisel, S. A., Neebe, E., & Bryant, D. (2000b). Relating Quality of Center-Based Child Care to Early Cognitive and Language Development Longitudinally. *Child Development, 71*(2), 339–357.

Burger, K. (2009). Frühkindliche Bildung und der Ausgleich von Bildungschancen [Early childhood care and education and equalization of educational opportunities]. In N. Flindt & K. Panitz (Eds.), *Frühkindliche Bildung. Entwicklung und Förderung von Kompetenzen* (pp. 67–74). Saarbrücken: Südwestdeutscher Verlag für Hochschulschriften.

Burger, K. (2010a). Frühkindliche Bildungsforschung: Nationale und internationale Bestandsaufnahme und Konsequenzen für Bildungspraxis und -politik in der Schweiz [Early childhood care and education: current state of national and international research and implications for educational practice and policy in Switzerland]. In M. Stamm & D. Edelmann (Eds.), *Frühkindliche Bildung, Betreuung und Erziehung. Was kann die Schweiz lernen?* (pp. 271–290). Zürich: Rüegger.

Burger, K. (2010b). How does early childhood care and education affect cognitive development? An international review of the effects of early interventions for children from different social backgrounds. *Early Childhood Research Quarterly, 25*, 140–165.

Burger, K. (2011a). The origins of early childhood education in Great Britain, France, and the United States of America: An international comparison. Manuscript submitted for publication.

Burger, K. (2011b). A quasi-experimental study into the relations between families' social and cultural background and children's crèche experience and global cognitive competence in primary school. *Early Child Development and Care*, iFirst Article 1-32. DOI: 10.1080/03004430.2011.590938

Burger, K. (2011c). Selektion und Bildungsungleichheiten: Fortschreibungen der Soziologie Pierre Bourdieus an einem Kolloquium der PH Fribourg [Selection and educational inequalities: up-dating the sociology of Pierre Bourdieu at a colloquium at the PH Fribourg]. *Vierteljahrsschrift für wissenschaftliche Pädagogik, 87*(2), 346-351.

Burger, K. (2012). A social history of ideas pertaining to childcare in France and in the United States. *Journal of Social History, 45*(4), 1005-1025.

Burger, K. (in press, a). Robert Owen's legacy across national borders. *Journal of Education Research*.

Burger, K. (in press, b). Societal conditions of child care and infant schooling in 19th-century France and United States. In J. A. Jaworski (Ed.), *Advances in Sociology Research* (vol. 12). Hauppage, NY: Nova Science Publishers.

Caille, J.-P. (2001). Scolarisation à 2 ans et réussite de la carrière scolaire au début de l'école élémentaire [School enrollment at 2 years and school success at the beginning of elementary school]. *Éducation & formations, 60*, 7-18.

Caldwell, B. (1991). Educare: new product, new future. *Developmental and Behavioral Pediatrics, 12*(3), 199–205.

Campbell, J. J., Lamb, M. E., & Hwang, C. P. (2000). Early child-care experiences and children's social competence between 1 1/2 and 15 years of age. *Applied Developmental Science, 4*(3), 166–175.

Campbell, F. A., Pungello, E. P., Miller-Johnson, S., Burchinal, M., & Ramey, C. T. (2001). The development of cognitive and academic abilities: Growth curves from an early childhood educational experiment. *Developmental Psychology, 37*(2), 231–242.

Canetti, E. (2005). *Die gerettete Zunge* (33. Aufl.). Frankfurt am Main: Fischer.

Capizzano, J., & Adams, G. (2000). *The hours that children under five spend in child care: variation across states* (No. B-8). Washington, DC: The Urban Institute.

Carlton, M. P., & Winsler, A. (1999). School readiness: The need for a paradigm shift. *School Psychology Review, 28*(3), 338–352.

Carneiro, P., & Heckman, J. J. (2003). *Human capital policy* (working paper 9495). Cambridge, MA: National Bureau of Economic Research.

Carnine, D. W. (1997). Bridging the research-to-practice gap. In J. W. Lloyd, E. J. Kameenui, & D. Chard (Eds.), *Issues in educating students with disabilities* (pp. 363–376). Mahwah, NJ: Lawrence Erlbaum.

Carr, M., & May, H. (1993). Choosing a model. Reflecting on the developmental process of Te Whariki: National early childhood curriculum guidelines in New Zealand. *International Journal of Early Years Education, 1*(3), 7–22.

Casale, R. (2005). Unverständliche Geschichten. Bemerkungen über das Verhältnis der Pädagogik zur Literatur. In H.-C. Koller & M. Rieger-Ladich (Hrsg.), *Grenzgänge. Pädagogische Lektüren zeitgenössischer Romane* (S. 19-34). Bielefeld: transcript.

Caughy, M. O., DiPietro, J. A., & Strobino, D. M. (1994). Day-care participation as a protective factor in the cognitive development of low-income children. *Child Development, 65*(2), 457–471.

Chevalier, A., Finn, C., Harmon, C., & Viitanen, T. (2006). *The economics of early childhood care and education* (technical research paper). National economic and social forum. Retrieved June 06, 2011, from http://www.nesf.ie/dynamic/pdfs/1-The-Economics-of-Early-Childhood-Care-and-Education.pdf.

Christian, K., Morrison, F. J., & Bryant, F. B. (1998). Predicting kindergarten academic skills: Interactions among child care, maternal education, and family literacy environments. *Early Childhood Research Quarterly, 13*(3), 501–521.

CIIP [Conférence intercantonale de l'instruction publique de la Suisse romande et du Tessin]. (1992). *Objectifs et activités préscolaires* [Preschool objectives and activities]. Neuchâtel: CIIP.

Clarke-Stewart, A. (1993). *Daycare* (Rev. ed.). Cambridge: Harvard University Press.

Clery, S. B., Lee, J. B., & Knapp, L. (1998). *Gender differences in earnings among young adults entering the labor market* (Statistical Analysis Report, NCES 98-086). Washington, D.C: National Center for Education Statistics.

Clifford, R. M., Barbarin, O., Chang, F., Early, D., Bryant, D., Howes, C., et al. (2005). What Is Prekindergarten? Characteristics of Public Prekindergarten Programs. *Applied Developmental Science,* (9), 126–143.

Cohen, A. J. (1996). A brief history of federal financing for child care in the United States. *The Future of Children, 6*(2), 26–40.

Committee on Early Childhood, Adoption, and Dependent Care. (2005). Quality early education and child care from birth to kindergarten. *Pediatrics, 115*(1), 187-191.

Contrepois, A. (2006). *Les jeunes enfants et la crèche: Une histoire* [The young children and the crèche : a history]. Paris: Éditions des Archives Contemporains.

Cook, T. D., Shadish, W. R., & Wong, V. C. (2008). Three conditions under which experiments and observational studies produce comparable causal estimates: New findings from within-study comparisons. *Journal of Policy Analysis and Management, 27,* 724-750.

Costa, D. L. (2000). From mill town to board room: The rise of women's paid labor. *Journal of Economic Perspectives, 14*(4), 101–122.

Côté, S. M., Boivin, M., Nagin, D. S., Japel, C., Xu, Q., Zoccolillo, M., et al. (2007). The role of maternal education and non-maternal care services in the prevention of children's physical aggression. *Archives of General Psychiatry, 64*(11), 1305–1312.

Côté, S. M., Borge, A. I., Geoffroy, M.-C., Rutter, M., & Tremblay, R. E. (2008). Nonmaternal care in infancy and emotional/behavioral difficulties at 4 years old: Moderation by family risk characteristics. *Developmental Psychology, 44*(1), 155–168.

Cowen, R. (2008). *International handbook of comparative education*. Berlin: Springer.

Cryan, J. R. (1992). Success outcomes of full-day kindergarten: More positive behavior and increased achievement in the years after. *Early Childhood Research Quarterly, 7*(2), 187–203.

Cryan, J. R., Sheehan, R., Wiechel, J., & Bandy-Hedden, I. G. (1992). Success outcomes of full-day kindergarten: More positive behavior and increased achievement in the years after. *Early Childhood Research Quarterly, 7,* 187-203.

Currie, J. (2001). Early childhood education programs. *Journal of Economic Perspectives, 15*(2), 213-238.

Curtis, R. C. (2009). *Desire, self, mind, and the psychotherapies: Unifying psychological science and psychoanalysis.* New York: Jason Aronson.

Dahlberg, G., & Moss, P. (2005). *Ethics and politics in early childhood education. Contesting early childhood series.* London: RoutledgeFalmer.

David, M., & Lézine, I. (1974). Early child care in France. *Early Child Development and Care, 4*(1), 5–148.

Day, D. (1983). *Early childhood education: a human ecological approach.* Glenview: Scott Foresman.

DeGarmo, D., Forgatch, M., & Martinez, C. (1999). Parenting of divorced mothers as a link between social status and boys' academic outcomes. *Child Development, 70,* 1231–1245.

Del Boca, D., & Locatelli, M. (2006). *The determinants of motherhood and work status: A survey* (Discussion Paper No. 2414). Bonn: Forschungsinstitut zur Zukunft der Arbeit. Retrieved July 03, 2011, from http://ftp.iza.org/dp2414.pdf.

Delour, M., Desplanques, L., Bonnefoi, M. C., Rufat, P., Fenieres, A., Patris, S., et al. (2004). La santé des enfants en crèche [The health of children in the day nursery]. In M. Roussey & O. Kremp (Eds.), *Pédiatrie sociale ou l'enfant dans son environnement. Progrès en pédiatrie 17, nouvelle série* (pp. 139–152). Rueil-Malmaison: Doin Editeurs.

DeLuca, V., & Rollet, C. (1999). *La pouponnière de Porchefontaine: L'expérience d'une institution sanitaire et sociale* [The day nursery of Porchefontaine : The experience of a sanitary and social institution]. Paris: L'Harmattan.

Dhuey, E. (2007). *Who benefits from kindergarten? Evidence from the introduction of state subsidization* (Job Market Paper). Santa Barbara, CA: Department of Economics, University of California.

DIW Berlin. (n.d.). *SOEP: Das Sozio-ökonomische Panel* [SOEP: The socio-economic panel]. Retrieved December 3, 2008, from http://www.diw.de/deutsch/soep/26628.html

Dollar, D., & Gatti, R. (1999). *Gender inequality, income, and growth: Are good times good for women?* (Policy research report on gender and development; working paper series, no. 1). Washington, D.C.: World Bank. Retrieved June 24, 2011, from http://darp.lse.ac.uk/frankweb/courses/EC501/DG.pdf.

Dollase, R. (2007). Gasteditorial: Bildung im Kindergarten und Früheinschulung. Ein Fall von Ignoranz und Forschungsamnesie [Guest editorial: Education in kindergarten and early schooling. A case of ignorance and research amnesia]. *Zeitschrift für Pädagogische Psychologie, 21*(1), 5-10.

Downs, S., Moore, E., McFadden, E. J., Michaud, S., & Costin, L. B. (2004). *Child welfare and family services: policies and practice.* Michigan: University of Michigan.

Driessen, G. W. J. M. (2004). A large-scale longitudinal study of the utilization and effects of early childhood education and care in the Netherlands. *Early Child Development and Care, 174*(7-8), 667-689.

Dubowy, M., Ebert, S., Maurice, J. von, & Weinert, S. (2008). Sprachlich-kognitive Kompetenzen beim Eintritt in den Kindergarten: Ein Vergleich von Kindern mit und ohne Migrationshintergrund [Linguistic-cognitive competencies at entry to kindergarten: A comparison between children with and without migration background]. *Zeitschrift für Entwicklungspsychologie und Pädagogische Psychologie, 40*(3), 124–134.

Duhn, I. (2008). Globalising childhood: Assembling the bicultural child in the New Zealand early childhood curriculum, Te Whariki. *International Critical Childhood Policy Studies, 1*(1), 82–105.

Duncan, G. J., Brooks-Gunn, J., & Klebanov, P. K. (1994). Economic deprivation and early childhood development. *Child Development, 65*(2), 296-318.

Duncan, G. J., Dowsett, C. J., Claessens, A., Magnuson, K., Huston, A. C., Klebanov, P., et al. (2007). School readiness and later achievement. *Developmental Psychology, 43*(6), 1428–1446.

Duncan, G. J., Ludwig, J., & Magnuson, K. A. (2007). Reducing poverty through preschool intervention. *Future of Children, 17*(2), 143–160.

Dunn, L. M., & Dunn, D. M. (1997). *Peabody Picture Vocabulary Test - third edition (PPVT-III).* Circle Pines, MN: AGS.

Durst, A. (2005). "Of women, by women, and for women": The day nursery movement in the progressive-era United States. *Journal of Social History, 39*(1), 141–159.

Early, D. M., Maxwell, K. L., Burchinal, M., Bender, R. H., Ebanks, C., Henry, G. T., et al. (2007). Teachers' education, classroom quality, and young children's academic skills: Results from seven studies of preschool programs. *Child Development, 78*(2), 558–580.

ECCE (1999). *European child care and education study. School-age assessment of child development: Long-term impact of pre-school experiences on school success, and family-school relationships* (Report submitted to European UnionDGXII: Science, Research and Development). RTD Action: Targeted Socio-Economic Research.

EDK. (2005). *Educare: betreuen – erziehen – bilden* [Educare: care – nurture – educate] (conference proceedings). Bern: Schweizerische Konferenz der kantonalen Erziehungsdirektoren. Retrieved June 29, 2010, from edudoc.ch/record/455/files/StuB24A.pdf?ln=de

EDK. (2010). *Effektive Besuchsdauer (Vorschule)* [Effective duration of attendance (preschool)]. Bern: Schweizerische Konferenz der kantonalen Erziehungsdirektoren. Retrieved July 8, 2010, from: www.ides.ch/dyn/15332.php

Ehrenspeck, Y., & Rustemeyer, D. (1996). Bestimmt unbestimmt. In A. Combe & W. Helsper (Hrsg.), *Pädagogische Professionalität. Untersuchungen zum Typus pädagogischen Handelns* (1. Aufl., S. 368–391). Frankfurt am Main: Suhrkamp.

Eisner, E. W. (1984). Can educational research inform educational practice? *The Phi Delta Kappan, 65*(7), 447–452.

Elicker, J., & Mathur, S. (1997). What do they do all day? Comprehensive evaluation of a full-day kindergarten. *Early Childhood Research Quarterly, 12,* 459–480.

Elkind, D. (1988). *Das gehetzte Kind: Werden unsere Kleinen zu schnell groß?* Hamburg: Kabel.

Elkind, D. (1989). *Wenn Eltern zuviel fordern: Die Rettung der Kindheit vor leistungsorientierter Früherziehung.* Hamburg: Hoffmann und Campe.

Elliott, C. D., Smith, P., & McCulloch, K. (1997). *Technical manual British Ability Scales II.* Windsor, Berkshire: NFER-NELSON Publishing Company.

Entwisle, D. R. (1995). The role of schools in sustaining early childhood program benefits. *The Future of Children, 5*(3), 133-144.

Entwisle, D. R., Alexander, K. L., & Olson, L. S. (1997). *Children, schools, and inequality.* Boulder: Westview Press.

EPPE. (2004). *The effective provision of pre-school education (EPPE) project* (Final Report). London: University of London, Institute of Education.

EPPE. (2008a). *Influences on children's attainment and progress in key stage 2: Cognitive outcomes in year 6* (Research Report DCSF-RR048). London: Department for Children, Schools and Families.

EPPE. (2008b). *Effective pre-school and primary education 3-11 project. Final report from the primary phase: Pre-school, school and family influences on children's development during key stage 2 (age 7-11)* (Research Report No DCSF-RR061). London: University of London, Institute of Education.

EPPNI. (2004). *Effective pre-school provision in Northern Ireland: Pre-school experience and literacy and numeracy development at the end of year 2 of primary school* (Technical Paper No. 10). Belfast: Department of Education, Department of Health, Social Services and Public Safety, and Social Steering Group.

Esser, H. (2006). *Migration, Sprache und Integration* [Migration, language, and integration] (AKI-Forschungsbilanz 4). Berlin: Arbeitsstelle Interkulturelle Konflikte und gesellschaftliche Integration (AKI), Wissenschaftszentrum Berlin für Sozialforschung (WZB).

Eurydice (2009). *Tackling social and cultural inequalities through early childhood education and care in Europe*. Brussels: European Commission. Retrieved July 30, 2010, from www.eurydice.org.

Evans, D. (2002). *Wörterbuch der Lacanschen Psychoanalyse*. Wien: Turia + Kant.

Evans, G. W., & Rosenbaum, J. (2008). Self-regulation and the income-achievement gap. *Early Childhood Research Quarterly, 23*(4), 504–514.

EYTSEN. (2003). *The Early Years Transition & Special Educational Needs (EYTSEN) Project* (Research report RR431). London: University of London, Institute of Education. Retrieved November 14, 2008, from http://www.dcsf.gov.uk/research/data/uploadfiles/RR431.pdf

FACES. (2006). *Family and child experiences survey: FACES 2000* (Technical Report). Washington, DC: Office of Planning, Research and Evaluation, U.S. Department of Health and Human Services. Retrieved January 23, 2009, from http://www.acf.hhs.gov/programs/opre/hs/faces/index.html

Fagnani, J. (2005). *Family policy in France: Old challenges, new tensions* (CESifo DICE Report). Munich: CESifo. Retrieved October 20, 2010, from http://www.ifo.de/pls/guestci/download/CESifo%20DICE%20Report%202005/CESifo%20DICE%20Report%202/2005/dicereport205-rm1.pdf

Fairbrother, G. P. (2005). Comparison to what end? Maximizing the potential of comparative education research. *Comparative Education, 41*(1), 5–24.

Fein, G., & Clarke-Stewart, A. (1973). *Day care in context*. New York: John Wiley.

Feinstein, R., Robertson, D., & Symons, J. (1999). Pre-school education and attainment in the National Child Development Study and British Cohort Study. *Education Economics, 7*(3), 209-234.

Fink, E. (1970). *Erziehungswissenschaft und Lebenslehre*. Freiburg i. Br.: Rombach.

Flitner, C. (2009). *Perspektiven in der familienergänzenden Kinderbetreuung* (Arbeits- und Sozialpolitik). Zürich: Denknetz. Retrieved April 10, 2011, from www.denknetz-online.ch/IMG/pdf/Flitner.pdf.

Fontaine, N. S., Torre, D. L., & Grafwallner, R. (2006). Effects of quality early care on school readiness skills of children at risk. *Early Child Development and Care, 176*(1), 99–109.

Foster, M. A., Lambert, R., Abbott-Shim, M., McCarty, F., & Franze, S. (2005). A model of home learning environment and social risk factors in relation to children's emergent literacy and social outcomes. *Early Childhood Research Quarterly, 20*(1), 13–36.

Foucault, M. (1978). *Dispositive der Macht: Über Sexualität, Wissen und Wahrheit* (Dt. Ausg.). Berlin: Merve Verlag.

Friebertshäuser, B., Rieger-Ladich, M., & Wigger, L. (2006). *Reflexive Erziehungswissenschaft: Forschungsperspektiven im Anschluss an Pierre Bourdieu* (1. Aufl.). Wiesbaden: VS Verlag für Sozialwissenschaften.

Fried, L. (2002). Qualität von Kindergärten aus der Perspektive von Erzieherinnen: Eine Pilotuntersuchung [Quality of kindergartens from the perspective of educators: A pilot investigation]. *Empirische Pädagogik, 16*(2), 191-209.

Fritschi, T., & Oesch, T. (2008). *Volkswirtschaftlicher Nutzen von frühkindlicher Bildung in Deutschland: Eine ökonomische Bewertung langfristiger Bildungseffekte bei Krippenkindern* [Economic return of early childhood education in Germany: An economic appraisal of long-term educational effects for children in nurseries]. Gütersloh: Bertelsmann Stiftung, BASS.

Fritschi, T., Strub, S., & Stutz, H. (2007). *Volkswirtschaftlicher Nutzen von Kindertageseinrichtungen in der Region Bern* [Economic returns of day-care facilities around Bern, final report] (Schlussbericht). Bern: Büro für arbeits- und sozialpolitische Studien. Retrieved November 21, 2008, from www.buerobass.ch/pdf/2007/volkswirt schaftlicher_nutzen_kita_kurzfassung.pdf

Frug, M. J. (1979). *Securing Job Equality for Women: Labor Market Hostility to Working Mothers*. Boston: University Law Review.

Fthenakis, W. E., & Textor, M. R. (Eds.). (1998). *Qualität von Kinderbetreuung: Konzepte, Forschungsergebnisse, internationaler Vergleich* [Quality of child care: Concepts, results from research, international comparison]. Weinheim: Beltz.

Fuchs, D., & Fuchs, L. S. (2001). One blueprint for bridging the gap: Project PROMISE (practitioners and researchers orchestrating model innovations to strengthen education). *Teacher Education and Special Education: The Journal of the Teacher Education Division of the Council for Exceptional Children, 24*(4), 304–314.

Fuchs, R. G. (1984). *Abandoned children: Foundlings and child welfare in nineteenth-century France*. Albany N.Y.: State Univ. of New York Press.

Fullerton, H. N. (1999). *Labor force participation: 75 years of change, 1950-98 and 1998-2025* (Labor force participation: monthly labor review). Washington, DC: Bureau of Labor Statistics.

Fusaro, J. A. (1997). The effect of full-day kindergarten on student achievement: A meta-analysis. *Child Study Journal, 27*(4), 269–280.

Fusaro, J. A., & Royce, C. A. (1995). A reanalysis of research data. *Perceptual and Motor Skills, 81*, 858.

Galobardes, B., Shaw, M., Lawlor, D. A., Lynch, J. W., & Smith, G. D. (2006). Indicators of socioeconomic position (part 1). *Journal of Epidemiology and Community Health, 60*, 7–12.

Gamel-McCormick, M., & Amsden, D. (2002). *Investing in better outcomes: The Delaware early childhood longitudinal study* (Report PS 030930). Newark: Center for Disabilities Studies, College of Human Services, Education, and Public Policy, University of Delaware. Retrieved November 23, 2008, from http://www.eric.ed.gov/ ERICDocs/data/ericdocs2sql/content_storage_01/0000019b/80/1b/87/9a.pdf

Gauvain, M. (1998). Thinking in niches: sociocultural influences on cognitive development. In D. Faulkner, K. Littleton, & M. Woodhead (Eds.), *Learning relationships in the classroom* (pp. 67–90). London: Routledge.

Gilliam, W. S., & Zigler, E. F. (2001). A critical meta-analysis of all evaluations of state-funded preschool from 1977 to 1998: Implications for policy, service delivery and program evaluation. *Early Childhood Research Quarterly, 15*(4), 441–473.

Gössling, J. (2008). *Selbstverhältnisse als Gegenstand der Erziehungswissenschaft: Zur Logik pädagogischen Handelns. Texte zur Theorie und Geschichte der Bildung* (Bd. 27). Berlin: LIT Verl.

Gonzales, P., Williams, T., Jocelyn, L., Roey, S., Kastberg, D., & Brenwald, S. (2009). *Highlights from TIMMS 2007: Mathematics and science achievement of U.S. fourth- and eighth-grade students in an international context.* Washington, D.C: National Center for Education Statistics.

Goodman, A., & Sianesi, B. (2005). Early education and children's outcomes: How long do the impacts last? *Fiscal Studies, 26*(4), 513-548.

Goodson, B. D., Layzer, J. I., St. Pierre, R. G., Bernstein, L. S., & Lopez, M. (2000). Effectiveness of a comprehensive, five-year family support program for low-income children and their families: Findings from the comprehensive child development program. *Early Childhood Research Quarterly, 15*(1), 5-39.

Goodwin, W. L., & Goodwin, L. D. (1996). *Understanding quantitative and qualitative research in early childhood education.* New York: Teachers College Press.

Gormley, W. T., JR, Phillips, D., & Gayer, T. (2008). Preschool programs can boost school readiness. *Science, 320*(5884), 1723–1724.

Gormley, W. T. J. &. G. T. (2005). Promoting school readiness in Oklahoma: An evaluation of Tulsa's Pre-K program. *The Journal of Human Resources, 40*(3), 533–557, from http://www.ssc.wisc.edu/jhr/2005ab/gormley3.htm.

Gormley, W. T., JR, Gayer, T., Phillips D., & Dawson, B. (2004). *The effects of Oklahoma's universal Pre-K program on school readiness: An executive summary.* Georgetown, from www.crocus.georgetown.edu/reports/executive_summary_11_04.pdf.

Gormley, W. T., Jr., Gayer, T., Phillips, D., & Dawson, B. (2005). The effects of universal pre-K on cognitive development. *Developmental Psychology, 41*(6), 872-884.

Granier, C. (1891). *Essai de bibliographie charitable.* Paris: Librairie Guillaumin et Cie.

Greenwood, C. R. (2001). Bridging the gap between research and practice in special education: Issues and implications for teacher preparation. *Teacher Education and Special Education: The Journal of the Teacher Education Division of the Council for Exceptional Children, 24*(4), 273–275.

Greenwood, C. R., & Abbott, M. (2001). The research to practice gap in special education. *Teacher Education and Special Education: The Journal of the Teacher Education Division of the Council for Exceptional Children, 24*(4), 276–289.

Grogan, S. (2000). Philanthropic women and the state: The société de charité maternelle in Avignon, 1802-1917. *French History, 14*(3), 295–321.

Guedeney, A., Grasso, F., & Starakis, N. (2004). Le séjour en crèche des jeunes enfants : sécurité de l'attachement, tempérament et fréquence des maladies. *Psychiatrie de l'enfant, XLVIII*(1), 259–312.

Guimarães, S., & McSherry, K. (2002). The curriculum experiences of pre-school children in Northern Ireland: Classroom practices in terms of child-initiated play and adult-directed activities. *International Journal of Early Years Education, 10*(2), 85-94.

Gull, D. F., & Burton, C. B. (1992). Age of entry, preschool experience, and sex as antecedents of academic readiness in kindergarten. *Early Childhood Research Quarterly, 7*(2), 175–186.

Gullo, D. F., & Burton, C. B. (1992). Age of entry, preschool experience, and sex as antecedents of academic readiness in kindergarten. *Early Childhood Research Quarterly, 7*(2), 175–186.

Gurteen, S. H. (1881). *What is charity organization?* Buffalo: Charity Organization Society of the City of Buffalo.

Hakuta, K. & D'Andrea, D. (1992). Some properties of bilingual maintenance and loss in Mexican background high-school students. *Applied Linguistics, 13*(1), 72-99.

Hamm, K., & Ewen, D. (2006). *From the beginning: Early Head Start children, families, staff, and programs in 2004* (Head Start Series, No. 7). Washington, DC: Center for Law and Social Policy.

Hammack, D. C. (1989). Private organizations, public purposes: Nonprofits and their archives. *The Journal of American Historians, 76*(1), 181–191.

Hansen, J. S. (2003). Early childhood education. In J. W. Guthrie (Ed.), *Encyclopedia of education* (2nd ed., pp. 615–621). New York: Macmillan.

Hanuschek, S. (2005). *Elias Canetti: Biographie*. München: Hanser.

Hatcher, B. A., Schmidt, V. E., & Cook, J. R. (1979). Full-day vs. half-day kindergarten: No difference. *PhiDeltaKappan, 61*, 68.

Hayden, J. (2000). *Landscapes in early childhood education: Cross-national perspectives on empowerment. A guide for the new millenium*. New York: Peter Lang.

Heckman, J. J. (2006). Skill formation and the economics of investing in disadvantaged children. *Science, 312*(5782), 1900–1902.

Hellekamps, S. (1998). Perspektivenwechsel. Überlegungen zum Verhältnis von Bildung und Roman. In: dies. (Hrsg.), *Ästhetik und Bildung. Das Selbst im Medium von Musik, Bildender Kunst, Literatur und Fotografie* (S. 103-117). Weinheim: Deutscher Studien Verlag.

Henry, G. T., Henderson, L. W., Ponder, B. D., Gordon, C. S., Mashburn, A. J., & Rickman, D. K. (2003). *Report of the findings from the early childhood study: 2001-02* (Report August 2003). Atlanta, GA: Andrew Young School of Policy Studies, Georgia State University. Retrieved July 12, 2009, from http://aysps.gsu.edu/publications/2003/earlychildhood.pdf

Henry, G. T., Rickman, D. K., Ponder, D., Henderson, L. W., Mashburn, A., & Gordon, C. S. (2004). *The Georgia early childhood study* (2001-2004 Final Report). Atlanta: Georgia State University, Andrew Young School of Policy Studies. Retrieved

November 27, 2008, from http://aysps.gsu.edu/publications/2005/EarlyChild hoodReport.pdf

Herry, Y., Maltais, C., & Thompson, K. (2007). Effects of a full-day preschool program on 4-year-old children. *Early Childhood Research & Practice, 9*(2). Retrieved June 05, 2011, from http://ecrp.uiuc.edu/v9n2/herry.html.

Hestenes, L. L., Kontos, S., & Bryan, Y. (1993). Children's emotional expression in child care centers varying in quality. *Early Childhood Research Quarterly, 8*(295-307).

Heywood, C. (1981). The market for child labour in nineteenth-century France. *History, 66*(216), 34–49.

Hild, M. &. V. A. (2001). *Roemer on equality of opportunity* (Social Science Working Paper 1128). Pasadena, CA: California Institute of Technology.

Hill, V. (2005). Through the past darkly: A review of the British Ability Scales Second Edition. *Child and Adolescent Mental Health, 10*(2), 87–98.

Hobbs, S., McKechnie, J., & Lavalette, M. (1999). *Child labor: A world history companion.* Santa Barbara: ABC-CLIO.

Hodgen, E. (2007). *Early childhood education and young adult competencies at age 16* (Report to the Ministry of Education). Wellington: New Zealand Council for Educational Research, Ministry of Education.

Hoff, E. (2006). How social contexts support and shape language development. *Developmental Review, 26*(1), 55-88.

Hoff, E., & Tian, C. (2005). Socioeconomic status and cultural influences on language. *Journal of Communication Disorders, 38*(4), 271-278.

Hofferth, S. L., West, J., Henke, R., & Kaufman, P. (1994). *Access to early childhood programs for children at risk* (National Household Education Survey). Washington, D.C.: U.S. Department of Education.

Honig, A. S. (1990). Research: A tool to promote optimal early child care and education. In A. S. Honig (Ed.), *Optimizing early child care and education* (pp. 1–10). New York: Gordon and Breach Science Publishers.

Howes, C. (1998). Relations between early child care and schooling. *Developmental Psychology, 24*(1), 53–57.

Howes, C., Burchinal, M., Pianta, R., Bryant, D., Early, D., Clifford, R., et al. (2008). Ready to learn? Children's pre-academic achievement in pre-kindergarten programs. *Early Childhood Research Quarterly, 23*, 27-50.

Howes, C., Phillips, D., & Whitebook, M. (1992). Thresholds of quality: Implications for the social development of children in center-based care. *Child Development, 63*, 449–460.

Howes, C., & Smith, E. W. (1995). Relations among child care quality, teacher behavior, children's play activities, emotional security, and cognitive activity in child care. *Early Childhood Research Quarterly, 10*, 381-404.

Howes, C., Burchinal, M. R., Pianta, R. C., Bryant, D., Early, D. M., Clifford, R. M., & et al. (2008). Ready to learn? Children's pre-academic achievement in pre-kindergarten programs. *Early Childhood Research Quarterly, 23*(1), 27–50.

References

Hradil, S. (2001). *Soziale Ungleichheit in Deutschland* [Social inequality in Germany]. Wiesbaden: VS Verlag für Sozialwissenschaften.

Humboldt, W. v. (1959). Über den Nationalcharakter der Sprachen. In C. Menze (Hrsg.), *Wilhelm von Humboldt. Bildung und Sprache. Eine Auswahl aus seinen Schriften* (S. 75–88). Paderborn: Schöningh.

Humboldt, W. v. (2002a). *Werke in fünf Bänden. Band I: Schriften zur Anthropologie und Geschichte* (4. Aufl.). Darmstadt: Wissenschaftliche Buchgesellschaft.

Humboldt, W. v. (2002b). *Werke in fünf Bänden. Band II: Schriften zur Altertumskunde und Ästhetik* (5. Aufl.). Darmstadt: Wissenschaftliche Buchgesellschaft.

Humboldt, W. v. (2002c). *Werke in fünf Bänden. Band III: Schriften zur Sprachphilosophie*. Darmstadt: Wissenschaftliche Buchgesellschaft.

Humboldt, W. v. (2002d). *Werke in fünf Bänden. Band IV: Schriften zur Politik und zum Bildungswesen* (6. Aufl.). Darmstadt: Wissenschaftliche Buchgesellschaft.

Humboldt, W. v. (2002e). *Werke in fünf Bänden. Band V: Kleine Schriften, Autobiographisches, Dichtungen, Briefe* (2. Aufl.). Darmstadt: Wissenschaftliche Buchgesellschaft.

Hurrelmann, K. (2000). *Gesundheitssoziologie: Eine Einführung in sozialwissenschaftliche Theorien von Krankheitsprävention und Gesundheitsförderung* [Sociology of health: An introduction to socio-scientific theories on the prevention of disease and the promotion of health] (4th ed.). Weinheim: Juventa.

Hustedt, J. T., Barnett, W. S., & Jung, K. (2008). *Longitudinal effects of the Arkansas Better Chance program: Findings from kindergarten and first grade* (Report NIEER). New Brunswick: Rutgers University, National Institute for Early Education Research. Retrieved August 12, 1008, from http://nieer.org/resources/research/Arkansas Longitudinal.pdf

Huttenlocher, J., Haight, W., Bryk, A., Seltzer, M., & Lyons, T. (1991). Early vocabulary growth: Relation to language input and gender. *Developmental Psychology, 27*(2), 236–248.

ILO-UNDP (2009). *Work and family: Towards new forms of reconciliation with social co-responsibility*. Geneva: International Labour Organization and the UN Development Programme.

Iten, R., et al. (2005). *Wie viele Krippen und Tagesfamilien braucht die Schweiz?: Kurzfassung der NFP52-Studie "Familienergänzende Kinderbetreuung in der Schweiz: aktuelle und zukünftige Nachfragepotenziale"*. Zürich: Infras, Mecop Universita svizzera italiana, Tassinari Beratungen. Retrieved August 15, 2011, from http://www.nfp52.ch/files/download/KurzfassungIten_d.pdf.

Jacobs, J., & Krause, M. (1989). *Der deutsche Bildungsroman: Gattungsgeschichte vom 18. bis zum 20. Jahrhundert*. München: Beck.

Jamieson, A., Curry, A., & Martinez, G. (1999, October). School enrollment *in the United States: Social and economic characteristics of students* (P20-533). Washington, DC: U.S. Census Bureau.

Jarousse, J.-P., Mingat, A., & Richard, M. (1992). La scolarisation maternelle à deux ans: Effets pédagogiques et sociaux. *Education et formations, 31*, 3–9. Retrieved June 02, 2011.

Jaumotte, F. (2003). Labour force participation of women: Empirical evidence on the role of policy and other determinants in OECD countries. *OECD Economic Studies, 2*(37), 52–108.

Joffe, C. E. (1977). *Friendly intruders: Child care professionals and family life.* Berkeley: University of California Press.

Jordan, N. C., Huttenlocher, J., & Levine, S. C. (1992). Differential calculation abilities in young children from middle and low-income families. *Developmental Psychology, 28*, 644–653.

Jung, S., & Stone, S. (2008). Sociodemographic and programmatic moderators of Early Head Start: Evidence from the national Early Head Start research and evaluation project. *Children & Schools, 30*(3), 149–157.

Kagan, S. L. (September 26, 2006). *American early childhood education: Preventing or perpetuating inequity?* (The Campaign for Educational Equity, Research Review No. 1). New York: Teachers College, Columbia University.

Kagan, S. L., & Kauerz, K. (2008). Preschool programs: Effective curricula. In R. E. Tremblay, R. Barr, & R. Peters (Eds.), *Encyclopedia on early childhood development* (pp. 1–5). Montréal: Centre of Excellence for Early Childhood Development.

Kagan, S. L., Tarran, K., Carson, A., & Kauerz, K. (2006). *The early care and education teaching workforce: At the fulcrum.* Houston: National Center for Children & Families. Retrieved July 27, 2010, from www.cornerstones4kids.org/images/teachers_report_0107.pdf.

Kagitcibasi, C., Sunar, D., & Bekman, S. (2001). Long-term effects of early intervention: Turkish low-income mothers and children. *Journal of Applied Developmental Psychology, 22*(4), 333–361.

Kagitcibasi, C., Sunar, D., Bekman, S., Baydar, N., & Celmalcilar, Z. (2009). Continuing effects of early enrichment in adult life: The Turkish Early Enrichment Project 22 years later. *Journal of Applied Developmental Psychology, 30*(6), 764–779.

Kaplan, A. (1964). *The conduct of inquiry. Methodology for behavioral science.* San Francisco: Chandler Pub. Co.

Karoly, L. A., Greenwood, P. W., Everingham, S. S., Houbé, J., Kilburn, M. R., Rydell, et al. (1998). *Investing in our children: What we know and don't know about the costs and benefits of early childhood interventions.* Santa Monica: Rand.

Karoly, L. A., Kilburn, M. R., & Cannon, J., S. (2005). *Early childhood interventions: proven results, future promise.* Santa Monica: Rand.

Keller, H. (2011). *Kinderalltag: Kulturen der Kindheit und ihre Bedeutung für Bindung, Bildung und Erziehung* [Children's everyday life: Cultures of childhood and their significance for bonding, care and eduction]. Berlin, Heidelberg: Springer.

Kelly, E. L. (2003). The strange history of employer-sponsored child care: interested actors, uncertainty, and the transformation of law in organizational fields. *The American Journal of Sociology, 109*(3), 606–649.

Kennedy, M. M. (1997). The connection between research and practice. *Educational Researcher, 26*(7), 4–12.

Kerlinger, F. N. (1977). The influence of research on education practice. *Educational Researcher, 6*(8), 5–12.

Kim, J., & Suen, H. K. (2003). Predicting children's academic achievement from early assessment scores: A validity generalization study. *Early Childhood Research Quarterly, 18*(4), 547–566.

KiTaS. (2008). *KiTaS-Richtlinien* [KiTaS-guidelines]. Zürich: Verband Kindertagesstätten der Schweiz. Retrieved September 14, 2009, from www.kitas.ch/fileadmin/user_ upload/intranetdokumente/geschaeftsstelle/KiTaS_RL_2008_01.pdf

Koegel, T. (2002). *Did the association between fertility and female employment in OECD countries really change its sign?* (working paper no. 2001-034). Rostock: Max Planck Institute for Demographic Research.

Konsortium Bildungsberichterstattung (2006). *Bildung in Deutschland: Ein indikatorengestützter Bericht mit einer Analyse zu Bildung und Migration* [Education in Germany: An indicator-based report with an analysis on education and migration]. Berlin: Bundesministerium für Bildung und Forschung.

Korenmann, S., Miller, J. E., & Sjaastad, J. E. (1994). *Long-term poverty and child development in the United States: Results from the NLSY* (Discussion paper No. 1044-94). Minnesota: Humphrey Institute of Public Affairs and Center for Population Analysis and Policy.

Korte, P. (2004). *Kontinuität, Krise und Zukunft der Bildung: Analysen und Perspektiven. Texte zur Theorie und Geschichte der Bildung* (Bd. 21). Münster: LIT.

Koven, S., & Michel, S. (1990). Womanly duties: Maternalist politics and the origins of welfare states in France, Germany, Great Britain, and the United States 1880-1920. *The American Historical Review, 95*(4), 1076–1108.

Krajewski, K., Renner, A., Nieding, G., & Schneider, W. (2008). Frühe Förderung von mathematischen Kompetenzen [Early training of quantity – number competencies in preschool]. *Zeitschrift für Erziehungswissenschaft, Sonderheft 11*, 91-103.

Kuhn, T. S. (1996). *The structure of scientific revolutions* (3rd ed.). Chicago: The University of Chicago Press.

La Berge, A. F. (1991). Medicalization and moralization: The creches of nineteenth-century Paris. *Journal of Social History, 25*(1), 65–87.

LaBrecque, R. T., & Sokolow, H. M. (1982). Pseudo-educational theory: How not to theorize in education. *Educational Theory, 32*(3-4), 143–155.

Lacan, J. (1973). *Schriften I*. Olten und Freiburg im Breisgau: Walter-Verlag.

Lacan, J. (1978). *Freuds technische Schriften* (Das Seminar, Buch I). Olten: Walter-Verlag.

Ladenthin, V. (1991). *Moderne Literatur und Bildung: Zur Bestimmung des spezifischen Bildungsbeitrags moderner Literatur*. Hildesheim: Olms.

Laevers, F. (2008). Experiential education: Making care and education more effective through well-being and involvement. In R. E. Tremblay, R. Barr, & R. Peters (Eds.), *Encyclopedia on early childhood development* (pp. 1–5). Montréal: Centre of Excellence for Early Childhood Development.

Lally, J. R. (2007). Infant care. In R. S. New & M. Cochran (Eds.), *Early childhood education: An international encyclopedia* (pp. 442–446). Westport, Conn.: Praeger.
Lamb, M. E. (1998). Nonparental child care: Context, quality, correlates, and consequences. In W. Damon, I. E. Sigel, & K. A. Renninger (Eds.), *Handbook of child psychology: Vol. 4. Child psychology in practice* (5th ed., pp. 73–133). New York: Wiley.
Landvoigt, T., Muehler, G., & Pfeiffer, F. (2007). *Duration and intensity of kindergarten attendance and secondary school track choice* (Discussion Paper No. 07-051). Mannheim: Zentrum für Europäische Wirtschaftsforschung.
Lanfranchi, A. (2002). *Schulerfolg von Migrationskindern* [School success of migrant children]. Opladen: Leske + Budrich.
Lanfranchi, A. (2010). Bildungsdisparitäten bei Migrationskindern: Für was ist die Schule zuständig, für was nicht? *Heilpädagogik online, 2*, 36–47.
Lascarides, V. C., & Hinitz, B. F. (2000). *History of early childhood education*. New York: Falmer Press.
Lee, V. E., & Burkam, D. T. (2002). *Inequality at the starting gate: Social background differences in achievement as children begin school.* Washington, DC: EPI book.
Leone, P. E., Christle, C. A., Nelson, M., Skiba, R., Frey, A., & Jolivette, K. (2003). *School failure, race, and disability: Promoting positive outcomes, decreasing vulnerability for involvement with the juvenile delinquency system.* Retrieved June 02, 2011, from www.edjj.org/Publications/list/leone_et_al-2003.pdf.
Leseman, P. P. M. (2002). *Early childhood education and care for children from low-income or minority backgrounds* (Paper for discussion at the OECD Oslo workshop, June 6-7). Oslo: OECD.
Leseman, P. P. M., & De Jong, P. F. (1998). Opportunity, instruction, cooperation and social-emotional quality predicting early reading achievement. *Reading Research Quarterly, 33*(3), 294–318.
Levin, M. E. (1981). Equality of opportunity. *The Philosophical Quarterly, 31*(31), 110–125.
Levy, D. U., & Michel, S. (2002). More can be less: Child care and welfare reform in the United States. In S. Michel & R. Mahon (Eds.), *Child care policy at the crossroads. Gender and welfare state restructuring* (pp. 239–266). London: Routledge.
Lewis, V. S. (1966). Stephen Humphreys Gurteen and the origins of charity organization. *The Social Service Review, 40*(2), 190–201.
Lindenmeyer, K. (2001). Children's Bureau, U.S. In J. M. Hawes & E. F. Shores (Eds.), *The family in America. An encyclopedia* (pp. 208–212). Santa Barbara, Calif.: ABC-CLIO.
Lipps, G., & Yiptong-Avila, J. (1999). From home to school: How Canadian children cope. *Education Quarterly Review, 6*(2), 51-57.
Little, K. B. (1994). *Maria M. Love: the life and legacy of a social work pioneer.* Buffalo: Western New York Heritage Institute, Canisius College.
Loeb, S., Bridges, M., Bassok, D., Fuller, B., & Rumberger, R. W. (2007). How much is too much? The influence of preschool centers on children's social and cognitive development. *Economics of Education Review, 26*(1), 52–66.

Lossing, B. J. (1884). *History of New York City: embracing an outline sketch of events from 1609 to 1830, and a full account of its development from 1830 to 1884.* New York: Perine Engraving and Pub. Co.

Love, J. M., Harrison, L., Sagi-Schwartz, A., van IJzendoorn, M. H., Ross, C., Ungerer, J. A., et al. (2003). Child Care Quality Matters: How Conclusions May Vary With Context. *Child Development, 74*(4), 1021–1033.

Lumsden, E., & Doyle, C. (2009). Working with families. In T. Waller (Ed.), *An introduction to early childhood. A multidisciplinary approach* (2nd ed., pp. 167–179). Los Angeles: SAGE.

Luster, T., & Dubow, E. (1992). Home environment and maternal intelligence as predictors of verbal intelligence: A comparison of preschool and school-age children. *Merrill-Palmer Quarterly, 38*, 151–175.

Lynch, K. A. (1988). *Family, class, and ideology in early industrial France: Social policy and the working-class family, 1825-1848. Life course studies.* Madison: Univ. of Wisconsin Press.

Mackenzie Oth, L. (2002). *La crèche est rentable, c'est son absence qui coûte* [Crèche is profitable, its absence costs]. Genève: Bureaux de l'égalité, Conférence latine des déléguées à l'égalité.

Magnuson, K. A., Meyers, M. K., Ruhm, C. J., & Waldfogel, J. (2004). Inequality in preschool education and school readiness. *American Educational Research Journal, 41*(1), 115-157.

Magnuson, K. A., Ruhm, C., & Waldfogel, J. (2007a). The persistence of preschool effects: Do subsequent classroom experiences matter? *Early Childhood Research Quarterly, 22*, 18–38.

Magnuson, K. A., Ruhm, C., & Waldfogel, J. (2007b). Does prekindergarten improve school preparation and performance? *Economics of Education Review, 26*(1), 33–51.

Magnuson, K. A., & Waldfogel, J. (2005). School readiness: closing racial and ethnic gaps. *The Future of Children, 15*(1), 169–196.

Mahoney, J. (2004). Comparative-historical methodology. *Annual Review of Sociology, 30*, 81–101.

Marbeau, J. B. F. (1845). *Des crèches; ou, moyen de diminuer la misère en augmentant la population.* Paris: Au comptoir des imprimeurs-unis, Quai Malaquais.

Marbeau, J. B. F. (1994). *The crèche (Vanessa, Nicolai, trans.).* Montréal (Original work published 1845).

Marcon, R. A. (1992). Differential effects of three preschool models on inner-city 4-year-olds. *Early Childhood Research Quarterly, 7*(4), 517-530.

Marjanovic Umek, L., Kranjc, S., Fekonja, U., & Bajc, K. (2008). The effect of preschool on children's school readiness. *Early Child Development and Care, 178*(6), 569–588.

Marotzki, W. (2006). Bildungstheorie und Allgemeine Biographieforschung. In H.-H. Krüger & W. Marotzki (Hrsg.), *Handbuch erziehungswissenschaftliche Biographieforschung* (2. Aufl., S. 59–70). Wiesbaden: VS Verlag für Sozialwissenschaften.

Mashburn, A. J., Pianta, R. C., Hamre, B. K., Downer, J. T., Barbarin, O. A., Bryant, D., et al. (2008). Measures of Classroom Quality in Prekindergarten and Children's

Development of Academic, Language, and Social Skills. *Child Development, 79*(3), 732–749.
Mason, A. (2004). Equality of opportunity and differences in social circumstances. *The Philosophical Quarterly, 54*(216), 368–388.
May, A. (2006). *Wilhelm Meisters Schwestern: Bildungsromane von Frauen im ausgehenden 18. Jahrhundert.* Königstein/Taunus: Helmer.
McCartney, K., Burchinal, M., Clarke-Stewart, A., Bub, K. L., Owen, M. T., Belsky, J., & NICHD Early Child Care Research Network (2010). Testing a series of causal propositions relating time in child care to children's externalizing behavior. *Developmental Psychology, 46*(1), 1–17.
McDermott, V. D. (2009). *Chicago Social Service Directory.* Charleston, SC: BiblioBazaar.
McLoyd, V. C. (1998). Socioeconomic disadvantage and child development. *American Psychologist, 53*(2), 185–204.
Meier, J. (March 2008). *"Frühkindliche Bildung als ein Schlüssel für gesellschaftliche Teilhabe"* [„Early childhood education and care as a key to societal participation"]. Gütersloh: Bertelsmann Stiftung. Retrieved November 19, 2009, from www.bertelsmann-stiftung.de/bst/de/media/xcms_bst_dms_24111_24272_2.pdf
Melhuish, E., & Petrogiannis, K. (Eds.) (2006). *Early childhood care and education: International perspectives.* New York: Routledge.
Melhuish, E., Phan, M. B., Sylva, K., Sammons, P., Siraj-Blatchford, I., & Taggart, B. (2008). Effects of the home learning environment and preschool center experience upon literacy and numeracy development in early primary school. *Journal of Social Issues, 64*(1), 95–114.
Mencken, H. L. (1990). *The American language: an inquiry into the development of English in the United States* (4th ed.). New York: Knopf.
Menze, C. (1965). *Wilhelm Humboldts Lehre und Bild vom Menschen.* Ratingen bei Düsseldorf: Henn.
Merrell, K. W. (1999). *Behavioral, social, and emotional assessment of children and adolescents.* Mahwah, NJ: Erlbaum Associates.
Meyers, M. K., Rosenbaum, D., Ruhm, C., & Waldfogel, J. (2004). Inequality in early childhood education and care: What do we know? In K. M. Neckerman (Ed.), *Social inequality* (pp. 223–270). New York: Russell Sage Foundation.
Mezey, J., Greenberg, M., & Schumacher, R. (2002). *The vast majority of federally-eligible children did not receive child care assistance in FY 2000.* Washington, DC: Center for Law and Social Policy, from ww.clasp.org/admin/site/publications_archive/files/0108.pdf
Micheaux, S., & Monso, O. (2007). *Faire garder ses enfants pendant son temps de travail* (N° 1132). Paris: Institut National de la Statistique et des Etudes Economiques.
Michel, S. (1999). *Children's interests - mothers' rights: The shaping of America's child care policy.* New Haven, CT: Yale Univ. Press.

Michel, S. (2001). Child care. In J. M. Hawes & E. F. Shores (Eds.), *The family in America. An encyclopedia* (pp. 146–156). Santa Barbara, Calif.: ABC-CLIO.
Michel, S. (2004). Child care. In G. Mink & A. O'Connor (Eds.), *Poverty in the United States. An Encyclopedia of History, Politics, and Policy* (pp. 149–156). Santa Barbara, California: ABC-CLIO.
Milosavljevic, V., & Tacla Chamy, O. (2007). *Incorporando un módulo de uso del tiempo a las encuestas de hogares: Restricciones y potencialidades*. Santiago de Chile: Naciones Unidas, CEPAL, Unidad Mujer y Desarrollo.
Ministère du Travail de l'Emploi et de la Santé (2010). *Bilan d'étape de la politique familiale*. Retrieved November 10, 2010, from www.travail-solidarite.gouv.fr/espaces, 770/famille,774/dossiers,725/accueil-du-jeune-enfant,1793/bilan-d-etape-de-la-politique,11822.html
Möde, E. (1995). *Das Begehren: Das Identitätsproblem in der Ethik der analytischen Psychotherapie* (2., überarb. Neuaufl.). München: Ed. Psychosymbolik.
Mollenhauer, K. (1987). Korrekturen am Bildungsbegriff? *Zeitschrift für Pädagogik, 33*(1), 1-20.
Mollenhauer, K. (1998). „Über die Schwierigkeit, von Leuten zu erzählen, die nicht recht wissen, wer sie sind". Einige bildungstheoretische Motive in Romanen von Thomas Mann. *Zeitschrift für Pädagogik, 44*, 487-502.
Molnar, A. (1985). The equality of opportunity trap. *Educational Leadership, 43*(1), 60–61.
Montie, J. E., Xiang, Z., & Schweinhart, L. J. (2006). Preschool experience in 10 countries: Cognitive and language performance at age 7. *Early Childhood Research Quarterly, 21*(3), 313–331.
Morgan, K. J. (2003). The politics of mothers' employment: France in comparative perspective. *World Politics, 55*(2), 259–289.
Morgan, K. J. (2005). The "production" of child care: How labor markets shape social policy and vice versa. *Social Politics, 12*, 243–263.
Morrison, G. S. (2006). *Fundamentals of early childhood education* (4th). Upper Saddle River, N.J: Merrill.
Moser, U., Bayer, N., & Berweger, S. (2008). *Summative Evaluation Grundstufe und Basisstufe* [Summative evaluation ,Grundstufe' and ,Basisstufe', interim report for EDK-OST] (Zwischenbericht zuhanden der EDK-OST). Zürich: Universität, Institution für Bildungsevaluation. Retrieved September 3, 2008, from www.ibe.uzh.ch/projekte/grund-undbasisstufe.html
Moser, U., Berweger, S., & Tresch, S. (2003). *Sprache und Mathematik bei Schuleintritt* [Language and mathematics at entry to school]. Zürich: Kompetenzzentrum für Bildungsevaluation und Leistungsmessung an der Universität Zürich.
Moser, U., Stamm, M., & Hollenweger, J. (2005). *Für die Schule bereit? Lesen, Wortschatz, Mathematik und soziale Kompetenzen beim Schuleintritt* [Ready for school? Reading, vocabulary, mathematics, and social competencies at school entry]. Aarau: Sauerländer.

Moss, P. (2006). Structures, understandings and discourses: possibilities for reenvisioning the early childhood worker. *Contemporary Issues in Early Childhood, 7*(1), 30–41.

Moss, P., & Dahlberg, G. (2008). Beyond quality in early childhood education and care – languages of evaluation. *New Zealand Journal of Teachers' Work, 5*(1), 3–12.

Moss, P., Krenn-Wache, M., Na, J., & Bennett, J. (2004). *Die Politik der frühkindlichen Betreuung, Bildung und Erziehung in der Bundesrepublik Deutschland: Ein Länderbericht der Organisation für wirtschaftliche Zusammenarbeit und Entwicklung*. Berlin: OECD.

Mozère, L. (1992). *Le printemps des crèches. Histoire et analyse d'un mouvement*. Paris: L'Harmattan.

Mozère, L. (2003). Family day care in France. In A. Mooney & J. Statham (Eds.), *Family Day Care: International Perspectives on Policy, Practice and Quality* (pp. 163–178). London: Jessica Kingsley Publishers.

Mueller, C. W., & Parcel, T. L. (1981). Measures of socioeconomic status: Alternatives and recommendations. *Child Development, 52*(1), 13-30.

Müller Kucera, K., & Bauer, T. (2000). *Volkswirtschaftlicher Nutzen von Kindertagesstätten: Welchen Nutzen lösen die privaten und städtischen Kindertagesstätten in der Stadt Zürich aus?* [Economic returns of day-care facilities: What benefit do the private and the municipal day-care facilities produce in the city of Zurich?] (Schlussbericht zuhanden des Sozialdepartementes der Stadt Zürich). Bern: Büro für arbeits- und sozialpolitische Studien. Retrieved May 23, 2008, from www.stadt-zuerich.ch/content/sd/ de/index/ueber_das_departement/strategie/kinderbetreuung/edspolitik5.html

Müller Kucera, K., & Bauer T. (2001). *Kindertagesstätten zahlen sich aus* (Edition Sozialpolitik Nr. 5a). Zürich: Sozialdepartement der Stadt Zürich.

Mulligan, G. M., Brimhall, D., & West, J. (2005). *Child care and early education arrangements of infants, toddlers, and preschoolers: 2001* (NCES 2006-039). Washington, DC: U.S. Department of Education, National Center for Education Statistics. Retrieved November 25, 2010, from http://nces.ed.gov/pubs2006/2006039.pdf

National Center for Education Statistics (NCES). (2003). *The condition of education*. Washington, D.C.: U.S. Government Printing Office.

NAYEC (1998). *Licensing and public regulation of early childhood programs: A position statement of the National Association for the Education of Young Children*. Washington, D.C.: National Association for the Education of Young Children.

NAYEC (2009). *Developmentally appropriate practice in early childhood programs serving children from birth through age 8* (position statement). Washington, D.C.: National Association for the Education of Young Children, from www.naeyc.org/files/naeyc/file/ positions/position%20statement%20Web.pdf.

Nelson, G., Westhues, A., & MacLeod, J. (2003). A meta-analysis of longitudinal research on preschool prevention programs for children. *Prevention & Treatment, 6*, 1-35.

Negrini, L., Sabini, S. , Knoll, A., & Stamm, M. (2011, June 22). *Wirkungen vorschulischer Settings auf den intellektuellen, sprachlichen und mathematischen Entwicklungsstand 3- bis*

4-jähriger Kinder - Teilergebnisse der Längsschnittstudie FRANZ [Effects of preschool settings on intellectual, linguistic, and mathematics proficiency levels of 3- to 4-year-old children – Results of the FRANZ longitudinal study]. Paper presented at the SGBF conference, Basel.

NICHD Early Child Care Research Network (1996). Characteristics of infant child care: Factors contributing to positive caregiving. *Early Childhood Research Quarterly, 11*, 269–306.

NICHD Early Child Care Research Network (1997). The effects of infant child care on infant-mother attachment security: Results of the NICHD study of early child care. *Child Development, 68*(5), 860–879.

NICHD Early Child Care Research Network (1998). Early child care and self-control, compliance and problem behavior at 24 and 36 months. *Child Development, 69*, 1145–1170.

NICHD Early Child Care Research Network (1999). Child care and mother-child interaction in the first 3 years of life. *Developmental Psychology, 35*, 1399–1413.

NICHD Early Child Care Research Network (2000). The relation of child care to cognitive and language development. *Child Development, 71*(4), 960–980.

NICHD Early Child Care Research Network (2001). Child care and family predictors of preschool attachment and stability from infancy. *Developmental Psychology, 37*(6), 847–862.

NICHD Early Child Care Research Network (2002a). Child-care structure, process, outcome: Direct and indirect effects of child-care quality on young children's development. *Psychological Science, 13*(2), 199–206.

NICHD Early Child Care Research Network (2002b). Early child care and children's development prior to school entry: Results from the NICHD study of early child care. *American Educational Research Journal, 39*(1), 133–164.

NICHD Early Child Care Research Network (2003). Does amount of time spent in child care predict socioemotional adjustment during the transition to kindergarten? *Child Development, 74*(4), 976–1005.

NICHD Early Child Care Research Network (2005a). Early child care and children's development in the primary grades: Follow-up results from the NICHD study of early child care. *American Educational Research Journal, 42*(3), 537–570.

NICHD Early Child Care Research Network (2005b). Predicting individual differences in attention, memory, and planning in first graders from experiences at home, child care, and school. *Developmental Psychology, 41*(1), 99–114.

NICHD Early Child Care Research Network (2006). Child-care effect sizes for the NICHD study of early child care and youth development. *American Psychologist, 61*(2), 99–116.

NICHD Early Child Care Research Network (2007). Age of entry to kindergarten and children's academic achievement and socioemotional development. *Early Education and Development, 18*(2), 337–368.

NICHD Early Child Care Research Network, & Duncan, G. J. (2003). Modeling the impacts of child care quality on children's preschool cognitive development. *Child Development, 74*(5), 1454–1475.

Niles, M. D., Reynolds, A. J., & Roe-Sepowitz, D. (2008). Early childhood intervention and early adolescent social and emotional competence: second-generation evaluation evidence from the Chicago longitudinal study. *Educational Research, 50*(1), 55-73.

Nipkow, K.-E. (1977). Bildung und Entfremdung. Überlegungen zur Rekonstruktion der Bildungstheorie. *Zeitschrift für Pädagogik*, (14. Beiheft), 205–229.

Norgaard, R. B. (1989). The case for methodological pluralism. *Ecological Economics, 1*(1), 37–57.

Norvez, A. (1990). *De la naissance à l'école. Santé, modes de garde et préscolarité dans la France contemporaine.* (Travaux et documents, cahier no 126). Paris: INED-PUF.

Nóvoa, A., & Yariv-Mashal, T. (2003). Comparative research in education: a mode of governance or a historical journey? *Comparative Education, 39*(4), 423–438.

NSW parenting centre (2003). *School readiness* (Discussion Paper 1). Retrieved May 05, 2011, from www.community.nsw.gov.au/docswr/_assets/main/documents/school_readiness.pdf.

Nutbrown, C. (2006). *Key concepts in early childhood education & care.* Thousand Oaks, CA: SAGE Publications.

OCDE (2003). *Education et accueil des jeunes enfants: Rapport préalable à la visite des experts en France.* Paris. Retrieved November 17, 2010, from www.oecd.org/dataoecd/60/38/34402477.pdf

O'Connor, S. M. (1990). Rationales for the institutionalization of programs for young children. *American Journal of Education, 98*(2), 114–146.

O'Connor, S. M. (1995). Mothering in public: The division of organized child care in the kindergarten and day nursery, St. Louis, 1886-1920. *Early Childhood Research Quarterly, 10*, 63–80.

OECD (2002). *Employment outlook.* Paris: OECD.

OECD Directorate for Education (2004). *Starting Strong: Curricula and pedagogies in early childhood education and care. Five curriculum outlines.* Paris: OECD. Retrieved June 09, 2011, from http://www.oecd.org/dataoecd/23/36/31672150.pdf.

OECD (2004). *Early childhood education and care policy in France* (OECD country note). Paris: Directorate for Education. Retrieved June 03, 2011, from http://www.oecd.org/dataoecd/60/36/34400146.pdf.

OECD (2006). *Starting Strong II: Early childhood education and care.* Paris: OECD Publishing.

OECD (2008). *Are we growing unequal? New evidence on changes in poverty and incomes over the past 20 years.* Paris: OECD. Retrieved August 21, 2011, from http://www.oecd.org/dataoecd/48/56/41494435.pdf.

OECD (2009). *Education at a glance 2009: OECD indicators* (UNESCO/OECD/ EUROSTAT database on education statistics). Retrieved July 1, 2010, from www.oecd.org/education/database.

OECD (2010a). *Factbook.* Paris: OECD.

OECD (2010b). *Education at a glance 2010: OECD indicators* (Indicator C1: Who participates in education). Retrieved August 16, 2011, from www.oecd.org/document/52/0,3746,en_2649_39263238_45897844_1_1_1_1,00.html

OECD (2010c). *PISA 2009 results: Overcoming social background*. [Paris]: OECD.

OECD (2010d). *Formal care and education for very young children. PF3.2 Enrolment in childcare and pre-schools*. Retrieved July 14, 2010, from www.oecd.org/els/social/family/database

OECD (2011a). *Growing unequal? Income distribution and poverty in OECD Countries*. Paris: OECD.

OECD (2011b). *Society at a glance: OECD social indicators*. Paris: OECD.

OECD (2011c). *Ageing: population pyramids in 2000 & 2050*. Paris: OECD. Retrieved June 02, 2011, from www.oecd.org/document/24/0,3746,en_2649_34637_2671576_1_1_1_1,00.html#publications.

OECD (2011d). Labour force statistics by sex and age - indicators. Paris: OECD. Retrieved April 10, 2011, from from stats.oecd.org.

Oelkers, J. (1985). *Die Herausforderung der Wirklichkeit durch das Subjekt: literarische Reflexionen in pädagogischer Absicht*. Weinheim: Juventa.

Oelkers, J. (1991). Bildung als Roman: Perspektiven des „Tristram Shandy". In: ders.: *Erziehung als Paradoxie der Moderne. Aufsätze zur Kulturpädagogik*. Weinheim: Deutscher Studien Verlag.

Osborn, A. F., & Milbank, J. E. (1987). *The effects of early education: A report from the Child Health and Education Study*. Oxford: Clarendon Press.

PACE (2002). *A stark plateau - California families see little growth in child care centers* (Policy Brief 02-2). Berkeley: Policy Analysis for California Education.

Pagel, G. (2007). *Jacques Lacan zur Einführung* (5. Aufl.). Hamburg: Junius.

Palermo, F., Hanish, L. D., Martin, C. L., Fabes R. A., & Reiser, M. (2007). Preschoolers' academic readiness: What role does the teacher-child relationship play? *Early Childhood Research Quarterly, 22*(4), 407–422.

Palley, E. (2010). Who cares for children? Why are we where we are with American child care policy? *Children and Youth Services Review, 32*, 155–163.

Plantenga, J., & Remery, C. (2009). *The provision of childcare services. A comparative review of 30 European countries*. Luxembourg: European Commission, Directorate-General for Employment, Social Affairs and Equal opportunities.

Pleines, J.-E. (1989). *Studien zur Bildungstheorie: 1971 - 1988*. Darmstadt: Wiss. Buchgesellschaft.

Pascal, C., & Bertram, T. (2001). Evaluating the costs and benefits of early childhood programmes. *European Early Childhood Education Research Journal, 9*(2), 21–44.

Pauen, S., & Pahnke, J. (2008). Mathematical skills in preschoolers: evaluating the effects of a short-time intervention. *Empirische Pädagogik, 22*(2), 193-208.

PAVO. (1977). *Verordnung über die Aufnahme von Kindern zur Pflege und zur Adoption* [Decree on the supervision of children for care and adoption]. Retrieved July 4, 2010, from www.admin.ch/ch/d/sr/2/211.222.338.de.pdf

Pfeffer, J. (1993). Barriers to the advance of organizational science: Paradigm development as a dependent variable. *The Academy of Management Review, 18*(4), 599–620.
Paxson, C., & Schady, N. (2007). Cognitive development among young children in Ecuador. The roles of wealth, health, and parenting. *The Journal of Human Resources, 42*(1), 49-84.
Payne, A. C., Whitehurst, G. J., & Angell, A. L. (1994). The role of home literacy environment in the development of language ability in preschool children from low-income families. *Early Childhood Research Quarterly, 9*(3-4), 427–440.
Peisner-Feinberg, E. S., Burchinal, M. R., Clifford, R. M., Culkin, M. L., Howes, C., Kagan, S. L., et al. (2001). The relation of preschool child-care quality to children's cognitive and social developmental trajectories through second grade. *Child Development, 72*(5), 1534-1553.
Peisner-Feinberg, E., & Schaaf, J. M. (2008). *Evaluation of the North Carolina More at Four Pre-kindergarten program: Children's longitudinal outcomes and program quality over time (2003-2007)*. Chapel Hill, NC: FPG Child Development Institute.
Pfeiffer, F., & Reuss, K. (2008). *Ungleichheit und die differentiellen Erträge frühkindlicher Bildungsinvestitionen im Lebenszyklus* [Inequality and the differential returns of investments in early childhood education in the life cycle] (Discussion Paper No. 08-001). Mannheim: Zentrum für Europäische Wirtschaftsforschung. Retrieved August 13, 2008, from http://opus.zbw-kiel.de/volltexte/2008/7098/pdf/dp08001.pdf
Phillips, D. A., Howes, C., & Whitebook, M. (1992). The social policy context of child care: Effects on quality. *American Journal of Community Psychology, 20*(1), 25–51.
Phillips, B., & Lonigan, C. (2009). Variations in the home literacy environment of preschool children: a cluster analytic approach. *Scientific Studies of Reading, 13*(2), 146–174.
Phillips, D., & Shonkoff, J. P. (Eds.) (2000). *From neurons to neighborhoods: The science of early child development*. Washington, D.C: National Academy Press.
Phillips, D., Voran, M., Kisker, E., Howes, C., & Whitebook, M. (1994). Child care for children in poverty: Opportunity or inequity? *Child Development, 65*, 472–492.
Phillipsen, L. C., Burchinal, M. R., Howes, C., & Cryer, D. (1997). The prediction of process quality from structural features of child care. *Early Childhood Research Quarterly, 12*, 281–303.
PISA. (2001). *Knowledge and skills for life: First results from the OECD programme for international student assessment (PISA) 2000*. Paris: OECD.
PISA. (2004). *Learning for tomorrow's world: First results from PISA 2003*. Paris: OECD.
PISA. (2007). *Science competencies for tomorrow's world*. Paris: OECD.
Plaisance, É., & Rayna, S. (2004). Early childhood schooling and socialization at french nursery school. *Prospects, 34*(4), 435–445.
Plucker, J. A., Eaton, J. J., Rapp, K. E., Lim, W., Nowak, J., Hansen, J. A., et al. (2004). *The effects of full day versus half day kindergarten: Review and analysis of national and Indiana data*. Indianapolis: Indiana Association of Public School Superintendents Information and Research Commission. Retrieved July 24, 2008, from http://www.eric.ed.

gov/ERICDocs/data/ericdocs2sql/content_storage_01/0000019b/80/1b/b9/a8. pdf

Pong, S.-l., & Hao, L. (2007). Neighborhood and School Factors in the School Performance of Immigrants' Children. *International Migration Review, 41*(1), 206–241.

Postman, N. (1982). *The disappearance of childhood.* New York: Delacorte Press.

Price, T. D., & Feinman, G. M. (1995). Foundations of prehistoric social inequality. In T. D. Price & G. M. Feinman (Eds.), *Foundations of social inequality* (pp. 3–4). New York: Plenum Press.

Prochner, L. (1996). Quality of care in historical perspective. *Early Childhood Research Quarterly, 11*, 5–17.

Prochner, L. (2003). The American creche: 'Let's do what the French do, but do it our way'. *Contemporary Issues in Early Childhood, 4*(3), 267–285.

Prost, A. (1984). L'évolution de la politique familiale en France de 1938 à 1981. *Le Mouvement Social, 129*, 7–28.

Pungello, E. P., Kainz, K., Burchinal, M., Wasik, B. H., Sparling, J. J., Ramey, C. T., & Campbell, F. A. (2010). Early Educational Intervention, Early Cumulative Risk, and the Early Home Environment as Predictors of Young Adult Outcomes Within a High-Risk Sample. *Child Development, 81*(1), 410–426.

Pungello, E. P., & Kurtz-Costes, B. (2000). Working women's selection of care for their infants: A prospective study. *Family Relations, 49*(3), 245–255.

Rabinovici, D. (1996). Warum die Milch vom Fleisch getrennt werden musste oder Die gerettete Zunge und das drohende Messer. In J. Pattillo-Hess & M. R. Smole (Hrsg.), *Canettis Aufstand gegen Macht und Tod* (S. 54–63). Wien: Löcker.

Rainwater, L., & Smeeding, T. M. (2003). *Poor kids in a rich country: America's children in comparative perspective.* New York: Russell Sage.

Ramey, C. T., & Ramey, S. L. (1998). Early intervention and early experience. *American Psychologist, 53*(2), 109–120.

Ramey, C. T., & Ramey, S. L. (2004). Early learning and school readiness: Can early intervention make a difference? *Merrill-Palmer Quarterly, 50*(4), 471–491.

Randall, V. (2000). *The Politics of Child Daycare in Britain.* Oxford: University Press.

Rauschenbach, T., & Schilling, D. (2007). *Erwartbare ökonomische Effekte durch den Ausbau der Betreuungsangebote für unter Dreijährige auf 750'000 Plätze bis 2013* [Expected economic effects of an extension of child care services for children under three years to 750.000 places until 2013]. München: Deutsches Jugendinstitut.

Rayna, S. (1992). L'accueil des jeunes enfants en crèche : quelques données récentes de la recherche. *Journal de Pédiatrie et de Puériculture, 5*(6), 346–352.

Reichenbach, R. (2007). *Philosophie der Bildung und Erziehung. Eine Einführung.* Kohlhammer: Stuttgart.

Reynolds, A. J., Mann, E., Miedel, W., & Smokowski, P. (1997). The state of early childhood intervention: Effectiveness, myths and realities, new directions. *Focus, 19*(3), 25–28.

Reynolds, A. J., Temple, J. A., Ou, S.-R., Robertson, D. L., Mersky, J. P., Topitzes, J. W., et al. (2007). Effects of a school-based, early childhood intervention on adult health and well-being. *Archives of Pediatrics & Adolescent Medicine, 161*(8), 730-739.
Reynolds, A. J., Temple, J. A., Robertson, D. L., & Mann, E. A. (2001). Long-term effects of an early childhood intervention on educational achievement and juvenile arrest: A 15-year follow-up of low-income children in public schools. *JAMA, 285*(18), 2339-2346.
Reynolds, A. J., Temple, J. A., Robertson, D. L., & Mann, E. A. (2002). Age 21 cost-benefit analysis of the Title 1 Chicago Child-Parent Centers. *Educational Evaluation and Policy Analysis, 24*(4), 267-303.
Reynolds, S. (1990). Who wanted the crèches? Working mothers and the birth-rate in France 1900-1950. *Continuity and Change, 5*(2), 173–197.
Reynolds, S. (1996). *France between the wars: Gender and politics*. London: Routledge.
Ricken, N. (2006). *Die Ordnung der Bildung: Beiträge zu einer Genealogie der Bildung* (1. Aufl.). Wiesbaden: VS Verlag für Sozialwissenschaften.
Riley, J. (2008). Early childhood education. In G. McCulloch & D. Crook (Eds.), *The Routledge international encyclopedia of education* (pp. 185–190). London ; New York: Routledge.
Robert Bosch Stiftung (2011). *Bildung und Gesellschaft* [Education and Society]. Retrieved August 15, 2011, from: www.bosch-stiftung.de.
Roberts, E., Bornstein, M. H., Slater, A. M., & Barrett, J. (1999). Early cognitive development and parental education. *Infant and Child Development, 8*, 49-62.
Robinson, V. M. J. (1998). Methodology and the Research-Practice Gap. *Educational Researcher, 27*(1), 17–26.
Rogoff, B. (2003). *The cultural nature of human development*. New York: Oxford University Press.
Rollet, C. (2001). La santé et la protection de l'enfant vues à travers les congrès internationaux (1880-1920). *Annales de la démographie historique, 1*, 97–116.
Rollet, C., & Morel, M. F. (2000). *Des bébés et des hommes*. Paris: Albin Michel.
Rose, E. R. (1999). *A mother's job: The history of day care, 1890-1960*. New York, NY: Oxford University Press.
Roseman, M. J. (1999). Quality child care: At whose expense? *Early Childhood Education Journal, 27*(1), 5–11.
Rossbach, H. G., Kluczniok, K., & Isenmann, D. (2008). Erfahrungen aus internationalen Längsschnittuntersuchungen [Experiences from international longitudinal studies]. In H. G. Rossbach, & Weinert, S. (Eds.), *Kindliche Kompetenzen im Elementarbereich: Förderbarkeit, Bedeutung und Messung* (Vol. 24, pp. 7-88). Berlin: Bundesministerium für Bildung und Forschung.
Rossbach, H. G., Kluczniok, K., & Kuger, S. (2008). Auswirkungen eines Kindergartenbesuchs auf den kognitiv-leistungsbezogenen Entwicklungsstand von Kindern

[The effects of attending a kindergarten on children's cognitive and performance-related development]. *Zeitschrift für Erziehungswissenschaft, Sonderheft 11*, 139-158.
Ruhloff, J. (2000). Wie ist ein nicht-normativer Bildungsbegriff zu denken? In C. Dietrich & H.-R. Müller (Hrsg.), *Bildung und Emanzipation. Klaus Mollenhauer weiterdenken* (S. 117–125). Weinheim: Juventa.
Rumberger, R. W., & Tran, L. (2006). *Preschool participation and the cognitive and social development of language-minority students* (CSE Technical Report 674 UC LMRI). Santa Barbara: University of California, Center for the Study of Evaluation and UC Linguistic Minority Research Institute. Retrieved December 2, 2008, from http://www.lmri.ucsb.edu/publications/06_rumberger-tran.pdf
Ruopp, R., & et al. (1979). *Children at the center: Summary findings and their implications*. (Final Report of the National Day Care Study). Cambridge, MA: Abt Associates, Inc.
Sagi-Schwartz, A., Koren-Karie, N., Gini, M., Ziv, Y., & Joels, T. (2002). Shedding further light on the effects of various types and quality of early child care on infant-mother attachment relationships: The Haifa study of early child care. *Child Development, 73*(4), 1166–1186.
SAKE Schweizerische Arbeitskräfteerhebung (2010). *Anteil Haushalte mit familienergänzender Kinderbetreuung nach Haushaltstyp und Alter des jüngsten Kindes, 2007*. Retrieved August 16, 2011, from BfS: www.bfs.admin.ch/bfs/portal/de/index/themen/20/05/blank/key/Vereinbarkeit/05.html.
Saluja, G., Scott-Little, C., & Clifford, R. M. (2000). Readiness for school: A survey of state policies and definitions. *Early Childhood Research & Practice, 2*(2). Retrieved May 02, 2011, from http://ecrp.uiuc.edu/v2n2/saluja.html.
Sammons, P., Elliot, K., Sylva, K., Melhuish, E., Siraj-Blatchford, I., & Taggart, B. (2004). The impact of pre-school on young children's cognitive attainments at entry to reception. *British Educational Research Journal, 30*(5), 691–712.
Sammons, P., Sylva, K., Melhuish, E., Siraj-Blatchford, I., Taggart, B., & Hunt, S. (2008a). *Effective pre-school and primary education 3-11 project (EPPE 3-11). Influences on children's attainment and progress in key stage 2: Cognitive outcomes in year 6* (Research Report DCSF-RR048). London: Department for Children, Schools and Families.
Sammons, P., Sylva, K., Melhuish, E., Siraj-Blatchford, I., Taggart, B., Hunt, S., & Jelicic, H. (August 2008b). *Effective preschool and primary education 3-11 project (EPPE 3-11): Influences on children's cognitive and social development in year 6* (Research brief DCSF-RB048-049). London: Department for children, schools and families.
Sammons, P., Sylva, K., Melhuish, E., Siraj-Blatchford, I., Taggart, B., & Jelicic, H. (2008c). *Effective pre-school and primary education 3-11 project (EPPE 3-11). Influences on children's development and progress in key stage 2: Social/behavioural outcomes in year 6* (Research Report No DCSF-RR049). Institute of Education, University of London.
Schady, N. (2006). *Early childhood development in Latin America and the Carribean* (Policy Research Working Paper No. 3605). Washington, DC: World Bank.
Schmid, T., Kriesi, I., & Buchmann, M. (2011). Wer nutzt familienergänzende Kinderbetreuung? Die Betreuungssituation 6-jähriger Kinder in der Schweiz [Who

uses extra-familial childcare? The care situation of 6-year-olds in Switzerland]. *Swiss Journal of Sociology, 37*(1), 9–32.

Schnabel, K., & Schwippert, K. (2000).Einflüsse sozialer und ethnischer Herkunft beim Übergang in die Sekundarstufe II und den Beruf. In J. Baumert, W. Bos, & R. Lehmann (Eds.), TIMSS/III, 1, (pp. 261-300).Opladen: Leske + Budrich.

Schneider, W., & Stefanek, J. (2004). Entwicklungsveränderungen allgemeiner kognitiver Fähigkeiten und schulbezogener Fertigkeiten im Kindes- und Jugendalter: Evidenz für einen Schereneffekt? [Developmental changes of general cognitive and school related skills during infancy and adolescence: evidence for a widening gap?]. *Zeitschrift für Entwicklungspsychologie und Pädagogische Psychologie, 36*(3), 147-159.

Schrader, M. (1975). *Mimesis und Poiesis: Poetologische Studien zum Bildungsroman*. Berlin, New York: Walter de Gruyter.

Schütz, G., & Wössmann, L. (2005a, October). *Chancengleichheit im Schulsystem: Internationale deskriptive Evidenz und mögliche Bestimmungsfaktoren* [Equal opportunities in the education system: International descriptive evidence and potential determinants] (Ifo working paper No. 17). Munich: Ifo Institute for Economic Research, University of Munich. Retrieved November 5, 2009, fromwww.ggg-bund.de/IfoWorkingPaper17.pdf

Schütz, G., & Wössmann, L. (2005b). *Wie lässt sich die Ungleichheit der Bildungschancen verringern?* [How can the inequality of educational opportunities be minimized?] (ifo Schnelldienst 21). Munich: Ifo Institute for Economic Research, University of Munich. Retrieved December 26, 2009, from www.cesifo-group.de/pls/guest/download/ifo%20Schnelldienst/ifo%20Schnelldienst%202005/ifosd_2005_21_3.pdf

Schulte-Haller, M. (2009). *Frühe Förderung. Forschung, Praxis und Politik im Bereich der Frühförderung: Bestandesaufnahme und Handlungsfelder*. Bern: Eidgenössische Kommission für Migrationsfragen.

Schweinhart, L. J., Montie, J., Xiang, Z, Barnett, W. S., Belfield, C. R., & Nores, M. (2005). *Lifetime effects: The High/Scope Perry Preschool study through age 40*. Ypsilanty, Michigan: High/Scope Press.

Schweinhart, L. J., & Weikart, D. P. (1988). Education for young children living in poverty: Child-initiated learning or teacher-directed instruction. *The Elementary School Journal, 89*(2), 212–225.

Schweinhart, L. J., & Weikart, D. P. (1997). The High/Scope Preschool curriculum comparison study through age 23. *Early Childhood Research Quarterly, 12*(2), 117–143.

Schweinhart, L. & Weikart, D. (1998). Why curriculum matters in early childhood education. *Educational Leadership, 55*(6), 57–60.

Schweitzer, S. (2002). *Les femmes ont toujours travaillé. Une histoire de leurs métiers, aux XIXème et XXème siècles*. Paris: Odile Jacob.

Scior, V. (2002). *Das Eigene und das Fremde. Identität und Fremdheit in den Chroniken Adams von Bremen, Helmolds von Bosau und Arnolds von Lübeck*. Berlin: Akademie Verlag.

Selbmann, R. (1984). *Der deutsche Bildungsroman*. Stuttgart: Metzler.
Selbmann, R. (Hrsg.). (1988). *Zur Geschichte des deutschen Bildungsromans*. Darmstadt: Wissenschaftliche Buchgesellschaft.
Sénéchal, M. (2006). Testing the home literacy model: Parent involvement in kindergarten is differentially related to grade 4 reading comprehension, fluency, spelling, and reading for pleasure. *Scientific Studies of Reading, 10*(1), 59–87.
Sergesketter, K., & Gilman, D. (1988). *The effect of length of time in kindergarten on reading achievement*. Indiana State University.
Seyda, S. (2009). Kindergartenbesuch und späterer Bildungserfolg. *Zeitschrift für Erziehungswissenschaft, 12*(2), 233–251.
Shaffer, D. R. (1994). *Social & personality development* (3rd ed.). Pacific Grove, Calif: Brooks/Cole Pub.
Shavelson, R. J. (1988). The 1988 Presidential Address Contributions of Educational Research to Policy and Practice: Constructing, Challenging, Changing Cognition. *Educational Researcher, 17*(7), 4–11.
Sheridan, S., Giota, J., Han, Y.-M., & Kwon, J.-Y. (2009). A cross-cultural study of preschool quality in South Korea and Sweden: ECERS evaluations. *Early Childhood Research Quarterly, 24*, 142–156.
Shin, H. B. (2005, May). *School enrollment - Social and economic characteristics of students: October 2003* (P20-554). Washington, DC: U.S. Census Bureau.
Shonkoff, J. P., & Meisels, S. J. (2006). *Handbook of early childhood intervention* (2. ed.). Cambridge, UK: Cambridge Univ. Press.
Shonkoff, J. P.; Phillips, D. A. (Eds.) (2000). *From neurons to neighborhoods: The science of early child development*. Washington, D.C: National Academy Press.
Sindelar, P. T., & Brownell, M. T. (2001). Research to practice dissemination, scale, and context: We can do it, but can we afford it? *Teacher Education and Special Education: The Journal of the Teacher Education Division of the Council for Exceptional Children, 24*(4), 348–355.
Siraj-Blatchford, I. (2004). Educational disadvantage in the early years: how do we overcome it? Some lessons from research. *European Early Childhood Education Research Journal, 12*(2), 5–20.
Siraj-Blatchford, I. (2009). Learning in the home and at school: how working class children 'succeed against the odds'. *British Educational Research Journal*. First published on: 17 June 2009 (iFirst).
Siraj-Blatchford, I., & Sylva, K. (2004). Researching pedagogy in English pre-schools. *British Educational Research Journal, 30*(5), 713–730.
Smith, S. A. (2002). *The Russian Revolution: a very short introduction*. United States: Oxford University Press.
Smolensky, E., & Gootman, J. A. (2003). *Working families and growing kids: Caring for children and adolescents*. Washington, D.C: National Academies Press.
Sontag, S. (1990). *Geist als Leidenschaft: Ausgewählte Essays zur modernen Kunst und Kultur* (2. Aufl.). Leipzig: Kiepenheuer.

Sparks, C. D. T. (1986). *The service, management, and physical features of a campus child care center - a plan for community colleges*. Dissertation, Texas Tech University.

Spiess, C. K., Büchel, F., & Wagner, G. G. (2003). Children's school placement in Germany: Does kindergarten attendance matter? *Early Childhood Research Quarterly, 18*(2), 255–270.

Spiess, C., Schupp, J., Grabka, M., Haisken-De New, J. P., Jakobeit, H., & Wagner, G. G. (2002). *Abschätzung der Brutto-Einnahmeneffekte öffentlicher Haushalte und der Sozialversicherungsträger bei einem Ausbau von Kindertageseinrichtungen* [Estimation of the gross revenues of public households and of the social insurance carriers in the case of an extension of day-care facilities] (Schriftenreihe Band 233). Berlin: Bundesministerium für Familie, Senioren, Frauen und Jugend. Retrieved January 13, 2009, from www.bmfsfj.de/Politikbereiche/kinder-und-jugend,did=6432.html

Spiess, C. K., & Tietze, W. (2002). Qualitätssicherung in Kindertageseinrichtungen: Gründe, Anforderungen und Umsetzungsüberlegungen für ein Gütesiegel [Quality assurance in pre-school day care: Reasons, requirements, and considerations for the implementation of a quality seal]. *Zeitschrift für Erziehungswissenschaft, 5*(1), 139-162.

Stamm, M. (2005a). *Zwischen Exzellenz und Versagen: Frühleser und Frührechner werden erwachsen* [Between excellence and failure: precocious readers and mathematicians become adults]. Chur/Zürich: Rüegger.

Stamm, M. (2005b). Bildungsaspiration, Begabung und Schullaufbahn: Eltern als Erfolgspromotoren? [Educational aspiration, talent and schooling: Parents as promoters of success?] *Revue suisse des sciences de l'éducation, 27*(2), 277–297.

Stamm, M. (2009a). *Begabte Minoritäten* [Gifted minorities]. Wiesbaden: VS Verlag für Sozialwissenschaften.

Stamm, M. (2009b, September 13). Unsere Sprösslinge werden durch die Kindheit gehetzt: Frühförderung durch Eltern und ein familienergänzendes Umfeld sind wichtig. Doch zu starker Leistungsdruck und Anpassung schaden den Kindern. *NZZ am Sonntag, 37*, 17.

Stamm, M. (2009c). Bildungsqualität in Vorschulsettings [Instructional quality in preschool settings]. *Zeitschrift für Grundschulforschung, 2*, 111–125.

Stamm, M. (2010a). *Frühkindliche Bildung, Betreuung und Erziehung* [Early childhood care and education]. Bern: UTB.

Stamm, M. (2010b). Frühkindliche Bildung: Fakten, Widersprüche und offene Fragen. *Frühförderung interdisziplinär, 4*, 147–153.

Stamm, M. (2010c). Vorschulkinder im Treibhaus? [Preschool children in the hothouse?] In L. Duncker, G. Lieber, N. Neuss, & B. Uhlig (Eds.), *Bildung in der Kindheit. Das Handbuch zum Lernen in Kindergarten und Grundschule* (pp. 126–131). Seelze: Klett.

Stamm, M. (2011a, January 24). Die Magie der Frühförderung: Über die Chancen und Grenzen der ausserfamiliären frühkindlichen Förderung [The magic of early intervention: on the chances and limits of extra-familial early intervention]. *NZZ*, 40.
Stamm, M. (2011b). Wieviel Mutter braucht das Kind? Theoretische Befunde und empirische Fakten zur Frage der Nützlichkeit oder Schädlichkeit von früher familienesterner Betreuung [How much mother does a child need? Theoretical results and empirical facts about the usefulness or harmfulness of day care]. *Diskurs Kindheits- und Jugendforschung, 1*, 17–29.
Stamm, M. (2011c). *Zur pädagogischen Qualität frühkindlicher Bildungsprogramme: Eine Kritik an ihrer ethnozentrischen Perspektive [On pedagogical quality of preschool programs: a critique of the ethnocentric perspective]*. Unpublished manuscript, Department of Education, University of Fribourg, Switzerland.
Stamm, M., Burger, K., & Reinwand, V. I. (2009). Frühkindliche Bildung als Prävention gegen Schulversagen? Empirische Befunde und kritische Anmerkungen zur frühpädagogischen Forschung. *Zeitschrift für Sozialpädagogik, 7*(3), 226–243.
Stamm, M., & Edelmann, D. (Eds.) (2010). *Frühkindliche Bildung, Betreuung und Erziehung: Was kann die Schweiz lernen?* [Early childhood care and education: What can Switzerland learn?] Zürich: Rüegger.
Stamm, M., Knoll, A., & Sabini, S. (2011). *FRANZ Studie: Erste Resultate* [FRANZ study: first results]. Fribourg: Departement Erziehungswissenschaften, Universität Fribourg. Retrieved August 18, 2011, from www.unifr.ch/pedg/franz/erste_resultate.htm?mainMenuItemToSlide=5.
Stamm, M., Reinwand, V. I., Burger, K., Schmid, K., Viehhauser, M., & Muheim, V. (2009). *Frühkindliche Bildung in der Schweiz. Eine Grundlagenstudie im Auftrag der UNESCO-Kommission Schweiz* [Early childhood education in Switzerland. A study on behalf of the Swiss Commission for UNESCO]. Fribourg: Universität Fribourg, Departement Erziehungswissenschaften.
Stamm, M., & Viehhauser, M. (2009). Frühkindliche Bildung und soziale Ungleichheit. Analysen und Perspektiven zum chancenausgleichenden Charakter frühkindlicher Bildungsangebote. *Zeitschrift für Soziologie der Erziehung und Sozialisation, 4*, 403–418.
State board of charities (1894). *Twenty-seventh annual report of the New York state board of charities for the year 1893*. Albany N.Y.: James B. Lyon.
Steussloff, A. G. (1994). *Autorschaft und Werk Elias Canettis: Subjekt – Sprache – Identität*. Würzburg: Königshausen und Neumann
Stipek, D. J., Feiler, R., Daniels, D. & Milburn, S. (1995) Effects of different instructional approaches on young children's achievement and motivation. *Child Development, 66*, 209–223.

Stipek, D. J., & Ryan, R. H. (1997). Economically disadvantaged preschoolers: Ready to learn but further to go. *Developmental Psychology, 33*(4), 711-723.

St. Pierre, R. G., Layzer, J. I., Goodson, B. D., & Bernstein, L. S. (1997). *The effectiveness of comprehensive, case management interventions: Findings from the national evaluation of the comprehensive child development program*. Cambridge: Research in Child Development and Family Studies. Retrieved September 24, 2008, from http://www.abtassociates.com/reports/paper6.pdf

Sui-Chu, E., & Willms, J. (1996). Effects of parental involvement on eighth-grade achievement. *Sociology of Education, 69*(2), 126–141.

Sweeting, A. (2005). The historical dimension: a contribution to conversation about theory and methodology in comparative education. *Comparative Education, 41*(1), 25–44.

Sylva, K., Melhuish, E., Sammons, P., Siraj-Blatchford, I., & Taggart, B. (2008). *Effective pre-school and primary education 3-11 project. Final report from the primary phase: Pre-school, school and family influences on children's development during key stage 2 (age 7-11)* (Research Report No DCSF-RR061). Institute of Education, University of London.

Sylva, K., Siraj-Blatchford, I., Taggart, B., Sammons, P., Melhuish, E., Elliot, K., & Totsika, V. (2006). Capturing quality in early childhood through environmental rating scales. *Early Childhood Research Quarterly, 21*, 76–92.

Sylva, K., Melhuish, E., Sammons, P., Siraj-Blatchford, I., Taggart, B., & Elliot, K. (2003). *The effective provision of pre-school education (EPPE) project: Findings from the pre-school period* (research brief no. RBX 15-03). Institute of Education, University of London.

Szreter, S. (2003). The population health approach in historical perspective. *American Journal of Public Health, 93*(3), 421–431.

Tabachnick, B. G., & Fidell, L. S. (2001). *Using multivariate statistics* (4th ed.). Boston: Allyn and Bacon.

Tabors, P. O., Roach, K. A., & Snow, C. E. (2001). Home language and literacy environment: Final results. In D. K. Dickinson & P. O. Tabors (Eds.), *Beginning literacy with language* (pp. 111–138). Baltimore, MD: Brookes.

Taylor, A. R., & Machida, S. (1994). The contribution of parent and peer support to Head Start children's early school adjustment. *Early Childhood Research Quarterly, 9*(3-4), 387–405.

Taylor, B. A., Dearing, E., & McCartney, K. (2004). Incomes and outcomes in early childhood. *The Journal of Human Resources, 39*(4), 980-1007.

Taylor, C. (1985). *Human agency and language. Philosophical papers: Vol. 1*. Cambridge: Cambridge Univ. Press.

Taylor Allen, A. (1988). "Let us live with our children": Kindergarten movements in Germany and the United States, 1840-1914. *History of Education Quarterly, 28*(1), 23–48.

Tenorth, H.-W. (1997). „Bildung" – Thematisierungsformen und Bedeutung in der Erziehungswissenschaft. *Zeitschrift für Pädagogik, 43*(6), 969-984.

Thiers, M. (1850). *Rapport général au nom de la commission de l'assistance et de la prévoyance publiques: Dans la séance du 26 janvier 1850.* Paris: Claye et Cie.
Thorndike, E. L. (1926). *The measurement of intelligence.* New York: Teacher's College, Columbia University.
Thorpe, K. J., Tayler, C. P., Bridgstock, R. S., Grieshaber, S. J., Skoien, P. V., Danby, S. J., & Petriwskyj, A. (2004). *Preparing for school: Report of the Queensland preparing for school trials 2003/4.* Queensland: School of Early Childhood QUT. Retrieved June 03, 2011, from http://eprints.qut.edu.au/10192/1/10192.pdf.
Tietze, W. (Ed.). (1998). *Wie gut sind unsere Kindergärten? Eine Untersuchung zur pädagogischen Qualität in deutschen Kindergärten* [What is the quality of our kindergartens like? An analysis of the pedagogical quality in German kindergartens]. Weinheim: Beltz.
Tietze, W., & Cryer, D. (1999). Current trends in European early child care and education. *Annals of the American Academy of Political and Social Science, 563,* 175–193.
Tietze, W., Cryer, D., Bairrão, J., Palacios, J., & Wetzel, G. (1996). Comparisons of observed process quality in early child care and education programs in five countries. *Early Childhood Research Quarterly, 11*(4), 447–475.
Tobin, J. (2005). Quality in early childhood education: An anthropologist's perspective. *Early Education & Development, 16*(4), 421–434.
Tout, K., Zaslow, M., & Berry, D. (2006). Quality and qualifications: Links between professional development and quality in early care and education settings. In M. Zaslow & I. Martinez-Beck (Eds.), *Critical issues in early childhood professional development* (pp. 77–100). Baltimore, MD: Brookes Publishing.
Treml, A. K. (2005). *Pädagogische Ideengeschichte: Ein Überblick.* Stuttgart: Kohlhammer.
Turney, K., & Kao, G. (2009). Pre-kindergarten child care and behavioral outcomes among children of immigrants. *Early Childhood Research Quarterly, 24,* 432–444.
Umek, L. M., Kranjc, S., Fekonja, U., & Bajc, K. (2006). Quality of the preschool and home environment as a context of children's language development. *European Early Childhood Education Research Journal, 14*(1), 131–147.
UNESCO. (2000). *Early childhood education: Need and opportunity* (Fundamentals of Educational Planning – 65). Paris: UNESCO.
UNESCO (2007). *Strong foundations: Early childhood care and education* (EFA global monitoring report). Paris: UNESCO.
UNESCO. (2008). *Education for all by 2015: Will we make it?* Paris: UNESCO.
UNICEF (2007). *Child poverty in perspective: An overview of child well-being in rich countries. A comprehensive assessment of the lives and well-being of children and adolescents in the economically advanced nations* (report card 7). Florence: UNICEF Innocenti Research Centre.
UNICEF (2008). *The child care transition: A league table of early childhood education and care in economically advanced countries* (report card 8). Florence: UNICEF Innocenti Research Centre.
United Nations (1990). *Convention on the rights of the child.* UNO. Retrieved May 13th, 2011, from www2.ohchr.org/english/law/pdf/crc.pdf.

UNO. (1990). *Convention on the rights of the child.* New York, Geneva: Office of the United Nations High Commissioner for Human Rights. Retrieved October 18, 2009, from www2.ohchr.org/english/law/crc.htm

Urban, D., & Mayerl, J. (2006). *Regressionsanalyse: Theorie, Technik und Anwendung* [Regression analysis: Theory, technique, and application] (2nd ed.). Wiesbaden: VS Verlag.

U.S. Census Bureau (2004). *Population estimates.* Retrieved November 5, 2010, from U.S. Census Bureau: www.census.gov/popest/age.html

U.S. Department of Health and Human Services (2005). *Head Start Impact Study: First year findings* (Head Start Research). Washington, D.C: Administration for Children and Families. Retrieved May 28, 2009, from www.acf.hhs.gov/programs/opre/hs/impact_study/.

U.S. Department of Health and Human Services (2009). *Head Start, Early Head Start programs to receive over $2 billion in Recovery Act funding,* from U.S. Department of Health & Human Services.

Vandell, D. L., & Corasaniti, M. A. (1990). Variations in early child care: Do they predict subsequent social, emotional, and cognitive differences? *Early Childhood Research Quarterly, 5*(4), 555–572.

Vandell, D. L., Henderson, V. K., & Wilson, K. S. (1988). A longitudinal study of children with day-care experiences of varying quality. *Child Development, 59*(5), 1286–1292.

Vandell, D. L., Belsky, J., Burchinal, M., Steinberg, L., & Vandergrift, N. (2010). Do effects of early child care extend to age 15 years? Results from the NICHD Study of Early Child Care and Youth Development. *Child Development, 81*(3), 737–756.

Van Tuijl, C., & Leseman, P. P. M. (2007). Increases in the verbal and fluid cognitive abilities of disadvantaged children attending preschool in the Netherlands. *Early Childhood Research Quarterly, 22*(2), 188–203.

Vaughn, B. E., Deane, K. E., & Waters, E. (1985). The impact of out-of-home care on child-mother attachment quality: Another look at some enduring questions. *Monographs of the Society for Research in Child Development, 50,* 110–135.

Victor, L. (2008). *Systematic reviewing.* Guildford, UK: Department of Sociology, University of Surrey. Retrieved August 16, 2011, from www.soc.surrey.ac.uk/sru/.

Vinovskis, M. A. (1993). Early childhood education: Then and now. *Daedalus, 122*(1), 151–176.

Von Matt, P. (2007). *Der Entflammte: über Elias Canetti.* München: Nagel & Kimche.

Vos, A. J., & Brits, V. M. (1990). *Comparative education and national education systems.* Durban: Butterworths.

Votruba-Drzal, E. (2003). Income changes and cognitive stimulation in young children's home learning environments. *Journal of Marriage and Family, 65,* 341–355.

Votruba-Drzal, E., Li-Grining, C. P., & Maldonado-Carreño, C. (2008). A developmental perspective on full- versus part-day kindergarten and children's academic trajectories through fifth grade. *Child Development, 79*(4), 957-978.

Waldfogel, J. (2002). Child care, women's employment, and child outcomes. *Journal of Population Economics, 15*(3), 527–548.
Waller, T. (2009). Modern childhood: contemporary theories and children's lives. In T. Waller (Ed.), *An introduction to early childhood. A multidisciplinary approach* (2nd ed., pp. 2–15). Los Angeles: SAGE.
Walsh, G., Sproule, L., McGuiness, C., Trew, K., Rafferty, H., & Sheehy, N. (2006). An appropriate curriculum for 4-5-year-old children in Northern Ireland: Comparing play-based and formal approaches. *Early Years: An International Journal of Research and Development, 26*(2), 201–221.
Walston, J. T., & West, J. (2004). *Full-day and half-day kindergarten in the United States: Findings from the early childhood longitudinal study, kindergarten class of 1998-99*. Washington, DC: U.S. Government Printing Office. Retrieved December 15, 2008, from http://nces.ed.gov/pubs2004/2004078.pdf
Warner, M. E. (2006). Overview: Articulating the economic importance of child care for community development. *Journal of the Community Development Society, 37*(2), 1–6.
Watanabe, K., Flores, R., Fujiwara, J., & Huong Tran, L. T. (2005). Early childhood development interventions and cognitive development of young children in rural Vietnam. *The Journal of Nutrition, 135*, 1918-1925.
Waterkamp, D. (1997). *Die vergleichende Erziehungswissenschaft zwischen Ethnozentrismus und globalem Denken*. Dresden: Dresdner Universitätsverl. & Universitätsbuchhandlung.
Weikart, D. P. (2000). *Early childhood education: need and opportunity* (Fundamentals of Educational Planning - 65). Paris: UNESCO. Retrieved June 10, 2011, from http://unesdoc.unesco.org/images/0012/001223/122380e.pdf.
Weinraub, M., Hill, C., & Hirsh-Pasek, K. (2001). Child care: options and outcomes. In J. Worell (Ed.), *Encyclopedia of women and gender. Sex similarities and differences and the impact of society on gender* (pp. 233–244). San Diego, Calif: Academic Press.
Weiss, C., & Bucavalas, M. J. (1980). Truth tests and utility tests: Decision-makers' frames of reference for social science research. *American Sociological Review, 45*, 302–313.
Weissbach, L. S. (1977). Child labor legislation in nineteenth-century France. *The Journal of Economic History, 37*(1), 268–271.
West, J., Hausken, E. G., & Collins, M. (1993). *Profile of preschool children's child care and early education program participation: National Household Education Survey* (NCES 93-133). Washington, D.C.: National Center for Education Statistics.
Whiting, B., & Edwards, C. (1992). *Children of different worlds. The formation of social behaviour*. Cambridge, MA: Harvard Univ. Press.
Widmer, P. (1997). *Subversion des Begehrens: Eine Einführung in Jacques Lacans Werk*. Wien: Turia und Kant.
Wiersma, W., & Jurs, S. G. (2005). *Research methods in education: an introduction* (8th ed.). Boston: Pearson.

Windelband, W. (1900). *Geschichte und Naturwissenschaft: Rede zum Antritt des Rectorats der Kaiser-Wilhelms-Universität Strassburg, gehalten am 1. Mai 1894*. Strassburg: J. H. Ed. Heitz.

Winsler, A., Tran, H., Hartman, S. C., Madigan, A. L., Manfra, L., & Bleiker, C. (2008). School readiness gains made by ethnically diverse children in poverty attending center-based childcare and public school pre-kindergarten programs. *Early Childhood Research Quarterly, 23*, 314-329.

Witte, A. D., & Trowbridge, M. (2005). The structure of early care and education in the United States: Historical evolution and international comparisons. *Tax Policy and the Economy, 19*, 1–37.

Wolgemuth, J. R., Cobb, R. B., Winokur, M. A., Leech, N., & Ellerby, D. (2006). Comparing longitudinal academic achievement of full-day and half-day kindergarten students. *The Journal of Educational Research, 99*(5), 260–270.

Wolter, S. C., Vellacott, M. C., Denzler, S., Grossenbacher, S., Kull, M., et al. (2007). *Bildungsbericht Schweiz 2006* [Education report Switzerland 2006]. Aarau: SKBF.

Woodhead, M. (2005). Early childhood development: A question of rights. *International Journal of Early Childhood, 37*(3), 79–98.

Wössmann, L. (2004). *How equal are educational opportunities? Family background and student achievement in Europe and the US* (CESifo working paper no. 1162). Ifo Institute for Economic Research, University of Munich. Retrieved January 05, 2009, from ftp://repec.iza.org/RePEc/Discussionpaper/dp1284.pdf.

Wrigley, J., & Dreby, J. (2005). Children and inequality. In M. Romero & E. Margolis (Eds.), *The Blackwell companion to social inequalities* (pp. 213–237). Malden, MA: Blackwell.

Yoshikawa, H. (1995). Long-term effects of early childhood programs on social outcomes and delinquency. *The Future of Children, 5*(3), 51–75.

Zaslow, M. J. (Ed.) (2011). *Quality measurement in early childhood settings*. Baltimore, Md: Paul H. Brookes Pub. Co.

Zhao, L., & Hu, X. (2008). The development of early childhood education in rural areas in China. *Early Years, 28*(2), 197-209.

Zigler, E., Gilliam, W. S., & Jones, S. M. (Eds.) (2006). *A vision for universal preschool education*. Cambridge, UK: Univ. Press.

Zigler, E., Gilliam, W. S., Jones, S. M., & Malakoff, M. (2006). The need for universal prekindergarten for children in poverty. In E. Zigler, W. S. Gilliam, & S. M. Jones (Eds.), *A vision for universal preschool education* (pp. 69–88). Cambridge, UK: Univ. Press.

Zigler, E. & Styfco, S.J. (1994). Head Start. Criticisms in a Constructive Context. *American Psychologist, 49*(2), 127-132.

Zill, N., Sorongon, A., Kim, K., & Clark, C. (2006). *FACES 2003 research brief. Children's outcomes and program quality in Head Start* (Report for the Administration for Children and Families). Washington: U.S. Department of Health and Human Services

(DHHS). Retrieved October, 7, 2008, from http://www.acf.hhs.gov/programs/opre/hs/faces/index.html.

Zupancic, M., & Kavcic, T. (2011). Factors of social adjustment to school: child's personality, family and pre-school. *Early Child Development and Care, 181*(4), 493–504.

Zvoch, K., Reynolds, R. E., & Parker, R. P. (2008). Full-day kindergarten and student literacy growth: Does a lengthened school day make a difference? *Early Childhood Research Quarterly, 23*, 94-107.

Zylan, Y. (2000). Maternalism redefined: Gender, the state, and the politics of day care, 1945-1962. *Gender & Society, 14*(5), 608–629.

VS Forschung | VS Research
Neu im Programm Erziehungswissenschaft

Gabi Elverich
Demokratische Schulentwicklung
Potenziale und Grenzen einer Handlungsstrategie gegen Rechtsextremismus
2011. 448 S. Br. EUR 39,95
ISBN 978-3-531-17858-5

Marcel Klaas / Alexandra Flügel / Rebecca Hoffmann / Bernadette Bernasconi (Hrsg.)
Kinderkultur(en)
2011. 329 S. Br. EUR 34,95
ISBN 978-3-531-16468-7

Sabine Klomfaß
Hochschulzugang und Bologna-Prozess
Bildungsreform am Übergang von der Universität zum Gymnasium
2011. 360 S. Br. EUR 39,95
ISBN 978-3-531-18127-1

Andreas Knoke / Anja Durdel (Hrsg.)
Steuerung im Bildungswesen
Zur Zusammenarbeit von Ministerien, Schulaufsicht und Schulleitungen
2011. 166 S. Br. EUR 24,95
ISBN 978-3-531-17888-2

Alexander Lahner
Bildung und Aufklärung nach PISA
Theorie und Praxis außerschulischer politischer Jugendbildung
2011. 363 S. Br. EUR 49,95
ISBN 978-3-531-18041-0

Andrea Óhidy
Der erziehungswissenschaftliche Lifelong Learning-Diskurs
Rezeption der europäischen Reformdiskussion in Deutschland und Ungarn
2011. 239 S. (Studien zur international vergleichenden Erziehungswissenschaft. Schwerpunkt Europa – Studies in International Comparative Educational Science. Focus: Europe) Br. EUR 39,95
ISBN 978-3-531-18113-4

Victor Tiberius
Hochschuldidaktik der Zukunftsforschung
2011. 371 S. Br. EUR 49,95
ISBN 978-3-531-18124-0

Erhältlich im Buchhandel oder beim Verlag.
Änderungen vorbehalten. Stand: Juli 2011.

Einfach bestellen:
SpringerDE-service@springer.com
tel +49 (0)6221 / 3 45 – 4301
springer-vs.de

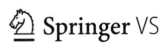